The Works of Chardri

The Life of the Seven Sleepers
The Life of St. Josaphaz
and
The Little Debate

MEDIEVAL AND RENAISSANCE
TEXTS AND STUDIES

VOLUME 462

THE FRENCH OF ENGLAND TRANSLATION SERIES
(FRETS)

VOLUME 9

THE WORKS OF CHARDRI

Three Poems in the French of Thirteenth-Century England

The Life of the Seven Sleepers
The Life of St. Josaphaz
and
The Little Debate

Translated by
Neil Cartlidge

FRETS Series Editors
Thelma Fenster and
Jocelyn Wogan-Browne

ARIZONA CENTER FOR MEDIEVAL

 ACMRS

AND RENAISSANCE STUDIES

Tempe, Arizona
2015

Published by ACMRS (Arizona Center for Medieval and Renaissance Studies)
Tempe, Arizona

Library of Congress Cataloging-in-Publication Data

Chardri, active 1189-1216.
  [Poems. Selections]
  The works of Chardri : three poems in the French of thirteenth-century
England : The life of the seven sleepers, The life of St. Josaphaz and The little
debate / Chardri ; translated by Neil Cartlidge.
      pages cm. -- (Medieval and renaissance texts and studies ; Volume 462)
(The French of England translation series (FRETS) ; Volume 9)
  Includes bibliographical references and index.
  ISBN 978-0-86698-513-0 (alk. paper)
  I. Cartlidge, Neil, 1967- translator. II. Title.
  PQ1441.C3A2 2015
  841'.1--dc23

                                                            2015001371

∞
This book is made to last. It is set in Adobe Caslon Pro,
smyth-sewn and printed on acid-free paper to library specifications.
Printed in the United States of America

In memory of
Paula Rosamund Harrison (née Daniels)
1971–2012

TABLE OF CONTENTS

Series Editors' Preface

We are very pleased to make available in FRETS the work of the late twelfth- or early thirteenth-century author who called himself Chardri, possibly an anagram of the name "Richard." Chardri's playfulness, wit, and commitment to brevity inform the three works in this volume, his entire French-language oeuvre as far as is known. *The Life of the Seven Sleepers* and *The Life of St. Josaphaz* are saints' lives on eastern themes, and *The Little Debate* is a bracing dispute between an old man and a youth on the existential gloom of human life. Neil Cartlidge's translations are the first into modern English, and are presented with an engaging and informative introduction, complete scholarly apparatus, and an appendix of original-language passages drawn from each of Chardri's three works. They will bring long overdue attention to Chardri's mastery of narrative and of medieval French poetic verse.

Chardri's works and the celebrated early Middle English debate poem, *The Owl and the Nightingale*, of which Professor Cartlidge is also the editor and translator, are extant in the same two thirteenth-century manuscripts. This pioneering volume on Chardri by a scholar fully immersed in the translingual nature of thirteenth-century literary production will help transform our understanding of Chardri and the multilingual culture in which he flourished.

Thelma Fenster
Jocelyn Wogan-Browne

TRANSLATOR'S PREFACE

This volume contains the first published translations (into any modern language) of the three lively but relatively little-known poems ascribed to a thirteenth-century Anglo-French writer calling himself only by the rather mysterious name of "Chardri." It is intended to bring Chardri's work to the attention of a much wider range of readers than he currently enjoys.

Durham University's Department of English Studies and Institute of Medieval and Early Modern Studies provided a stimulating and supportive environment throughout the duration of this project. I am particularly grateful to my fellow medievalists in English Studies, Corinne Saunders, Elizabeth Archibald, David Ashurst and Mike Huxtable, all of whom have given me more help and encouragement over the years than I can possibly measure or repay.

Various versions of these translations have been shared since 2007 with Durham undergraduate students taking my "special topic" module 'From Conquest to Plague: English Literature, 1066–1348'. I owe thanks to all of them for their comments and criticisms.

A term's research-leave granted by the University in Epiphany 2013 enabled me to bring this book to completion.

Beyond Durham, I am grateful to Judith Weiss and John Hirsh, both of whom gave me useful advice at key points in the project's development. Most of all, I am indebted to the Series Editors, Thelma Fenster and Jocelyn Wogan-Browne, both for offering me the opportunity to translate all of Chardri's works together in the first place, and for suggesting so many valuable improvements to my text.

I should also like to thank the Bodleian Library; the British Library; Jesus College, Oxford; and the Vatican Library for allowing me access to manuscripts in their care.

Finally, Kate Thomas and our daughters, Carrie and Imogen Thomas, have as usual made everything possible — and everything worthwhile.

Neil Cartlidge

ABBREVIATIONS AND SHORT REFERENCES

Manuscripts

C London, British Library MS Cotton Caligula A. 9 (*Josaphaz*, fols 195r–216r; *Seven Sleepers*, fols 216v–229v; *Little Debate*, fols 249r–261v) = "**L**" in Koch and Merrilees

J Oxford, Jesus College MS 29, part 2 (*Seven Sleepers*, fols 207v–222v; *Josaphaz*, fols 223r–244r; *Little Debate*, fols 244v–257v) = "**O**" in Koch and Merrilees

V Rome, Vatican Library MS Reg. lat. 1659, part 2 (*Little Debate*, fols 91r–98r)

Series

ANTS   Anglo-Norman Text Society
EETS OS   Early English Text Society Original Series
EETS SS   Early English Text Society Supplementary Series

Editions of Chardri's works

Koch
Chardry's Josaphaz, Set Dormanz und Petit Plet: Dichtungen in der Anglo-Normannischen Mundart des XIII. Jahrhunderts, ed. John Koch (Heilbronn: Henninger, 1879)

Merrilees, *Little Debate*
Le Petit Plet, ed. Brian S. Merrilees, ANTS 20 (Oxford: Blackwell for ANTS, 1970): includes an image of **C**, fol. 250r, containing *Petit Plet*, vv. 100–171

Merrilees, *Seven Sleepers*
La Vie des Set Dormanz by Chardri, ed. Brian S. Merrilees, ANTS 35 (London: Westfield College for ANTS, 1977): includes an image of **C**, fol. 216v, containing *Set Dormanz*, vv. 1–63

Rutledge
T.J.S. Rutledge, 'A Critical Edition of *La vie de seint Josaphaz*; a Thirteenth-Century Poem by the Anglo-

Norman Poet Chardri,' Ph.D. diss., University of
Toronto, 1973

Editions of other CJ-texts

Brook & Lesley	*Laʒamon: 'Brut'*, ed. G.L. Brook and R.F. Leslie, 2 vols, EETS OS 250, 277 (London, 1963, 1978).
Cartlidge, *O&N*	*The Owl and the Nightingale: Text and Translation*, ed./trans. Neil Cartlidge, (Exeter: Exeter University Press, 2001, repr. 2003)
Ker	*The Owl and the Nightingale: Reproduced in Facsimile from the Surviving Manuscripts: Jesus College Oxford 29 and British Museum Cotton Caligula A. IX*, ed. Neil Ker, EETS OS 251 (Oxford, 1963): includes an image of J, fol. 257v, containing *Le Petit Plet*, vv. 1736–80
Morris	*An Old English Miscellany containing A Bestiary, Kentish Sermons, Proverbs of Alfred, Religious Poems of the Thirteenth Century*, ed. Richard Morris, EETS OS 49 (London, 1872)

Sources and Analogues

Allgeier	Arthur Allgeier, "Untersuchungen zur syrischen Überlieferung der Siebenschläferlegende," *Oriens Christianus* N.S. 4 (1915): 279–97, 5 (1915): 10–59, 6 (1916): 1–43, 7/8 (1918) 33–87: contains an edition and translation (into German) of the earliest Syriac version of the Seven Sleepers legend
BJL	*Barlaam et Iosaphat: versión vulgata latina: con la traducción castellana de Juan de Arce Solorceno (1608)*, ed./trans. (into Spanish) Óscar de la Cruz Palma, Nueva Roma 12 (Consejo Superior de Investigaciones Científicas, Universitat Autònoma de Barcelona: Madrid, 2001)
Distiches of Cato	*Minor Latin Poets*, ed./trans. J. Wight Duff and Arnold M. Duff, (London: Heinemann, 1934) 585–639; cf. also *Le Livre de Catun*, ed. Tony Hunt, ANTS Plain Text Series 11 (London: ANTS, 1994)
Elliott	*The Apocryphal New Testament: A Collection of Apocryphal Christian Literature in an English Translation based*

	on *M.R. James*, trans. J.K. Elliott (Oxford: Clarendon Press, 1993; repr. 2009)
Hirsh	*Barlam and Iosaphat: A Middle English Life of Buddha: Edited from MS Peterhouse 257*, ed. John C. Hirsh, EETS OS 290 (Oxford, 1986)
L$_1$	"Passio Septem Dormientium," ed. Michael Hüber, *Beitrag zur Visionsliteratur und Siebenschläferlegende des Mittelalters: Eine literargeschichtliche Untersuchung: I. Teil: Texte*, Beilage zum Jahresbericht des humanistischen Gymnasiums Metten (1902–1903), pp. 39–78
Lang, *Balavariani*	David Marshall Lang, trans., *The Balavariani (Barlaam and Josaphat): A Tale from the Christian East translated from the Old Georgian*, with an introduction by Ilia V. Abuladze (London: Allen and Unwin, 1966)
Palmer	*'De remediis fortuitorum' and the Elizabethans*, ed. R.G. Palmer (Chicago: Institute of Elizabethan Studies, 1953)
Ryan	*Jacobus de Voragine: The Golden Legend: Readings on the Saints*, trans. William Granger Ryan, 2 vols. (Princeton: Princeton University Press, 1993)

Cited Works of Reference

AND	*Anglo-Norman Dictionary*, ed. David Trotter et al., at www.anglo-norman.net
BHL	*Bibliotheca hagiographica latina antiquae et mediae aetatis*, ed. Société des Bollandistes, Subsidia Hagiographica 6 (Bruxelles: Société des Bollandistes, 1898-1901), with supplements in Subsidia Hagiographica 12 (1911) and 70 (1986)
Dean	Ruth J. Dean, with the collaboration of Maureen B.M. Boulton, *Anglo-Norman Literature: A Guide to Texts and Manuscripts* (London: ANTS, 1999): Chardri's works are items 265 (*Little Debate*), 532 (*Josaphaz*), and 534 (*Seven Sleepers*)
Morawski, *Proverbes*	Joseph Morawski, *Proverbes français antérieurs au XVe siècle*, Classiques français du moyen âge 47 (Paris: Champion, 1925)
Morawski, *Diz*	Joseph Morawski, *Les Diz et Proverbes des Sages* (Paris: Les Presses universitaires de France, 1924)

OED   *Oxford English Dictionary*, ed. James A.H. Murray et
                                 al. (London, 1884-1928); Supplement (1933); 2nd ed.
                                 (1989); now online at www.oed.com
PL   *Patrologia Latina*, ed. Jacques-Paul Migne, 217 vols.
                                 (1844–1855), plus 4 vols. of indexes (1862–65); now
                                 online at http://pld.chadwyck.co.uk

Frequently Cited Studies

Cartlidge, "Composition"   Neil Cartlidge, "The Composition and Social
                                 Context of MSS Jesus College Oxford 29 (II)
                                 and BL Cotton Caligula A.ix," *Medium Ævum*
                                 66 (1997): 250–69
Cartlidge, "Imagining X"   Neil Cartlidge, "Imagining X: a Lost Early Ver-
                                 nacular Miscellany," in *Imagining the Book*, Medi-
                                 eval Texts and Cultures of Northern Europe 7,
                                 ed. John J. Thompson and Stephen Kelly (Turn-
                                 hout: Brepols, 2005), 31–44
Cartlidge, *Medieval Marriage*   Neil Cartlidge, *Medieval Marriage: Literary
                                 Approaches 1100–1300* (Cambridge: Brewer,
                                 1997)
Hüber, *Wanderlegende*   Michael Hüber, *Die Wanderlegende von den
                                 Siebenschläfern: Eine literargeschichtliche Untersuc-
                                 hung* (Leipzig: Harrassowitz, 1910)
Peri, *Religionsdisput*   Hiram Peri, *Der Religionsdisput der Barlaam-
                                 Legende: ein Motiv abendländischer Dichtung*, Acta
                                 Salmanticensia, Filosofía y Letras vol. 14, no. 3
                                 (Salamanca: University of Salamanca, 1959)
Sonet   Jean Sonet, *Le Roman de Barlaam et Josaphat*,
                                 2 volumes (vol. 1: Louvain: Bibliothèque de
                                 l'Université, 1949; vol. 2: Namur: Bibliothèque
                                 de la Faculté de Philosophie et Lettres/Paris:
                                 Vrin, 1950)

All quotations from the Bible are taken from the Douai-Rheims translation of
the Vulgate, which is available online at www.drbo.org.

INTRODUCTION

Chardri's Significance

The man who called himself "Chardri" is one of the most distinctive, self-assured, and entertaining of all medieval English writers before Chaucer, but his work is currently so little known that he barely features in literary histories of this period. It is difficult to imagine that this would have been the case had he chosen to write in Middle English, rather than the French of England. Had he used the "national" vernacular, then the appeal of his work would surely have been generally recognised long ago, and he would perhaps have been a relatively canonical figure by now. Certainly, no assessment of the richness and sophistication of English literary culture in the thirteenth and fourteenth centuries can claim to be entirely complete unless it takes Chardri's work into account.

Chardri explicitly identifies himself as the author of two poems that offer particularly free and imaginative retellings of legends about Christian saints. Both of these legends are among the most remarkable products of the complex cultural interchanges that took place between East and West throughout the Middle Ages. *The Life of the Seven Sleepers* (*La Vie des Set Dormanz*) recounts the legend of seven young men from the city of Ephesus (in what is now the south-western corner of Turkey), who are rescued from persecution at the hands of the third-century Roman emperor Decius only by a miraculous sleep that lasts for over three and a half centuries. This story was very widely current in medieval Christianity, but it has an important place in Islamic tradition as well, for it appears in the Qur'an.[1] Its central motif, that of the preternaturally long sleep, remains current in western culture in the form of tales like Charles Perrault's "Sleeping Beauty in the Wood" and Washington Irving's "Rip van Winkle."[2] Chardri's other hagiographical work, *The Life of St. Josaphaz* (*La Vie de seint*

---

[1] Sura 18: in *The Qur'an: A Modern English Version*, trans. Majid Fakhry (Reading: Garnet, 1997), 178–85, esp. 178–79. See further Louis Massignon, "Les 'Sept Dormants' Apocalypse d'Islam," in *Opera Minora*, ed. Y. Moubarac, 3 vols. (Beirut: Dar Al-Maaref, 1963), 3: 104–118.

[2] For Perrault's "La Belle au Bois Dormant," see *Perrault: Contes*, ed. Pierre Collinet (Paris: Gallimard, 1981), 129–30, trans. Christopher Betts, *Charles Perrault: The Complete Fairy Tales* (Oxford: Oxford University Press, 2009), 83–97. For an edition of "Rip van Winkle," see *American Gothic: An Anthology 1787–1916*, ed. Charles L. Crow (Oxford:

Josaphaz), is a version of a legend derived from early Buddhism.[3] Its protagonist, Josaphaz, is essentially a Christianised version of the Buddha himself. Here he appears as a beautiful young prince of India, who is converted to Christianity by a wise man called Barlaam, and then subjected to a series of deceptions and temptations at the hands of his doting but tyrannical father. Eventually, Josaphaz manages to escape from his father's control, and he goes on to establish his new faith, Christianity, as the national religion of his country. The third of the three texts translated here, *The Little Debate* (*Le Petit Plet*), is a philosophical dialogue conducted by two idealised figures, an Old Man and a Young Man, who together present lively and dramatically contrasting responses to the problem of human suffering in the world. The ascription of this text to Chardri has not been challenged since it was first suggested in 1800.

As it happens, these three poems survive together in medieval manuscripts only in conjunction with two Middle English texts that have occupied prominent positions in the literary history of England for over 150 years: *The Owl and the Nightingale* and Laȝamon's *Brut*.[4] *The Owl and the Nightingale* is the earliest extant long comic poem in the English language; and it survives only in the same two medieval books that also preserve all three of the texts ascribed to Chardri. Laȝamon's *Brut* is the earliest extant English-language version of Geoffrey of Monmouth's legendary history of the island of Britain (and therefore the first English-language text to feature appearances by such figures as King Arthur, Old King Cole, Cymbeline, and Lear). It too survives alongside Chardri's works in one of these two books. As a writer, Chardri bears comparison with the *Owl*-poet in his command of energetic and idiomatic dialogue, his eye for colourful

Blackwell, 1999), 19–29. See also Stith Thompson, *Motif Index of Folk Literature*, 6 vols (Bloomington IN: Indiana University Press, 1955–1958), 2: 349–50.

[3] According to Jean Sonet (59), "On ne peut plus parler de ressemblance, il faut conclure à l'identité . . . C'est la même légende qui a survécu pendant tant de siècles et dans des milieux aussi différents" ("One can no longer talk about a resemblance [between the *Josaphaz*-legend and the Buddha's]: one has to accept that they are identical . . . This is the same legend that has survived across so many centuries and in such a diverse set of milieux"). More cautiously, Óscar de la Cruz (**BJL**, 24) emphasises that the legend's originally Buddhist core acquired a number of distinct accretions: "Es evidente, por lo menos, que el admisible origen budista del [*Barlaam et Iosaphat*] sólo hace referencia a una pequeña parte del total de la novela (los cincos primeros capítulos)" ("It is evident, at least, that only a small part of the whole narrative (the first five chapters) can legitimately be referred to a Buddhist origin"). The name Josaphaz is ultimately a corruption of the phrase "Bodhi-sattva" ("'the Buddha-elect', or 'one who aspires to be Buddha'": see Hirsh, 183; de la Cruz, **BJL**, 15). Its form is likely to have been influenced by the name of the biblical king Josaphat (Matt. 1: 8), as Hirsh notes.

[4] *The Owl and the Nightingale* first appeared in a modern edition in 1838 and the *Brut* in 1847. Both have been established presences in histories of English literature ever since. For editions, see Cartlidge, *O&N*, and Brook & Lesley.

detail, his lively sense of humour, and his subtlety and variety of tone. He also bears comparison with Laȝamon in his control of narrative pace and structure, his relish for the exotic and the marvellous, and the breadth of his geographical and historical horizons. However, his claims to literary-critical attention go far beyond simply offering an Anglo-French context for these two Middle English poems. He is a fluent, acute and attractive poet in his own right: never prolix or ponderous, despite the avowedly moral purposes for which he wrote, and capable of finding moments of fun even among the conventional horrors of hagiography.[5]

All three of his works recognise, and often movingly dramatise, the human experience of anxiety, doubt, bereavement, and fear, but perhaps the most distinctive characteristic that they have in common is what seems to be a remarkable commitment to optimism. For Chardri it is axiomatic that God's government is always benign, so that serving God with a good heart is inevitably a kind of win-win situation.[6] Even though life on earth is naturally beset with temptations and adversities, yet in the end he appears to endorse the view that "no one can be in the wrong if he strives to cheer himself up."[7] It is perhaps in line with this rather sprightly attitude towards life that he shows such a pronounced interest in the powers and prerogatives of youth, suggesting at one point that he himself is still notably young. This could perhaps be taken as a tongue-in-cheek remark, a joke at his own expense rather than a biographical fact, but in either case it suggests considerable confidence in his own identity.[8] This self-confidence also extends to the assertion in the *Little Debate* of what looks like a rather exaggerated sense of English national superiority (at vv. 1255–72). No doubt this too is meant to be provocative, but it is still striking that it is Chardri who gives voice to it, rather

---

[5] Not many literary historians have ever offered a judgment on Chardri's qualities as a writer. Among those who have are Sonet, who says (154) that "l'auteur a un style agréable, alerte, imagé: sa composition se lit sans fatigue car il sait noter le détail qui pique l'attention" ("the author has an agreeable style, lively and colourful: his compositions are not tiring to read, because he knows how to make use of those details that sustain attention"); and Josef Merk (in *Die literarische Gestaltung der altfranzösischen Heilegenleben bis Ende des 12. Jahrhunderts* [Affoltern am Albis: Weiss, 1946], 228–30), for whom "Chardry beherrscht die knappe, sachliche Erzählung, die treffend nur das zum Verständnis der Geschichte Notwendige bringt . . . Chardry besitzt also eine knappe, aber angenehme und flüssige Erzählungsweise" ("Chardri is a master of the brisk, factual narrative that deftly includes only what is necessary for understanding the story . . . he possesses a brisk, but pleasant and fluent, narrative style").

[6] See, e.g., *Josaphaz*, vv. 2917–20: "Whoever wishes to serve God will receive blessings both on heaven and on earth—because as long as he lives he will be well liked by people here on earth, and when he dies he will go directly to God."

[7] *Little Debate*, vv. 1765–66. Chardri's poetry also gives voice to the idea that being happy is the best way to deal with one's enemies: "The more that you're happy, the more annoyed you'll make your enemies" (*Little Debate*, vv. 1673–74).

[8] *Little Debate*, vv. 18–20.

than Laȝamon or the *Owl*-poet, given that he is the only of these three poets *not* to write in the English language.

Manuscripts, Transmission, and Date of Composition

The two medieval books that contain all three of Chardri's works are London, British Library MS Cotton Caligula A.9 (henceforth C) and Oxford, Jesus College MS 29, part 2 (J).[9] As well as *The Owl and the Nightingale*, C and J also preserve six other Middle English poems, all of them religious poems of a decidedly austere cast: *Death's Wither-Clench, An Orison to our Lady, Doomsday, The Last Day, The Ten Abuses*, and *A Little Sooth Sermon*. A seventh such text now found only in C (*Will and Wit*) probably once existed once in J, even though it is now lost.[10] All of these works together form what I have elsewhere suggested could usefully be described as the "CJ-group."[11] Outside this group, C also preserves one of the two surviving copies of Laȝamon's *Brut* (the only one of these two to survive the Ashburnham House fire of 1731 without any significant damage),[12] as well as a brief survey of English kings up to the accession of King Henry III of England, which is written in French prose.[13] Apart from the CJ-group, J also contains a widely circulated French poem on manners and morals (the *Doctrinal*

---

[9] For descriptions and discussions of these manuscripts and their contents, see Ker, ix–xx; Betty Hill, "The history of Jesus College, Oxford, MS 29," *Medium Aevum* 32 (1963): 203–13; Merrilees, *Little Debate*, xi–xiv; Margaret Laing, *Catalogue of Sources for a Linguistic Atlas of Early Middle English* (Cambridge: Brewer, 1993), 69–70; Cartlidge, "Composition"; Cartlidge, *Medieval Marriage*, 160–99; and Cartlidge, *O&N*, xxvii–xxxi; John Scahill, "Trilingualism in Early Middle English Miscellanies: Languages and Literature," *Yearbook of English Studies* 33 (2003): 18–32, esp. 28–30. In the case of J, the manuscript in question forms only the second part of the extant book, having been bound with an "unrelated manuscript of much later date" (Ker, xi). J's copies of Chardri's works have suffered from some significant damage. Lines 751–873 and 1382–1509 of *Josaphaz* and vv. 440–567 of the *Little Debate* are all missing due to the loss of leaves after fols 228, 232 and 247 respectively (Ker, x, xii).

[10] The loss is probably due to the disappearance of a folio that once existed before what is now J, fol. 181. All these texts are edited by Morris, 156–92; see also Carleton Brown, *English Lyrics of the XIIIth Century* (Oxford: Clarendon Press, 1932), 15–18, 42–54, 56–60, 65, and Karl Reichl, *Religiöse Dichtung im englischen Hochmittelalter: Untersuchung und Edition der Handschrift B.14.39 des Trinity College in Cambridge* (Munich: Fink, 1973), 408–36, 470–75.

[11] Cartlidge, *Medieval Marriage*, 160.

[12] The two manuscripts are edited together (in a facing-page format) by Brook & Lesley.

[13] *Li Rei de Engleterre: ein anglonormannischer Geschichtsauszug*, ed. John Koch (Berlin: Gärtner, 1886); see also Christian Foltys, *Brutus, Li Rei de Engleterre, Le Livere de Reis de Engleterre* (Berlin: Free University of Berlin, 1962); Dean, no. 13.

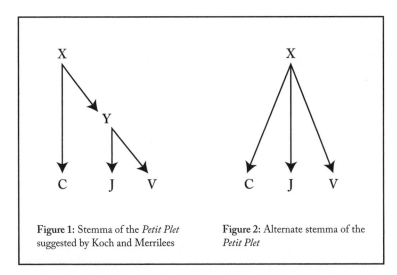

Figure 1: Stemma of the *Petit Plet* suggested by Koch and Merrilees

Figure 2: Alternate stemma of the *Petit Plet*

Sauvage),[14] a dramatization of the confrontation between the Four Daughters of God taken from the first part of the Anglo-Norman *Vie de Tobie* by Guillaume le Clerc,[15] and a number of other shorter Middle English poems, all of them either moral or religious. They include *The Passion of Our Lord*, *The Proverbs of Alfred*, the *Poema Morale*, and the *Luue-Ron* of Thomas of Hales.[16] There is also a third copy of the *Petit Plet*—and of the *Petit Plet* only, not either of Chardri's saints' lives—in the Vatican Library, MS Reg. 1659 (henceforth V).[17] Here Chardri's poem is preserved along with a number of proverbs about women and a 414-fragment of a didactic poem called the *Petite Philosophie*.[18]

Of these three manuscripts, C and J can be shown to derive from a common exemplar, which is conventionally described as "X."[19] Koch and Merrilees suggest that another lost exemplar lies between J and X, and that V was also derived

---

[14] *Doctrinal Sauvage*, ed. Aimo Sakari, Studia Philologica Jyväskyläensia 3 (Jyväskylä: University of Jyväskylä, 1967); Dean, no. 244.

[15] Ed. R. Reinsch, in *Archiv für das Studium der neueren Sprachen und Literaturen* 62 (1879): 375–96; Dean, no. 468.

[16] For these Middle English poems, see Morris, 37–155.

[17] For a description, see Merrilees, *Little Debate*, xiv–xv. As with J, V makes up only the second part of the book into which it is now bound, which is "composed of two distinct and originally separate parts" (Merrilees, *Little Debate*, xiv).

[18] *La Petite Philosophie*, ed. W.H. Trethewey, ANTS 1 (Oxford: Blackwell, 1939); Dean, no. 325.

[19] The textual evidence provided by Chardri's texts supports this assumption. As Merrilees points out there are "probably errors common to all three manuscripts, which suggest existence of a faulty copy (X) prior to [the three surviving manuscripts] but later than the original"; and there are similar "common faults" in the two saints' lives

from it; but they offer no very strong evidence that such a manuscript ("Y") ever existed, and it seems to me most likely that C and J were both copied directly from X, and that V too derives independently from X.[20] In other words, the stemma depicted in Figure 2 above seems to me to provide just as plausible an explanation of the evidence as the one depicted in Figure 1.

In the absence of any firm evidence for Chardri's identity, it is difficult to say when exactly he was at work. His poems cannot be any younger than the manuscripts in which they survive, but none of these, unfortunately, can be dated with any precision. V is generally described as a fourteenth-century manuscript, while C and J have been ascribed to the second half of the thirteenth century. In fact, the evidence that C and J were written before 1300 (which is entirely palaeographical) hardly seems clear or decisive enough to rule out the possibility that they too are fourteenth-century books.[21] This means that, as things stand, it is impossible to say more than that Chardri's career should probably placed somewhere in the thirteenth century.[22] There is no evidence at all for the order in

---

(Merrilees, *Seven Sleepers*, 9; Rutledge, 3). On X, and its likely appearance, see Cartlidge, "Imagining X."

[20] Merrilees, *Little Debate*, xvi–xvii; Koch, ix–xi. Merrilees lists "ten evident errors" that he thinks prove that J and V "form a solid group against" C, but this seems to me a very slender basis on which to postulate the existence of a lost intermediate exemplar between X and JV. It may indicate only that in certain respects the C-scribe was willing to handle the lost common exemplar more intelligently than the scribes of the other two manuscripts, solving textual problems in X that they do not. It might seem that an obstacle to my position can be found at v. 378, where V writes two lines not found in C (or printed in either editors' text), and J writes just the first of these two lines: *Morir mestut certes bieau frere / Mes io ne say en quele manere* V; *Murir mestet certes beu frere* J. This might seem to suggest that JV have a descent separate from C. In fact, it seems to me just as likely that the cause of this set of variations is an ambiguity in X. Accidentally copying v. 339 again at this point ("Morir m'estoet certes, beau frere", as Merrilees prints it), the X-scribe somehow failed to cancel it clearly. The result was that J copied it anyway, even though there is no rhyming line for it, and V not only copied it, but then invented a (rather feeble) rhyming line to go with it. Only C recognised the line as an error, and (correctly) omitted it. See further Cartlidge, "Imagining X," 34–37.

[21] The two manuscripts must be younger than *The Owl and the Nightingale*, which I have argued may well have been written after 1272: see Neil Cartlidge, "The Date of *The Owl and the Nightingale*," *Medium Ævum* 65 (1996): 230–47 and "Nicholas of Guildford and *The Owl and the Nightingale*," *Medium Ævum* 79 (2010): 14–24.

[22] Rutledge asserts (1) that "linguistic evidence fixes the date of composition of *La Vie de Seint Josaphaz* at between 1190 and 1220" and that "non-linguistic internal evidence suggests 'termini' of 1212 and 1215." The linguistic evidence is hardly clear enough to permit any such precision; and the "non-linguistic internal evidence" that Rutledge adduces seems to me wholly unconvincing. It means placing far too much weight on the reference to the city of Pavia in *Josaphaz*, v. 722; and on the fact that Chardri's works "do not seem influenced by" (110) the outcomes of the Fourth Lateran Council of 1215.

which he wrote his three surviving works.[23] In the absence of any better principle, they appear in this book in the same order as they do in the manuscript used as the base for all of the editions of Chardri's work so far: that is, **C**.

Authorship and Implied Audience

Nothing is known about Chardri apart from what the poems themselves tell us. There is no historical record of anyone called "Chardri"; and in itself the name makes no sense. However, it is not a place-name. It is most obviously interpreted as an anagrammatic inversion of the two syllables of the name "Richard".[24] However, this is not much of a clue to Chardri's real identity, since, as it happens, Richard was an extremely common name in thirteenth-century England. It may have been some kind of stage-name or *nom de plume*. In form, it perhaps refers implicitly to the several versions of the Tristan-and-Isolt legend in which Tristan is said to hide his identity by adopting a pseudonym formed from a reversal of the syllables of his name (i.e. "Tantris").[25] When he does so, he also takes on the role of courtly entertainer or fool; and it may be that, in basing own pseudonym on the model of "Tantris", Chardri was pointedly drawing attention to his own social role. It is possibly no coincidence that Tristan appears prominently among the examples of morally dubious subject-matter that he offers at the beginning of the *Seven Sleepers*.[26]

Merrilees is more cautious, suggesting only that "the linguistic characteristics of the *Petit Plet* allow a tentative dating near the turn of the twelfth century" (*Little Debate*, xxxii) and that "the language of the *Set Dormanz* gives no grounds for believing its date is much earlier or later" (*Seven Sleepers*, 7).

[23] Merrilees is prepared to speculate on this issue in *Seven Sleepers*, 7. He suggests the order *Josaphaz–Seven Sleepers–Little Debate*, on the grounds that the progressively freer treatment of sources shown here corresponds with the likely order of composition. He also says that he is "inclined to place the *Set Dormanz* later than *Josaphaz* [. . .] because it seems to reflect the author's greater facility in poetic composition." Rutledge (110–111) prefers *Little Debate–Seven Sleepers–Josaphaz*. He suggests that the *Little Debate* "was probably written either first (judging from its originality) or last, after Chardri had wearied of hagiographies." None of these arguments seems to me particularly compelling.

[24] Merrilees, *Seven Sleepers*, 8.

[25] See, for example, *La Folie Tristan (Berne)*, vv. 124–25 and *La Folie Tristan (Oxford)*, v. 317, both texts ed. Samuel N. Rosenberg in *Early French Tristan Poems*, ed. Norris J. Lacy, 2 vols (Cambridge: Brewer, 1998), 1: 226, 272. *La Folie Tristan (Oxford)* is translated by Judith Weiss in *The Birth of Romance in England: The 'Romance of Horn', The 'Folie Tristan', The 'Lai of Havelock', and 'Amis and Amilun'*, FRETS 4 (Tempe AZ: ACMRS, 2009), 139–53.

[26] *Seven Sleepers*, v. 54.

There seems little doubt that it was for audiences in England that Chardri was working, rather than for ones in France, for he goes out of his way to flatter the English at the expense of the French.[27] He tells us that women who are "full of virtue and kindness, simplicity and good manners, and whose natures are loyal" are much more frequently to be found "in England, than in France."[28] Indeed, he goes on:

> Of all the realms that exist, England is pre-eminent. And in what way, do you think? In every kind of enjoyment and elegant behaviour! If the women there are so well brought up, it shouldn't be any surprise if there are lots of knights there (together with all the other men who follow them), who are superlatively valiant, elegant and noble — except that heavy drinking often mars the decorousness of their lives.[29]

Chardri's praise for the inhabitants of England is clearly far too extravagant to be taken entirely seriously, but it is still perhaps francophone audiences in England who are much more likely to have enjoyed it than any one else. Even the one flaw that Chardri pretends to be willing to admit, a tendency towards *beverie* (or "heavy drinking"), is presented implicitly as a mere peccadillo, and perhaps an excusably sociable one too in the kind of convivial contexts in which poetry like Chardri's is likely to have been performed.[30] It need not follow from this that Chardri was necessarily born in England himself, or that he always thought of himself as English. Indeed there is some evidence to the contrary in the way that he attributes to the English (*li Engleis*) what seems to be a particularly crass proverb: "a dog, wife or horse should be praised in proportion to how much affection you have for it."[31] Perhaps Chardri is suggesting that the kind of bluff, outdoorsy chauvinism implied by this saying's equation between dogs, horses, and wives is a characteristically "English" attitude. However, what is most significant here is that he specifically says *"the* English" ("li Engleis"), not *"we* English" ("nos Engleis"). Whoever "the English" are, it is not a group that he himself identifies with at this point; and the most likely explanation for this, I think, is that here *li Engleis* refers specifically to those who *speak* English — for whom English is a preferred language in a way that it is not for him. What Chardri emphasises is that this is a proverb that he has translated from the English language. In other words what is at issue at this point is not different national identities (the inhabitants of England as opposed to the inhabitants of France), but different linguistic communities (those who speak English as opposed to those who speak French).

---

[27] The one possible indication that Chardri knew something of the continent as well is his reference to St. Riquier in the *Little Debate*, v. 299.

[28] *Little Debate*, vv. 1251–56.

[29] *Little Debate*, vv. 1263–72.

[30] See note to *Little Debate*, vv. 1271–72.

[31] *Little Debate*, vv. 1279–80.

The implication of this, in turn, is that, as a French-speaker living in England, Chardri was happy to be "English" *vis-à-vis* the inhabitants of France, and "not English" *vis-à-vis* all those in England who did not speak French. Such ambivalence was by no means atypical of England's French-speaking communities.[32]

The literary horizons of Chardri's intended audiences are implied, to some extent, by the range of supposedly entertaining but morally unimproving tales that he lists in the *Seven Sleepers* as being in competition with his own work. He refers first of all to the "fables of Ovid", which is presumably a reference to Ovid's *Metamorphoses*. Then comes a reference to "Tristan" (as we have seen), together with another name from chivalric romance, "Galerun." After that come two figures from medieval animal-fiction, Renart (the fox) and Hersente (the she-wolf).[33] At the end of *Josaphaz*, Chardri also admits that most people would more readily hear about Roland, Oliver, and the battles fought by Charlemagne's comrades-in-arms (the "duze pers"), than about the passion of Christ.[34] If Chardri's original audiences really did spend a significant part of their time on texts of this kind (when they were not listening to Chardri himself, that is), then they themselves can hardly have been professionally religious.[35] In other words, they

---

[32] This point is effectively demonstrated by Ian Short, in "'Tam Angli quam Franci': Self-Definition in Anglo-Norman England," *Anglo-Norman Studies* 18 (1996) 153–75. See also Elizabeth Salter, *English and International: Studies in the Literature, Art and Patronage of Medieval England*, ed. Derek Pearsall and Nicolette Zeeman (Cambridge: Cambridge University Press, 1988), 1–28; and Hugh M. Thomas, *The English and the Normans: Ethnic Hostility, Assimilation, and Identity 1066–c.1220* (Oxford: Oxford University Press, 2005), 377–90; Ardis Butterfield, *The Familiar Enemy: Chaucer, Language, and Nation in the Hundred Years War* (Oxford: Oxford University Press, 2009), 3–35. There is also some evidence for the extent of Chardri's geographical horizons in the list of Christian lands that he gives in *Josaphaz*, vv. 58–65: "Lombardy and France, England and Normandy, Brittany and Hungary, Burgundy and Germany, Russia and Spain, Lorraine and Poitou, Flanders and Anjou, Ireland and the Auvergne."

[33] See further *Seven Sleepers*, notes to vv. 51 and 54–55.

[34] *Josaphaz*, vv. 2934–35. I have elsewhere argued that "Even in making a claim for the greater value of hagiography, Chardri's tone is casually dismissive rather than morally censorious; this might well suggest the stance of a professional entertainer, necessarily accommodating self-advertisement with respect for the various tastes of his patrons" (Cartlidge, "Composition," 253). As I also pointed out in this essay, one of the Middle English texts in J ("The Passion of Our Lord," ed. Morris, 37–57) likewise refers to the Twelve Peers in the course of claiming to offer edifying matter ("Nis hit nouht of karlemeyne ne of þe Duzeper" (v. 3). It was perhaps a conventional motif: see also Walter Map, *De nugis curialium*, ed. and trans. M.R. James, R.A.B. Mynors and C.N.L. Brooke (Oxford: Clarendon, 1983), 404.

[35] Hiram Peri states that Chardri himself was "obviously no clergyman" ("offenbar kein Geistlicher": *Religionsdisput*, 54), which I think oversteps the limits of the evidence. Chardri's works may seem to be pitched at a lay audience, but this is no reason for thinking he himself must have been a member of the laity.

were probably lay-people; and the very fact that they are imagined as having so much opportunity for leisure-time reading suggests that they were also relatively wealthy and of relatively high social status. The likely implication of this is that the intended audience belonged to the aristocracy.[36] This, of course, is also a deduction that could be made from the very fact that Chardri chose to write in French at all, since French, as it was used in England in this period, was largely a language of privilege and power.

It is only in *Josaphaz* and *Seven Sleepers* that the author explicitly identifies himself as "Chardri";[37] which means that the case for Chardri's authorship of the *Little Debate* is essentially only circumstantial, but it is nevertheless very strong.[38] It rests, firstly, on the fact that, in all of the manuscripts in which *Josaphaz* and *Seven Sleepers* are known to have existed, the *Little Debate* was copied along with them;[39] and, secondly, on a number of linguistic, stylistic and thematic similarities between the three poems. For example, the historical phonology implied by the three texts' use of rhyme is consistent enough both to suggest that they could all have been written by one individual, and to differentiate them from other thirteenth-century Anglo-Norman works.[40] There are a number of vocabulary items common to both Chardri's saints' lives and the *Little Debate* that are either

---

[36] Some support for this might also be perceived in the rather snobbish views on the flightiness of cityfolk that is expressed by the narrator in *Seven Sleepers*, vv. 1221–24. Socially elitist attitudes are also expressed by other voices in Chardri's work: for example, the proverb cited by the Young Man in *Little Debate*, vv. 837–38, and Decius's assertion of the distinctness of the aristocracy (by education as well as birth) in *Seven Sleepers*, vv. 296–302. However, the sharp criticism of *les hauz* ("the great") in *Seven Sleepers*, vv. 1857–80, might be taken to indicate that Chardri's access to the aristocracy did not extend to the very highest ranks, the magnates (Cartlidge, "Composition," 256).

[37] *Josaphaz*, v. 2953; *Seven Sleepers*, v. 1892. Chardri's claims to authorship of these two poems is also supported by the fact that they have much in common, including the duplication or near-duplication of whole lines (e.g. *Seven Sleepers*, v. 154/*Josaphaz*, vv. 819, 2773; *Seven Sleepers*, vv. 557–8/*Josaphaz*, vv. 1349–50; *Seven Sleepers*, vv. 197–98/*Josaphaz*, vv. 2063–64), some unusual turns of phrase (e.g. *Seven Sleepers*, v. 1868/*Josaphaz*, v. 2188) and some distinctive arguments phrased in rather similar ways (e.g. *Seven Sleepers*, vv. 617–20/*Josaphaz*, vv. 1943–44; *Seven Sleepers*, vv. 161–64/*Josaphaz*, vv. 145–48).

[38] Chardri's authorship of the *Little Debate* has not been challenged since it was first suggested by the Abbé de la Rue in 1800 (Merrilees, *Little Debate*, xxviii).

[39] These manuscripts include, not just the surviving manuscripts C and J, and their putative exemplar X, but also the lost Titchfield Abbey manuscript, Q.III, which, when listed in 1400 contained a *Vita septem dormientium*, a *Vita sancti Iosaphat*, and an *Altercacio inter iuuentutem et senectutem*. See Cartlidge, "Composition," 251, and "Imagining X," 40. For editions of the catalogue, see R.M. Wilson, "The Medieval Library of Titchfield Abbey," *Proceedings of the Leeds Philosophical and Literary Society* 5 (1940): 150–77, 252–76; David N. Bell, *The Libraries of the Cistercians, Gilbertines and Premonstratensians*, Corpus of British Medieval Library Catalogues 3 (London, 1992), 180–254.

[40] Merrilees, *Little Debate*, xxix–xxx.

relatively unusual or else used in relatively unusual ways.[41] There are some recurring turns of phrase, not in themselves so distinctive as to rule out the possibility of multiple authorship, but still supporting the general impression that all three works share the same idiolect.[42] Sometimes there are coincidences of phrasing even in contexts that are otherwise rather different. For example, the *Little Debate*'s (not very consoling) observation that a dead person will rot no matter how sweet his diet happened to be comes remarkably close (in formulation, if not in sentiment) to Maximian's warning to Decius in the *Seven Sleepers*, that his idols will rot and he will die, no matter how he succours them.[43] All three poems have identifiable sources, but in each case they are reworked with remarkable freedom and self-confidence. Most striking of all, however, is the way in which the three poems share a number of very distinct thematic emphases.

Thematic Emphases

Chardri seems to have been particularly interested in the idea of a natural association between youth and wisdom. The *Little Debate* is explicitly presented as a dialogue between a Young Man ("L'Enfant") and an Old Man ("Li Veillard")—in what is perhaps a significant departure from his source, where the contestants are called *Ratio* and *Sensus* (or "Reason" and "Sensuality"). In Chardri's poem, it is the Young Man who proposes to teach the Old Man something of his wisdom, rather than, as one might expect, the other way around. The poem is a particularly striking instance, in other words, of a widespread topos in medieval culture:

---

[41] For example: *waucrer*, "to wander about, drift" in *Little Debate*, v. 1584, and *Josaphaz*, v. 1298; *chanter*, "to persuade, preach, discuss" in *Little Debate*, v. 553, *Seven Sleepers*, v. 877, and *Josaphaz*, vv. 869 etc.; *bataille*, "ordeal, fuss" in *Little Debate*, v. 1144, and *Josaphaz*, v. 1107.

[42] For example: the use of the *cenele* (the haw) as a measure of worthlessness in *Little Debate*, v. 970 and *Josaphaz*, v. 2081; the phrase *fet de dreit le tort*, in *Little Debate*, vv. 1074 and 1220, and *Josaphaz*, v. 133; the juxtaposition of St. Augustine and St. Gregory as representative Church Fathers (*Josaphaz*, v. 7; *Petit Plet*, v. 799). There are a few lines in the *Little Debate* that closely resemble some lines in the *Seven Sleepers*: i.e. *Little Debate*, v. 317 ("Quanke s'en vent, pus s'en revet") and *Seven Sleepers*, v. 817 ("Cum l'un s'en vet, l'autre s'en vent"); *Little Debate*, v. 329 ("Cil ki nasqui, aprés morra") and *Seven Sleepers*, v. 819 ("Cum l'un s'en moert, e l'autre nest"). There is also at least one such correspondence between the *Little Debate* and *Josaphaz*: i.e. *Josaphaz*, vv. 647–48 ("S'il plus vit, murir l'estoet / Nul hoem par el passer ne poet") and *Little Debate*, vv. 330 ("Passer par el pas no porra") and 339 ("Morir m'esteot certes"). None of these coincidences is individually compelling, but the case is cumulative.

[43] *Little Debate*, vv. 447–48: "Vus serrez mort e pus porri, / Ja tant suef ne seez norri"; *Seven Sleepers*, vv. 403–4: "Il purrirunt et vus murrez, / En queu manere les succurrez."

the "puer-senex", the young man who is (paradoxically) wise beyond his years.[44] By the end of the *Little Debate*, the Young Man has succeeded in convincing his opponent of his sagacity, and is duly credited with victory in the debate. The Old Man even acknowledges that:

> Compared to your intelligence and articulacy I certainly don't have any at all. I'm not saying this to you simply as a compliment. You have a great deal of intelligence and good sense. If anyone tells me that a light-hearted young man can't possibly be intelligent and rational, I'd contradict him unhesitatingly, since without doubt this contest has enabled me to find what I was seeking. Good sense suits a young man very well.

Few, if any, readers of the poem are likely to give ready acceptance to the Old Man's assessment of his opponent, for it is undeniable that many of the Young Man's arguments are either relatively commonplace, tendentious, and/or downright callous. Nevertheless it is clearly with the Young Man that Chardri at least pretends to identify most closely at the beginning of this poem, since at this point he promises that none of his readers will "hear any lies from me, for in a young man a great deal of wisdom can often be found."[45] The implication of this is that he too is a "young man", and perhaps a young man of the same thoughtful, yet courtly, cast of mind as the Young Man who speaks in the poem (although of course he may have been playing on the possibility that his intended audience may not have thought him very young at all, or, for that matter, very wise). He is even prepared to defend young people for their readiness to have fun by accusing the elderly of hypocrisy:

> If young people like to have a good time, then you shouldn't blame them too much for their attitude, as long it doesn't get extravagant. You did the same when you were young. It's typical of old people, when they are old, to become utterly hostile to everything they liked when they were young.[46]

All of these emphases are paralleled in the two saints' legends. Youth's liking for a good time is given a remarkably sympathetic treatment even in the legend of *Josaphaz*, despite the unworldly austerity that that text generally advocates:

> No one can blame a youngster for wanting to have fun: this is how it is with everybody when they are young. Unfortunately it often happens that the old reproach the young for doing exactly what they themselves were even more intent on doing, when they were young long ago.[47]

---

[44] See E.R. Curtius, *European Literature and the Latin Middle Ages*, trans. Willard R. Trask (Princeton: Princeton University Press, 1953; repr. 1990), 98–101.

[45] *Little Debate*, vv. 18–20.

[46] *Little Debate*, vv. 111–18. The argument is clearly inspired by the *Distiches of Cato*, I. 16.

[47] *Josaphaz*, vv. 577–83.

Josaphaz is also at least as interested as the *Little Debate* is in the association between youth and wisdom. The saintly prince Josaphaz could certainly be seen as another instance of the "puer-senex." In the end he even succeeds in giving religious instruction to his own father:

> Then the boy was able to give his father instruction, patiently teaching him his beliefs, and baptising him, just as it was his duty to do. The son received his father from the font . . .[48]

From the very outset, however, the text emphasizes Josaphaz's learning and intelligence. His father is determined to stop his son from facing the harsh realities of life, and yet he allows him access to all the learned "arts" (with the exception of theology, of course) and to all the scientific knowledge available in the Orient (vv. 449–52). Quite early on in the story, we see one of Josaphaz's servants taking careful note that the young man is dangerously "astute" (*cointe*, v. 470). Indeed, Josaphaz's success in converting his own father could be seen as the culmination of a series of encounters with conspicuously venerable, learned, elderly men, each of whom might be seen as a temporary or surrogate father-figure.[49] Throughout all this, Josaphaz's own youth is repeatedly emphasised. He is described over and over again in the text as a "boy"—i.e. *enfant*, the same word that is used to denote the Young Man in the *Little Debate*. We are told that Josaphaz was only 25 years old when he gave up his kingdom (vv. 2865–66), but even at the very end of the text, after another 35 years spent in the desert, he is still described as "Josaphaz, l'enfant" (v. 2929).

The youthfulness of Chardri's saintly Seven Sleepers is also explicitly emphasised. They are almost always described as *enfant*, *vaslet* or *bacheler*; and the tyrannical Emperor Decius says that it is their youth that motivates him, initially, to show leniency towards them: "it would seem to me a great pity," he says to Maximianus, the leader of the Seven, "if I were compelled to set my mind on disgracing such very fine young men [*si tres bele juvente*]."[50] Like Josaphaz and the Young Man in the *Little Debate*, Maximianus is explicitly cast as a teacher. At the beginning of the story he attempts to instruct Decius about Christianity (vv. 336–414), but he

---

[48] *Josapahaz*, vv. 2453–56.

[49] These would include Barlaam, the man who introduces Josaphaz to Christianity, as well as the two pagan sages ultimately converted by Josaphaz—Nachor (who converts at v. 1599) and Theodas (who converts at v. 2252). Even the "old man with a beard as white as hawthorn" who predicts Josaphaz's Christianity shortly after his birth (vv. 206–27) might be seen as belonging to this pattern.

[50] *Seven Sleepers*, vv. 422–24. This is a detail that Chardri takes over from his Latin source, L₁ (V, 46), where the emperor tells the Seven that "it would not be just for you to waste your youth in torments or for the charm of your beauty to be dissipated" ("Non enim iustum est perdere aetates vestras in tormentis, et tabefieri decorem pulchritudinis vestrae").

is unsuccessful despite the fact that he is apparently so eloquent (*ben disant*) that he temporarily reduces the tyrannical emperor to an abashed silence. After his miraculous resurrection, 362 years later, we find him asserting that this event should be interpreted specifically as a "demonstration" (*mustrance*) of theological truth. He argues that it was arranged by God "so that the heresy might be exposed, and so that you might be more certain in your belief" (vv. 1693–96).

All three texts also suggest that youth has a particular connection, not just with wisdom, but also with beauty. In the *Little Debate*, the Young Man is associated with beauty to the extent that he is discovered in a particularly beautiful place, the *locus amoenus* of his orchard.[51] The two saints' lives identify youth with beauty even more directly; and indeed it is largely because of their preeminent beauty that the protagonists of these texts exert power over the people around them. Of the young Josaphaz we are told that "the more he grew, the more handsome he became: he was a particularly graceful young man" (vv. 171–72). When he is moved by pity for Barlaam, we are told that tears fell, not just from his eyes, but "from his *beautiful* eyes [*des beaus ouz*]" (v. 864). The girls who are placed in his tower in order to seduce him are so intensely inflamed by love for him because "young Josaphaz" was "the most beautiful man then alive [*le plus bel ki fust vivant*]" (v. 1806). This beauty is of a distinctly passive kind, a matter of being looked at and desired rather than doing anything to earn such amorous attention, but there are clear parallels for such an ideal of masculine beauty even among the chivalric heroes of Anglo-French secular romance. In the *Romance of Horn*, for example, the young Horn is said to be beautiful "like an angel." Here we are told that the pagan king Rodmund, having captured Horn and his companions, "carefully observed their lovely faces and their bearing . . . But Horn surpassed them all in every fair feature, as God in His Trinity intended him to, who moved the king's heart to spare them [from execution]."[52] Chardri's *Seven Sleepers* also lays considerable emphasis on its protagonists' physical beauty. The seven young men are compared with new-blown roses, hawthorn-flowers and summer sunshine. When they wake from their long sleep, for example, we are told that "their complexions were as bright and beautiful as roses in first bloom."[53] Even the cruel Decius is specifically said to be reluctant to punish these young men out of respect for their beauty—because "he did not want to see the bodies of such

---

[51] *Little Debate*, vv. 45–76. On the term *locus amoenus*, see Curtius, *European Literature*, 195–200.

[52] See Judith Weiss's tranlsation of *Horn* in *The Birth of Romance in England*, 46–47.

[53] *Seven Sleepers*, vv. 947–48. See also vv. 623–24 (new-blown roses); vv. 1553–54 (hawthorn), vv. 1666–68 (sunshine). Again there are some precedents for such imagery in the Latin vulgate texts. L_1 says that the Sleepers' faces were like roses ("facies eorum tanquam rosa florens": XVIII, 73) and sunshine ("facies eorum tanquam sol": XVIII, 75). The "roses in bloom" also appear in the *Golden Legend* (Ryan, 2: 17).

very beautiful people subjected to torture."[54] The reason he decides to have them walled up in their cave, so we are told, is because it spares him from seeing their beauty harmed, a motif that recalls King Rodmund's response to Horn.

The outward beauty of Josaphaz and the Seven Sleepers is clearly an index of their holiness, a marker of their inner virtue and grace, but it nevertheless might seem rather paradoxical that Chardri should emphasise it to the extent that he does, given that one of his other recurrent concerns is the discrepancy between the outward adornment of idols and their inner valuelessness. He seems to sense no contradiction between his condemnation of Emperor Decius for filling his temple made "of grey marble [and] hard stone" with images of his gods "lavishly decorated with silver, with gems and with beaten gold" and his celebration of the eventual beautification of the Seven Sleepers' cave, "the huge cave gilded all over [and] enclosed not with beams of wood, but with marble and limestone."[55] Nor does he offer any criticism of King Barachie for treating the bodies of Barlaam and Josaphaz as a "treasure" and having them ceremoniously "enclosed in gold and silver."[56] It could be argued that the difficulty of defining the relationship between outer form and inner truth, or between materiality and God's grace, is for Chardri a key concern. When the Young Man urges his interlocutor to "take heart and be happy" because of the beauty of the flowers in the meadow around them ("as if this meadow. . . is in itself in possession of perfect joy, taking pleasure in its own way"), this is not a call to mere hedonism, or an attempt to suggest that appreciating the beauties of this world justifies ignoring the demands of the next. Rather, the Young Man's point is that the flowers' beauty is an indication of the immanence of God's power within nature, so that it is actually the Old Man's discontent with the order of things, not the Young Man's readiness to enjoy himself, that set him at odds with God's will. For Chardri, the very orderedness of the created world is itself a self-sufficient argument for the unerringness and absoluteness of God's power. He makes this particularly clear at the beginning of the *Seven Sleepers*, in a majestic passage inspired by Psalm 146:

> The power of God, that lasts forever and is forever pure and unerring, should not be left unspoken. No one is surprised when God makes the weather warm or icy, cloudy, clear or windy, whether on land or at sea, because everyone is used to seeing the changes that he brings about with his power. Yet, if only we were able to consider it deeply enough (and if God were willing to help us, for we could never succeed unless he helped us), then we would find it astonishing. For which of us could easily measure the number of the stars in the sky, or the height of the firmament, that shines

---

[54] *Seven Sleepers*, vv. 751–52. L₁ says only that Decius "did want to injure them" ("cum nollet laedere eos": IX, 52). See also *Seven Sleepers*, vv. 644–58.

[55] *Seven Sleepers*, vv. 103, 123, 1791–94.

[56] *Josaphaz*, vv. 2891–906. Arvennir's body is placed in shroud that is pointedly "not made of brocade or samite, or fastened with either silver or gold" (*Josaphaz*, vv. 2498–99).

so clear and bright, or the extent of all the earth or the expanse of the ocean so deep? Anyone who ventured to talk at all about it could only marvel.[57]

From this perspective (as Chardri goes on to argue) it is obviously foolish to be incapable of "thinking about anything else except the misfortunes that we see occurring in this world."[58] This, of course, happens to be precisely the form of "foolishness" to which the Old Man stubbornly clings throughout the *Little Debate*.

There is one particular sense in which Chardri might be said to be particularly interested in the relationship between God's grace and the materiality of the created world. This concerns the fate of human bodies after death. The Old Man expresses considerable anxiety on this point. What worries him, he says, is the possibility that his body might be left unburied, "left lying out in the open for everybody to see":

> Then many people would be offended by its stench and nakedness; and it would be terribly humiliating for me if my body weren't quickly placed in the ground. The birds would pluck me apart and the fierce wolves would devour me, and all the dogs as well; and for me that would be a terrible ordeal.[59]

The Young Man replies with what is, in effect, a bald summary of the standard Augustinian response to questions about the theological status of funeral observances.[60] Anxieties about the fate of the physical body after death, and particularly about the possibility of being "plucked apart" or "devoured", were perhaps inevitably intensified by the gradual refinement of Christian beliefs about the nature of the resurrection on Judgment Day, according to which "all of [the dead] will rise with their own bodies, which they now wear."[61] It was only natural for people to interpret "the destruction of the body" as a challenge to "faith in the resurrection," especially if faith in the resurrection necessarily involved accepting that human bodies could be, and would be, completely restored on the Last Day in substance as well as shape.[62] On this point, medieval doctrine was ultimately shaped by debates about the nature of the body that had taken place in late antiquity (with particular reference to Christ's incarnation and the resurrection on Judgment Day). Indeed, as Caroline Walker Bynum observes, "the literature of

---

[57] *Seven Sleepers*, vv. 1–10, 17–22. This passage is later ironically recalled in vv. 249–52, when Decius' courtiers attempt to suggest that the Emperor is "ruler of the whole circumference of the world, of the animals as well as the land, the birds in the air and the fish swimming in the ocean." Chardri also asserts God's power in similar terms in both the *Little Debate* and *Josaphaz* as well: see *Seven Sleepers*, n. to vv. 1–10.

[58] *Seven Sleepers*, vv. 29–31.

[59] *Little Debate*, vv. 623–32.

[60] See *Seven Sleepers*, nn. to vv. 632, 637–40, 647, 660–68.

[61] See *Seven Sleepers*, n. to v. 1593.

[62] See *Seven Sleepers*, n. to v. 637–40.

late antiquity throbs with fear of being fragmented, absorbed, and digested."[63] The legend of the *Seven Sleepers* is specifically presented as an antidote to such fears. It even imagines that these fears were so substantial as to have constituted a real threat to fifth-century Christianity: a "great and powerful heresy" perpetuated by "false, deluded folk" who insist "it cannot be [. . .] that a dead man might ever rise again [. . .] nor will he ever be resurrected in the flesh."[64] The particular demonstration (*mustrance*) provided by the reawakening of the Seven Sleepers, is (as Maximianus explains at vv. 1692–1727) that it does indeed lie within God's power to restore to the dead their own, original, living bodies—whatever these "false, deluded folk" might assert to the contrary. The relevance of all this to the anxieties expressed by the Old Man in the *Little Debate* is perhaps underlined by the fact that Chardri's description of the passing of time after the Seven Sleepers are walled up in their cave focuses on the inevitability of mortality so closely that its phrasing closely resembles that of the *Little Debate*.[65]

Throughout Chardri's works human bodies (and particularly their destruction, disintegration and decay) loom disproportionately large. The *Little Debate* foregrounds the "stench and the putrefaction" of rotting bodies. In the *Seven Sleepers*, Maximianus insists that Decius's idols will rot and that he will die; and then, when Malchus asks for Decius to be summoned, he is told that "it's now nearly four hundred years since he rotted in the earth."[66] In *Josaphaz*, when the boy-saint threatens the sage Nakor, what he emphasises is the dismemberment to which he intends to subject the old man's corpse: "I swear I'll cut out your tongue with my bare hands [. . .] I'll rip out your heart and I'll never show you any mercy until I can give your heart to the dogs outside, along with the rest of your body; and you can be certain that I'll treat your corpse as shamefully as I possibly can!"[67] Chardri also gives particularly sympathetic and effective treatment to what could be regarded as one of the definitive scenes in the legend of Barlaam and Josaphaz (and an element in it that can be traced all the way back to the origins of the legend in Buddhist texts such as the *Buddhacarita*): that is, the young man's series of encounters with figures representing physical fragility, indignity, and suffering to which human bodies are subject.[68] First he meets a leper and a blind man, and then a man who is said to be "very old indeed" (*de mut grant age*). Chardri describes in graphic detail the impact of the years on this man's body:

---

[63] Caroline Walker Bynum, *The Resurrection of the Body in Western Christianity, 200–1336* (New York: Columbia University Press, 1995), 112.

[64] *Seven Sleepers*, vv. 856–72. See further n. to v. 872.

[65] See *Seven Sleepers*, vv. 813–20; and *Petit Plet*, vv. 296–64, esp. 317, 329, 353–56.

[66] *Little Debate*, v. 403; *Seven Sleepers*, vv. 1438–39; *Seven Sleepers*, vv. 1487–94.

[67] *Josaphaz*, vv. 1487–92.

[68] See *Josaphaz*, n. to vv. 590–94.

His face was wrinkled; his hair was all white; his arms hung down like a
saddle-cloth; his back was curved like a hunchback's; his head drooped forwards; there were no teeth in his mouth; he had a dreadful stammer; there
was mucus hanging from his nose; his eyes were full of tears; and he never
had any relief from any of this. He tottered along like a drunkard.[69]

The moral that Josaphaz's companion chooses to draws from the appearance of this
figure is, again, phrased in such a way as to recall the *Little Debate*: "Nobody can
escape death."[70] In this context, there is considerable dramatic force in Josaphaz's
observation that "this life is a very bitter thing, whatever anyone says, when we all
face death and no one can escape it."[71] In effect, *Josaphaz* here offers a direct response to the specific problem that the Old Man happens to set the Young Man
at the beginning of the *Little Debate*: the difficulty of dealing with the emotional
stress caused by fear of death. The description of the extremely old man in *Josaphaz* also recalls the *Little Debate*'s discussion of the miseries and indignities of old
age: the way in which "because of their maladies and fatigue, old people have to be
looked after by somebody else, just as a nurse looks after a child—ministering to it
in every way, putting it to bed and getting it up, looking after it as it eats and as it
cries."[72] In addition to this, all three texts contain catalogues of the different ways
in which human bodies are subject to dismemberment and destruction by merci-
less pagan persecutors. The *Little Debate* refers to "a hundred thousand saints [who]
have been granted joy," explaining that "some were drowned, some were burned in
the fire, some were eaten by bears or leopards."[73] Neither Josaphaz, Barlaam, or the
Seven Sleepers themselves ever suffer such a fate (indeed, none of them die by violence), but Chardri's accounts of their lives are nevertheless full of tortures and ex-
ecutions. In the *Seven Sleepers* we are given a whole list of the cruelties from which
the Sleepers seek refuge in their cave:

> . . .some [Christians] were hanged, some were drawn, some were flayed and
> then killed, some were drowned, some were burned, some were tortured
> in every part by hunger, some succumbed to cold, some were devoured by
> beasts, some were roasted, some were boiled, some were buried alive, some
> died from their sufferings, many were torn apart.[74]

Josaphaz answers this with Arvennir's treatment of the hapless philosophers who
fail to overcome Nakor's arguments for Christianity:

---

[69] *Josaphaz*, vv. 624–34.
[70] *Josaphaz*, v. 648; *Little Debate*, v. 330.
[71] *Josaphaz*, v. 649–54.
[72] *Little Debate*, vv. 205–210.
[73] *Little Debate*, vv. 637–40.
[74] *Seven Sleepers*, vv. 169–78

Some of them he subjected to cruel beatings. More than a hundred of them had their eyes put out at his command. He ordered that some should have their hands cut off, others their feet, just as he pleased. According to my source, there was not a single one of them who got away from there without dreadful injury.[75]

All of this might seem difficult to reconcile with my suggestion that Chardri is a notably "optimistic writer", but its impact is mitigated both by Chardri's recurrent insistence that God's providence is both absolute and benign, and by the depth of sympathy that he reveals for those who express weakness or fear in the face of suffering. For Chardri, even the Seven Sleepers are not so much models of superhuman fortitude as human beings with a plausible share of frailty and irresolution. Although the Latin text on which his poem seems to be based states that the seven young men went into the cave only in order to pray for the strength of mind to face martyrdom at the emperor's hands, Chardri clearly implies that they were thinking about trying to escape it altogether.[76] He also tends to amplify the saints' timidity. When one of the Seven, Malchus, goes into the city under cover in order to spy and buy provisions, and there hears all about Decius's harsh treatment of the Christians, "he was more afraid then he had ever been in his life [. . .] full of heartfelt anxiety about how he could escape without the pagans catching him."[77] Having hurriedly procured some bread, Malchus returns to his companions "using all his cleverness" (*par sa veisdie*);[78] and together they all weep with fear, trembling "in every limb, anguished and perspiring."[79] This is an appealingly *un*superhuman reaction to the imminent threat of pain and death that the Seven now face. At this point in the narrative Chardri clearly expects his readers to be able to identify with the seven young men, to imagine how they might feel were they ever in a similar predicament themselves. When his protagonists all fall asleep soon afterwards, Chardri stresses that this is only a natural physiological response to stress.[80] It is perhaps also at least implicit that this marks the beginning of a miracle designed to illustrate God's compassion, as well as his omnipotence:

> Indeed it was God who guided them, and put them to sleep, just as he pleased.
> [. . .] He who wrought the sea and the earth and heaven, granted them such

---

[75] *Josaphaz*, vv. 1620–26; see also vv. 1287–96.

[76] See note to *Seven Sleepers*, vv. 469–84.

[77] *Seven Sleepers*, vv. 566–67, 570–72. L_1 says only that Malchus was fearful ("timens", VII, 49).

[78] *Seven Sleepers*, v. 573.

[79] *Seven Sleepers*, vv. 591–94. In L_1 the Seven trembled ("tremuerunt").

[80] See note to *Seven Sleepers*, vv. 617–20. There is no precedent for this suggestion in L_1.

repose in order to show everybody else a miracle. No one has ever heard the like of it. This miracle God brought about by means of his power . . .[81]

Chardri's sense of the intrinsic ridiculousness of human folly and frailty (and of the extensiveness of God's tolerance for it) is so highly developed that he is even prepared to find room in his two saints' lives for a certain amount of what can only be described as situation comedy. When Malchus returns to the city to buy bread, without knowing that 362 years have elapsed in the meantime, the first thing that he sees is "a beautiful and impressively big cross standing above the gate." Understandably, "he stopped dead, he was so amazed": indeed, "he was so shocked that he almost fell over."[82] We next see him wondering at some length whether he might be suffering some sort of hallucination. In the end he discounts this possibility, on the very reasonable grounds that he happens to be feeling rather peckish.[83] A little later on, when he realises that he has excited the suspicion of the bakers from whom he was trying to buy bread, the feelings that he expresses to himself at this point are strikingly unsaintly:

Now they've seen me, now they've noticed me, now they suspect me, these bakers—these treacherous rogues. Now please God they all had their eyes poked out—and let me be a league away on horseback![84]

In *Josaphaz*, the attendant who is given the chance to see Barlaam's precious stone, but only on the condition that he is chaste and sinless, reacts with a degree of consternation that is, in the context, distinctly amusing:

No way! [*Ne mie a gas!*] Don't show it to me then, good brother, for I'm a dirty sinner, and I've been so my whole life![85]

When the saint finally makes his escape from the tower, his servants initially assume that he has not appeared simply because he is having a lie-in. Eventually, however, they agree that "it's certainly time he was getting up," rather as if Josaphaz were an indolent teenager lurking in his bedroom. When they do at last enter his room, we then see them earnestly arguing among themselves about whether or not they dare unseal the letter that he has left behind for them. Much of the pleasure of reading Chardri's saints' lives is in the little details, the realistic touches that bring such scenes to life. So, for example, Malchus is ticked off by Maximianus for buying little loaves, rather than big ones which (he says) would have been a much better buy (which is possibly

---

[81] *Seven Sleepers*, vv. 621–22, 627–31. This expands on L₁'s assertion that all this occurred "per dispositionem Dei" (XI, 54).
[82] *Seven Sleepers*, vv. 1041–42. In L₁ Malchus is merely "amazed" ("miratus", XIV, 62).
[83] There is no parallel for this reasoning in L₁.
[84] *Seven Sleepers*, vv. 1159–66. These sentiments seem to be original with Chardri.
[85] *Josaphaz*, vv. 735–38.

one reason why Malchus is still hungry the following morning).[86] The money that Malchus tries to give the bakers is not only of an ancient stamp, but also "shiny."[87] When Barlaam dresses up as merchant (with a precious stone to sell), he makes sure to carry a pack (*male*) "as if it contained his wares [*sa mercerie*]."[88] And when Josaphaz escapes from the tower, the letter that he leaves behind is found propped up on his pillow (*desus sun oriller*).[89] All of these details are original with Chardri and all of them add, subtly but substantially, to the dramatic impact of these scenes.

The *Little Debate* is not a narrative, and so offers less scope for situation-comedy of this kind, but there is an equivalent for it in the dramatic relationship between its two interlocutors, which is expressed in a dialogue that is often notably colourful and robust. So, for example, the Young Man's initial response to the Old Man's attempts at intimating his mortality is scathingly contemptuous:

> Only someone who'd never heard any sermonising—someone ignorant of his ABC [*abecé*] as well as all the other letters—would have anything to learn from you. Your tongue is as lavish with precepts as a priest's on Sunday.[90]

When the Old Man complains that he is afraid of dying young (rather illogically given that he is by definition now too old to die young), his interlocutor apparently takes great offence at what he sees as the Old Man's own flippancy. "You shouldn't be deceitful [. . .] you shouldn't joke," he says [*ne mentez pas . . . ne vus serreit mie a gas*].[91] The Young Man also objects to the Old Man's complaint that he has lost his children, not because he doubts the truth of it, but because he seems to think that it is rather unsporting of the Old Man to introduce such a thorny topic only at such a late stage in the debate: "Why have you concealed it from me, and not mentioned it before?" he says, with apparent irritation.[92] Even when trying to address his opponent's anxieties directly, his language can be very bracing, if not downright brutal, as, for example, when he attempts to deal with the Old Man's grief for his wife by telling him:

> Leave off your grieving and remember that you're a man! You shouldn't weep like a sulky child for some apple.[93]

---

[86] *Seven Sleepers*, vv. 986–87: "The loaves that you brought us yesterday were small: you left behind the big ones that it would have been a better buy." Here Chardri is developing the suggestion in L₁ that Malchus buys small loaves ("modicos panes", VII, 49) because he is in such a hurry to get out of the city.

[87] *Seven Sleepers*, v. 990: *blancs*, literally: "white." This detail is not paralleled in L₁.

[88] *Josaphaz*, vv. 700–701.

[89] *Josaphaz*, vv. 2605.

[90] *Little Debate*, vv. 182–86.

[91] *Little Debate*, vv. 561–62.

[92] *Little Debate*, vv. 1093–94.

[93] *Little Debate*, vv. 1528–31.

The language used by the Young Man, in particular, is often memorably pungent, as for example when he says that God will provide "beef with the horns
attached"; or when he compares women to "February of the thirteen moods"; or
when he suggests that a friend cannot be regarded as entirely trustworthy "until
you have properly tested the planks."[94]

Sources and Influences

1. *The Seven Sleepers*

The legend of the *Seven Sleepers* has an extremely long history and is very widely
diffused.[95] It can be traced back at least to the fifth century; and there are extant
Christian versions of the legend not just in Syriac, Greek, Coptic and Armenian,
but also outside the Christian tradition, in Persian and Arabic.[96] There are several medieval Latin versions,[97] which in turn gave rise to an extensive tradition in
the vernacular languages, including French, German, Italian, Spanish, Swedish,
Irish and English.[98] According to Merrilees, Chardri's is one of no fewer than

---

[94] *Little Debate*, vv. 910, 1298 and 1644.

[95] See Merrilees, *Seven Sleepers*, 1–3; and, at more length, John Koch,
*Die Siebenschläferlegende, ihre Ursprung und ihre Verbreitung: Eine mythologisch-
literaturgeschichtliche Studie* (Leipzig: Reissner, 1883); Hüber, *Wanderlegende*; Louis
Massignon, "Le Culte liturgique et populaire des VII dormants martyrs d'Ephèse
(Ahl Al-Kahf): Trait d'union Orient-Occident entre l'Islam et la Chrétienté," in *Opera
Minora*, 3: 119–80.

[96] There is some debate about whether the legend was first set down in Greek or in
Syriac. Allgeier argued for the Syriac, but see Peeters, "Le texte original de la Passion
des Sept Dormants," *Analecta Bollandiana* 41 (1923) 369–85; and Ernest Honigmann,
"Stephen of Ephesus (April 15, 448–Oct. 29, 451) and the legend of the Seven Sleepers,"
in idem, *Patristic Studies* (Vatican City: Biblioteca Apostolica Vaticana, 1953), 125–68.

[97] BHL 2313–20. The Latin texts are analysed by Hüber, in *Wanderlegende*, 59–91.
They include versions of the story by Gregory of Tours and Paul the Deacon. A version
also appears in Jacobus de Voragine's *Golden Legend* (trans. Ryan, 2: 15–18).

[98] For the Seven Sleepers in Old English, see Ælfric of Eynsham, *Catholic Homilies
II*, XXVII, vv. 222–23, ed. Malcolm Godden, *Ælfric's Catholic Homilies: The Second Series*,
EETS SS 5 (London, 1979), 247–48; and the longer version (of unknown authorship)
in *Ælfric's Lives of Saints*, ed. W.W. Skeat, EETS, 76, 82, 94, 114 (London, 1881–1900;
repr. as 2 vols., 1966), 1: 488–541, more recently edited by Hugh Magennis as *The
Anonymous Old English Legend of the Seven Sleepers*, Durham Medieval Texts 7 (Durham:
Department of English Studies, 1994). In Middle English, there are ten manuscripts
of the *South English Legendary* that contain a version of the Seven Sleepers story: see
Manfred Görlach, *The Textual Tradition of the South English Legendary* (Leeds: School of
English, 1974), 184. See also Hüber, *Wanderlegende*, 155–73.

nineteen different versions in Old French alone.[99] It seems that Chardri's immediate source is most likely to have belonged to the L_1 tradition, one of the several
recensions of the so-called "vulgate" Latin version of the legend.[100] However, it is
difficult to be entirely certain of Chardri's source, because he makes "a very free
adaptation of the material available" and "at no point, except perhaps for individual lines, can the *Set Dormanz* be considered a translation."[101] There are a few
moments when Chardri seems to be following the Latin text quite closely;[102] but
these are the exceptions, rather than the rule. On the whole what is most striking is just how much Chardri adds to the relatively spare narrative offered by the
vulgate texts.

In particular, L_1 offers no precedent for several specific emphases that are
clearly fundamental to Chardri's understanding of the tale. For him, the miracle
of the 362-year sleep is significant above all because it is an illustration of the extent of God's omnipotence. He insists on this perspective from the outset, with
a prologue celebrating the manifestness of God's absolute power in the world
(vv. 1–50), for which there is no parallel in the Latin; he also allows Maximianus to assert his belief in God's role as Creator (vv. 385–400), again without
any parallel in the corresponding passage in L_1; and when the Seven Sleepers finally awake after their long sleep he says explicitly that it was God who brought
this about "by means of his great power" (*par la sue grant vertu*, v. 934), where
the Latin says only that this happened "because God wished it."[103] Similarly, L_1
also provides no precedent for Chardri's interpretation of the story as a reflection
on the folly of idolatry. The emperor's idols are mentioned,[104] but their appearance is not described in detail, as they are in Chardri (vv. 99–128); and, although
Maximianus tells the emperor in L_1 that he will not bow before his idols,[105] it is
only in Chardri's version that he also takes the opportunity to say how much he
despises them (vv. 336–56).

---

[99] Brian S. Merrilees, "La Vie des Septs Dormanz en ancien français," *Romania* 95
(1974): 362–80. This includes a "version provençale."

[100] On this point, see Hüber, *Wanderlegende*, 189; Merk, *Literarische Gestaltung*, 233;
and Merrilees, *Seven Sleepers*, 3–6. L_1 = BHL 2316: I have used the edition by Hüber.
There is also an edition (with translation), based on a single manuscript (London, BL MS
Egerton 2797), by Hugh Magennis, in *The Anonymous Old English Legend*, 74–91.

[101] Merrilees, *Seven Sleepers*, 5. Cf. also Koch (xvii), who says that Chardri's is the
longest and most complete of all the medieval versions still extant ("die längste und
vollständigste bearbeitung ist die Chardry's").

[102] See, e.g., notes to vv. 135, 189–92.

[103] L_1: "ex voluntate Dei" (XII, 58).

[104] L_1: "praecepit, ut sacrificarent cum eo idolis" (I, 40).

[105] L_1: "ante idola non declinamur" (IV, 46).

2. *Josaphaz*

Like the legend of the Seven Sleepers, the legend of Barlaam and Josaphat has a long and complex history.[106] Nearly 150 distinct versions of the legend have been identified, in a range of different Asian, European, and African languages.[107] It has been generally accepted ever since the 1850s that the legend's origins lie in early Buddhism. The narrative that lies at its core—i.e. "the prediction of asceticism at Josaphat's birth and his subsequent encounter with the four omens, his temptation by women once he has announced his faith, and his renunciation of his kingdom"[108]—is found (with variations) in several of the lives of the Buddha that circulated in the first few centuries CE, such as the second-century *Buddhacarita* (or *Acts of the Buddha*) ascribed to the Sanskrit writer, Aśvaghoṣa.[109] From this starting-point in Buddhism, the story seems to have travelled westwards via translations into Turkish, Persian, Arabic and Georgian, gathering various narrative accretions as it went.[110] It was apparently in Georgian that the

---

[106] For surveys and general accounts of the legend's history, see Ernst Kuhn, "Barlaam und Josaphat: Eine bibliographisch-literargeschichtliche Studie," *Abhandlungen der philosophisch-philologischen Classe der Königlichen Bayerischen Akademie der Wissenschaften* 20 (1897): 1–88; Peri, *Religionsdisput*; Abuladze, 'Introduction', in Lang, *Balavariani*; Hirsh, xv–xxviii; Monique B. Pitts, "Barlaam and Josaphat: A Legend for All Seasons," *Journal of South Asian Literature* 16 (1981): 1–17; Philip Almond, "The Buddha of Christendom: A Review of the Legend of Barlaam and Josaphat," *Religious Studies* 23 (1987): 391–406; de la Cruz, BJL, 23–27; Constanza Cordoni, "Barlaam und Josaphat in der europäischen Literatur des Mittelalters," Ph.D. diss., University of Vienna, 2010. As Sonet says, the legend's extraordinarily wide diffusion is "staggering" ("On reste stupéfait devant la diffusion extraordinaire qui fut la sienne": 5). Lang observes that "versions of the Barlaam and Josaphat story [. . .] survive in virtually all countries of Christendom from Iceland to Ethiopia, from Poland to the Philippines" (*Balavariani*, 10). Almond goes so far as to say that "it enjoyed a popularity attained perhaps by no other legend" (391).

[107] See the table of affiliation provided by Hiram Peri as an endpiece to *Der Religionsdisput*.

[108] Hirsh, xvi.

[109] E.H. Johnston, trans., *The Buddhacarita: or, Acts of the Buddha* (Calcutta, 1936; repr. New Delhi: Oriental Books, 1972).

[110] See Willi Bang, "Manichäische Erzähler," *Le Muséon* 44 (1931): 1–35; W.B. Henning, "Persian Poetical Manuscripts from the Time of Rūdakī," in *A Locust's Leg: Studies in Honour of S.H. Taqizadeh*, ed. idem and E. Yarshater (London: Lund, 1962), 89–104; Daniel Gimaret, trans., *Le Livre de Bilawhar et Būḏāsf selon la version arabe ismaélienne* (Geneva: Droz, 1971) and Gimaret, ed., *Kitāb Bilawhar wa Būḏāsf* (Beirut: Dar El-Machreq, 1986); Lang, *Balavariani*, and also Lang, "*The Life of the Blessed Iodasaph*: A New Oriental Christian Version of the Barlaam and Ioasaph Romance (Jerusalem, Greek Patriarchal Library: Georgian MS 140)," *Bulletin of the School of Oriental and African Studies* 20 (1957): 389–407.

Barlaam-and-Josaphat legend was first Christianised.[111] This Georgian text also seems to have provided the basis for what is the ancestor of all the European Barlaam-and-Josaphat texts, the Greek version traditionally ascribed to St. John Damascene (and therefore supposed to belong to the eighth century).[112] This ascription is not now generally accepted, although the association with St. John may have contributed to the authority that this Greek text went on to enjoy. The "Damascene" text was itself the basis for two translations into Latin made in the eleventh century: the so-called "Naples" and "vulgate" versions.[113] This "vulgate" Latin text served in turn as the fountainhead for a very large number of different reworkings of the story throughout the Middle Ages and beyond—including Chardri's.[114] There are over a hundred different versions of the legend still extant in European languages, including German, Spanish, English, Italian, Dutch,

---

[111] See Lang, *Balavariani*, 12: "It is one of the many remarkable features of the Barlaam and Josaphat legend that one of the vital links in its passage from East to West is to be sought in the literary world of medieval Georgia, a Christian kingdom in the Caucasus which had served since the fourth century as a bastion of Christendom among the Infidels. The Georgians, who took the story direct from the Arabs, were apparently the first to give it a specifically Christian flavour. Theirs was the first Christian Church to include St Iodasaph—in reality the Bodhisattva prince of India—in the number of its saints and celebrate his festival with hymns and anthems, dating back to the tenth and eleventh centuries." There are two medieval versions still extant in Georgian: it is the longer one of the two (trans. Lang, *Balavariani*) that apparently provides the source for the Greek text. The shorter version, which is probably an abridgement, is also translated by Lang as *The Wisdom of Balahvar: A Christian Legend of the Buddha* (London: Allen & Unwin, 1957).

[112] Robert Volk, ed., *Die Schriften des Johannes von Damaskos*, vol. 6, part 2: *Historia animae utilis de Barlaam et Ioasaph (spuria)*, Patristische Texte und Studien 60 (Berlin: de Gruyter, 2006).

[113] BHL 979. The vulgate version begins 'Cum cepissent monasteria construi. . .': see the edition by Óscar de la Cruz Palma (**BJL**). Sixty-two manuscripts containing copies of this text were identified by Sonet (76), although there are likely to be many more, as he acknowledged ("Ce nombre s'augmentera problablement. . ."). Some additions were made by de la Cruz, **BJL**, 52–53. See also Hiram Peri (Pflaum), "La plus ancienne traduction latine du roman grec de Barlaam et Josaphat et son auteur," *Studi mediolatini e volgari* 6/7 (1959): 169–89. There were also other versions in Latin, including one in Jacobus de Voragine's *Golden Legend* (trans. Ryan, 2: 355–67).

[114] Cf. de la Cruz (**BJL**, 15: "El número de versiones, traducciones y epítomes evidencia una enorma repercusión en la tradición medieval y una amplia transcendencia en la literatura posterior" ("The [sheer] number of versions, translations, and epitomes is evidence of [the legend's] enormous impact on the medieval tradition and of its considerable importance to literature subsequently"). Hirsh (xv) ranks the Barlaam-and-Josaphat legend—along with "the traditions of Alexander and the Marvels of the East"—as one of the three key story traditions through which "the medieval West came to know the East."

Catalan, Occitan, Norwegian, Danish, Swedish, Romanian, Italian, Portuguese, Irish, and Russian.[115] Chardri's poem is one of ten different versions of the story in Old French alone.[116]

The popularity of the story in medieval Christendom might seem surprising given that the original kernel apparently lies in another religion entirely. "That Buddha should become a Christian saint," suggests Rutledge, "is quite extraordinary." Yet, as he himself goes on to argue, the legend actually harmonises Christian and Buddhist perspectives with relatively little discomfort, if only because both theologies have "a common enemy, the world, which by means of sensual pleasure and a thirst for power, prevents man from attaining salvation." Indeed, "the Buddhist emphasis on self-denial finds a sympathetic counterpart in the person of the medieval Christian hermit-monk." For Rutledge, it is not just Josaphat who should be read as a reimagining of the Buddha, but Barlaam as well, since in the Christian adaptation of the Buddha story, the Buddha is effectively "split into two people"—that is, "Josaphat, the passive contemplator, and Barlaam, the active guide to happiness."[117] On its long journey westwards, the legend also seems to have absorbed some influence from Manicheism: to the extent that Barlaam, in particular, has been interpreted as wandering holy man of a distinctly Manichean cast, one of the so-called *electi*. Yet the Manichean elements are not so clearly marked as to make the legend jar in any way with either Buddhism or Christianity.[118] In its contempt for wealth, power, and pleasure, and its idealisation of wisdom, asceticism, and unworldliness, the Barlaam-and-Josaphat legend is clearly compatible with the ideals of all three religions.

Chardri's *Josaphaz* is "by far the most independent of the French versions."[119] Indeed, it is one of the most distinctive of all the medieval treatments of the legend. Most of Chardri's interventions in the Barlaam-and-Josaphat legend work in the direction of intelligent compression.[120] As Koch explains, Chardri's version of the legend differs from all other medieval versions in that "he addresses the dogmatic aspects of the text only fleetingly, and all the various similes, fables and exempla designed to support the dogmatism are simply removed, so as to allow a much fuller and more comprehensive attention to the narrative aspects of the Latin vulgate text."[121] This means that Chardri chose to omit not just the

---

[115] Peri, *Religionsdisput*, 22; for references to all these texts, see Peri's bibliography, 244–62.

[116] Sonet, 136–90.

[117] Rutledge, 2, 11.

[118] On these points, see Hirsh, xxiii–xxviii; Almond, 404–6.

[119] Merrilees, *Seven Sleepers*, 2.

[120] Cf. Sonet, 153: "Cette version est de toutes les versions métriques du *Barlaam*, la plus condensée."

[121] Koch, xv: "Vielmehr zeichnet sich dieser von allen anderen dadurch aus, daß er das dogmatische element nur andeutungsweise behandelt, und alle zur unterstützung

extended accounts of Christian preaching that fill the vulgate, but all of the il-
lustrative parables that had become an integral part of the Barlaam-and-Josaphat
tradition, the so-called apologues.[122] These apologues have had their own distinct impact on western literature. For example, the story of the Archer and the
Nightingale (**BJL**, pp. 212–14) is the ultimate source of the Old French *Lai de
l'Oiselet* and of John Lydgate's poem *The Churl and the Bird*.[123] The tale of the
Four Caskets (**BJL**, pp. 166–68) was used by Shakespeare as the basis for the
plot of the *Merchant of Venice*.[124] However, none of these apologues can be found
in Chardri's *Josaphaz*. This is apparently due to his consistent strategy of elimi-
nating anything from the story that tends to obscure or retard the narrative of
Josaphaz's life.[125] Indeed, not only does Chardri remove the apologues and the
"dogmatic" material: he also tends to omit all of the material in the legend without any direct relevance to Josaphaz's own immediate experience of events.[126] It
seems that he was determined to present the legend as a biography: as a coher-
ent account of a single individual's life, rather than as a framework supporting a
rather diverse collection of pious material (which is effectively what the vulgate
text amounts to be).

Although Chardri generally tends to reduce and simplify the narrative that
he found in his source, he does also makes some significant additions to it. These
are all in the direction of heightening the drama of particular scenes by inserting
extra colour, gloss, and detail. So, for example, the scene in which the fifty-five
astronomers offer prophecies of greatness at the cradle of the infant Josaphaz is,
in Chardri's version, much more fully realised. The Latin simply says that each
of the astronomers was asked to state separately ("edicere singulos") what would

---

desselben angewendeten gleichnisse, fabeln und beispiele geradezu wegläßt, dafür in
dem erzählenden teil der legende aber genau und umständlich der lat. Vulgata folgt." A
similar analysis is offered by Peri, *Religionsdisput*, 54.

[122] On the apologues and their significance, see W.F. Bolton, "Parable, Allegory
and Romance in the Legend of Barlaam and Josaphat," *Traditio* 14 (1958): 359–66.

[123] Lenora D. Wolfgang, *Le Lai de l'Oiselet: An Old French Poem of the Thirteenth
Century: Edition and Critical Study*, Transactions of the American Philosophical Society
80/5 (Philadelphia, 1995), esp. 7–8; Neil Cartlidge, "The Source of John Lydgate's 'The
Churl and the Bird'," *Notes and Queries* 242 (1997): 22–24.

[124] Geoffrey Bullough, *Narrative and Dramatic Sources of Shakespeare*, 8 vols.
(London: Routledge, 1961–1975), 1: 458.

[125] As Koch observes, this is presumably the explanation for the fact that the title
given to this text in both manuscripts refers only to Josaphaz ("la vie de seint Josaphaz"
C; "la vie seynt Josaphaz" J), rather than Barlaam and Josaphaz together (which is more
usual in other versions of the legend). As he says, "the king's son is the real hero of the
legend" ("Der königssohn ist der eigentliche held der legende": Koch, xv).

[126] For example, the story of the two monks (**BJL**, 142–44); of the extended account
of the defiance and martyrdom of the hermits captured by Arachis (**BJL**, 348–58); the
conference between Arvennir and Theodas (**BJL**, 452).

happen to the child, and that all of them promised that he would be wealthy and powerful ("dicebant illum magnum esse futurum in diuitiis et potentia").[127] By contrast, Chardri pictures them coming forward one after the other:

> One of them said that he would be more powerful than any king or count or marquis then in the entire world, no matter if the whole globe were searched.

> Another said, "He'll be strong and sturdy, surpassing every knight in courage."

> The third said, "This child will be the most valiant man in the world and, not to mention anything else, the wisest under the heavens."[128]

> The fourth said, "This is how he'll be: he'll be fabulously rich." So one said this, another said that . . .[129]

This sequence is broken only by the sudden intervention of "the old man with a beard as white as hawthorn", whose very appearance reduces the court to an awed silence. The dramatic momentum that Chardri generates at this particular point in the narrative is entirely original with him. The Latin text says only that "one astrologer more excellent than the others" then spoke ("vnus autem de astrologis excellentior cunctis ait"). Similarly, Chardri's provides a much more fully imagined account of the saints's nocturnal escape from his own palace (in vv. 2587–2630).[130] The Latin provides no precedent for the sealing of his letter, its placing on the pillow, the secret postern-gate through which Josaphaz escapes, or the comical uncertainty of his servants the following morning. On a smaller scale, Chardri adds to the Latin various small details that help to make the narrative more powerful. For example, it is only Chardri who chooses to identify the species of animal that attacks the unfortunate man who later identifies himself as a "therapist" (the *mire de parole*). Where the Latin refers only to a "bestia", Chardri specifically says that it was a wolf.[131] He also draws a much more vivid picture of the king's attempts to communicate secretly with Nakor, his supposed stooge in the debate with the philosophers. Where the Latin says vaguely that the king

[127] BJL, 130.

[128] 202 **under the heavens** *suz la chape del cel*: literally, "under the sky's cape." Cf. *Little Debate*, v. 1303.

[129] *Josaphaz*, vv. 193–205.

[130] Cf. Koch, 186: "Diese ganze scene ist von unserm dichter viel weiter ausgemalt als im lat. texte" ("This entire scene is much more colourfully depicted by our poet than by the Latin text").

[131] *Josaphaz*, v. 285; BJL, 134.

tried to communicate with him by hints ("per enigmata"), Chardri tells us that he was "winking" at him. [132]

3. *The Little Debate*

The basic outline for the *Little Debate* is provided by a short moral text known as *De remediis fortuitorum* (*On Remedies against Misfortunes*). It seems likely that Chardri was working directly from this text, which was widely circulated in the Middle Ages—largely because it was attributed throughout this period (and up until the seventeenth century) to the Roman philosopher and man of letters, Lucius Annaeus Seneca (ca. 4 BCE–65 CE). [133] There are over 250 surviving manuscripts of *De remediis*, the earliest of them dating to the eighth century; and significant use of it can be shown to have been made by William of Conches, Vincent of Beauvais, Roger Bacon, and Petrarch, among others. [134] It consists of a brief dialogue between two figures called *Sensus* ("Sensuality") and *Ratio* ("Reason"), in which Sensus suggests a series of occasions for human unhappiness, anxiety, or grief, and *Ratio* responds by offering a corresponding set of rational arguments for adopting a philosophical attitude (a literally stoical attitude) towards them. In effect, *De remediis* asks to be read as a poetic meditation on the human condition, a meditation specifically designed to promote fortitude in the face of adversity. [135] The whole debate, however, is characterised by extreme brevity: an attempt to reduce *Sensus*'s big questions about the nature of human suffering to a procession of conspicuously pithy (and perhaps implicitly quotable) "sentences." So, for example, the very first issue that the two speakers address is the inevitability of death. *Sensus* declares simply "Morieris" ("Thou shalt dye") to which *Ratio* responds "Ista hominis natura est: non pœna" ("This is the nature of man, and nat punysshement"). *Sensus* repeats this word "Morieris" nine times thereafter, and *Ratio* gives nine other arguments against the anxiety implicit

---

[132] *Josaphaz*, v. 1557; **BJL**, 416.

[133] For discussion of this text's authorship, see Robert J. Newman, "Rediscovering the *De remediis fortuitorum*," *American Journal of Philology* 109 (1988) 92–107. Newman acknowledges that "the objections to Senecan authorship of the [*De remediis fortuitorum*] are strong," but still thinks that there is some evidence that "points to Seneca as the most probable author" (93). I have worked from the most recent edition of the *De remediis*, by R.G. Palmer, which also includes the translation printed in 1547 by the grammarian Robert Whittington.

[134] Newman, "Rediscovering," 92, n. 1.

[135] Newman argues ("Rediscovering," 98, n. 17) that *De remediis fortuitorum* was originally conceived as a *meditatio* in a specifically Senecan sense. "By the *meditatio*," he explains, "the Stoic hoped to rid himself of the fear of future events by illustrating to himself ahead of time that they are not evil. In contrast to the *consolatio*, the *meditatio*, although employing similar techniques, is concerned with future evils." He cites Seneca, *Ep.* 24.2 and *Nat.* 6.39.12.

within it, each of them just as laconic. Among them is the argument that life is a pilgrimage: "peregrenatio est vita: multa cum deambulaueris, deinde redeundum est"("this lyfe is but a pylgrymage: after thou hast walked a great waye, after thou must returne agayne").[136] After repeatedly insisting on his fear of dying, *Sensus* then moves on to talk about the experience of dying, specifically instancing the sufferings of someone struck down by swords: "Sed sæpe ferieris et multi in te gladii concurrent" ("But thou shalt be ofte stryken, and many swordes shall rushe into the"). To this *Ratio* replies, "Quid refert an multa sint vulnera? Non potest amplius quam vnum esse mortiferum" ("What skylleth it [i.e. what difference does it make]? wheder there be many woundes, there can nomore but one be a death wounde").[137]

Chardri's treatment of these themes is much more expansive, but it clear that he is following essentially the same movements of thought. In other words, he seems to have read *De remediis fortuitorum*, in effect, as a set of bullet-points providing the basis for what becomes, in his own hands, a much more detailed and sympathetic discussion.[138] *Sensus*'s anxiety about the inevitability of death is translated into the words spoken by the Old Man in the *Little Debate*, vv. 295–98:

> One thing I'll say to begin with. Here's the sum of it: I'm going to die. I can't avoid it, you know, and because of it I'm deeply troubled at heart.

The Young Man's responses clearly build on the ideas suggested by *Ratio*. So for example, in v. 304 he emphasises that death "ne deit pas peine estre nomee" ("shouldn't be described as a punishment"), reflecting *Ratio*'s insistence that it is "non pœna." Likewise, in vv. 361–64 we see him using the metaphor of life as a pilgrimage:

> As long as you're here on earth, your life is just a pilgrimage; and, when you die, you'll be returning to your natural state at last.

The scenario that pseudo-Seneca's *Sensus* goes on to imagine (of death by multiple sword-strokes), then re-emerges in Chardri's text, together with *Ratio*'s attempted rationalization of this scenario, as the basis for vv. 380–89:

> THE OLD MAN: ". . . If I received many blows from an axe or cuts from a sword, or if I were chopped into small pieces, I'd find that a terrible ordeal."

---

[136] Palmer, 30–31. Here I have repunctuated Palmer's text (as I do too in some of the subsequent quotations).

[137] Palmer, 34–35.

[138] It is perhaps precisely in recognition of the cultivated brevity of the *Little Debate*'s source that it is called the *Little Debate*—for it is not, in itself, a notably "little" text.

THE YOUNG MAN: The young man replied: "May God, who made the world, save me! I'll tell you my opinion concerning what you've just asked me. No matter how many times you were injured by weapons in this world, whether in peace or in war, you couldn't lose your life more often than once . . ."

These are just a few examples to show how Chardri used the *De remediis fortuitorum* as a framework for the construction of his own poem. The list of anxieties that Chardri's protagonists discuss is in almost all respects the same as that of *De remediis fortuitorum*—i.e. "death, death by violence, death in a foreign country, death before one's time or without burial . . . sickness . . . other men's ill opinions of oneself . . . and finally . . . the loss of children, friend and wife."[139] However, he does make one significant departure from this model. The culminating misfortune, for Chardri, is not the loss of a wife, as in *De remediis fortuitorum*, but the loss of a friend. It could be that in this way he is trying to indicate his awareness of the importance of the ideal of friendship to the Senecan moral tradition within which he was working.[140] However, it could also be read as suggesting some degree of misogyny on Chardri's part. It is certainly true that, while the *De remediis fortuitorum* discusses marriage in less than fifty words, the *Little Debate*'s treatment extends to over three hundred lines, most of them more or less directly critical of wives. Chardri's editor, Brian Merrilees, sees this as a serious misjudgment, arguing that "the poet has harmed the balance of his work with his long diatribe against women."[141] This is perhaps unnecessarily harsh. After all, it is not the voice of the "the poet" that we are supposed to hear in this "diatribe", but only that of the Young Man (with whom Chardri need not be identifying at this particular point). What the Young Man says is only part of a debate, and it inspires a robust and (on the whole much more compelling) response by the Old Man. However, it is certainly the case that, in developing the argument between the Old Man and the Young Man from the relatively slender suggestions provided by *De remediis*, Chardri does at this point draw heavily on the broad tradition of medieval satire directed against women. Like Chaucer, he makes conspicuous use of a text by a man who has been described as "the *éminence grise* behind the medieval tradition of antifeminist literature," St. Jerome.[142] The clearest resonances are with those sections of St. Jerome's antimatrimonial treatise (known as *Adversus Jovinianum*) that are actually excerpted from what Jerome himself referred to as the "golden

---

[139] Merrilees, *Little Debate*, xxiv.

[140] On this complex tradition, see Brian Patrick Maguire, *Friendship and Community: The Monastic Experience 350–1250* (1988; repr. Ithaca: Cornell University Press, 2010); Reginald Hyatte, *The Arts of Friendship: The Idealization of Friendship in Medieval and Early Renaissance Literature* (Leiden: Brill, 1994); Verena Epp, *Amicitia: Zur Geschichte personaler, sozialer, politischer und geistlicher Beziehungen im frühen Mittelalter*, Monographien zur Geschichte des Mittelalters 44 (Stuttgart: Hiersemann, 1999).

[141] Merrilees, *Little Debate*, xxiv.

[142] Jill Mann, *Feminizing Chaucer* (Cambridge: Brewer, 2002), 39.

book" ("aureolus . . . liber") of Theophrastus: a work criticising marriage that does not survive *except* for the passages that St. Jerome preserved.[143] Alongside this learned, Latin tradition of antifeminist satire, Chardri may also have made use of some contemporary vernacular texts dramatising the conflict between the genders, such as Anglo-Norman poems like 'Gilote et Jehane' and the 'Estrif de deus dames'.[144] Indeed, it may be that he played up the Young Man's misogyny, not because he had any investment in the idea of gender-conflict as a social reality, but because he wanted to link the *Little Debate* to the specifically literary tradition represented by poems like 'Gilote et Jehane'—a tradition in which the differences of perspective created by gender are only one aspect of a complex, witty, and often deliberately provocative debate about social and sexual relationships.

While the speakers in *De remediis fortuitorum* are scarcely more than moral conveniences, the *Little Debate* tends towards becoming a genuine drama of character. The Young Man may ultimately be the one who is acknowledged as the victor in the debate, but he is far from being entirely convincing. Indeed his arguments are often undermined by his own palpable complacency, his confidence in his own logical cleverness and his lapses in charity. Many of his arguments are conspicuously strained and/or inhumane. For example, his attempt to console the Old Man for the death of his wife by suggesting that she is unlikely to have lived up to his high estimation of her had she lived—on the grounds that all women are untrustworthy by definition—is not only repellent in itself, but hardly very well calculated to make the Old Man feel any better. In effect, he attempts to answer the Old Man's profound and apparently very real sense of loss with what amounts to a series of misogynistic clichés; and the Old Man has no difficulty at all in making clear just how wide of the mark they are:

> She was my loyal wife; and I have every right to grieve for her. She was the very sweetest lady there was and the most generous I ever knew. She was faithful and pure. Her beauty surpassed that of the briar-rose. She had a very large share in every virtue that you could name and she surpassed all other women, just as a sapphire surpasses pebbles.[145]

---

[143] St. Jerome's extracts from Theophrastus are found in *Adversus Jovinianum*, Book I, chapter 47. For an edition of this, together with extended commentary and discussion, see Ralph Hanna III and Traugott Lawler, ed. and trans., *Jankyn's Book of Wikked Wyves: Volume 1: The Primary Texts: Walter Map's "Dissuasio", Theophrastus' "De nuptiis", Jerome's "Adversus Jovinianum"* (Athens, GA: University of Georgia Press, 1997). Translations of these extracts can also be found in *Women Defamed and Women Defended: An Anthology of Medieval Texts*, ed. Alcuin Blamires (Oxford: Oxford University Press, 1992), 70–73. The clearest resonance of Jerome/Theophrastus is to be found in the *Little Debate* at vv. 1491–1508; but see also vv. 1146–54, 1365–66, 1455–58 and 1479–88. For a more extended discussion of Chardri's attitude to women, see Cartlidge, *Medieval Marriage*, 168–73.

[144] See notes to vv. 1396, 1401–02 and 1405–06.

[145] *Little Debate*, vv. 1183–92.

This speech has an air of conviction that is conspicuously lacking from the Young Man's own arguments. Similarly, the Young Man's argument that beggars have less need to grieve for their children than kings do (*Little Debate*, vv. 1125–28) — if only because they are driven by lust (*dedut*) to produce too many of them — hardly suggests any very convincing grasp of human psychology; and it is in any case difficult to see how such an argument is likely to persuade the Old Man that his own bereavements weigh any less deeply. The Young Man's arguments in relation to this issue actually tend to work against him. His observation that kings as well as beggars lose their children is hardly very consoling: instead it serves only to emphasise the inevitability and universality of human mortality, in a fashion that only seems to justify the Old Man's gloomy view of the world. At the same time, it is probably fair to say that the Young Man's opponent is possibly not a great deal more attractive than he is. The Old Man is self-obsessed, stubbornly morose, and patently jealous of other people's happiness, but he does at least have the excuse that life seems to have dealt him an unusually large share of disasters. The effect of this contrast of characters is to leave the debate much more finely balanced than the two protagonists themselves ultimately believe it to be. On the face of it the very structure of Chardri's poem implies an acceptance of the assumption central to his source, which is that human reason can be used for therapeutic effect, providing "remedies" for misfortune in the form of a series of consolatory "proofs." Yet what tends to emerge from the drama of the poem itself is a sense that the experience of grief and suffering is in the end always so powerful that no intellectual argument for patience in adversity can, in itself, ever seem entirely sufficient.[146]

Relationship with *The Owl and the Nightingale*

The Owl and the Nightingale survives only in company with the three works ascribed to Chardri; and there are a number of general perspectives that all four poems share. For example, both the *Owl*-poet and Chardri seem particuarly willing to allow room for the expression of a certain amount of snobbery. While the narrator in the *Seven Sleepers* condemns cityfolk for their stupidity and the Young Man in the *Little Debate* expresses scorn for beggars who have too many children, the Nightingale offers a contemptuous caricature of yokels driven wild by summertime lust.[147] On the other hand, both poets are also willing to take a sharply critical stance against the ruling classes. The *Owl*-poet permits the Wren and the Nightingale to accuse bishops of corruption and nepotism, while the

---

[146] This argument would come close to that of Chaucer's *Book of the Duchess*, which also dramatises both the need for consolation and the inevitability of its inadequacy.

[147] *Seven Sleepers*, vv. 1221–24; *Little* Debate, vv. 1124–28; The *Owl and the Nightingale*, vv. 509–16.

narrator of the *Seven Sleepers* lays charges of usury, simony, and lechery (among other things) against the nobility as well as the senior clergy.[148]

The relationship between *The Owl and the Nightingale* and the *Little Debate* is particularly close.[149] Both are unusually substantial debate-poems of just under 1800 lines in length (1794 and 1780 lines respectively). Both describe an encounter between two contrasting personalities (one persistently gloomy and pessimistic, the other sunnier, but also notably complacent and self-regarding). Both poems have an unusually wide range of tone, ranging from the sheer pettiness of the Young Man's initial response to the Old Man's "sermonising", and of the Nightingale's attack on the Owl for being ugly—right the way through to moments of genuine pathos, such as the Old Man's fierce insistence on the validity of his grief for his lost wife, and the Nightingale's movingly sympathetic depiction of the sorrows of the betrayed maiden.[150] The two poems also have a number of specific themes in common. For example, the Young Man's declaration that "I'd rather go to God smiling" could perhaps be taken to correspond with the Nightingale's emphasis on the "merriness" of heaven ("hu murie is þe blisse of houene").[151] Conversely, the Owl's response to the Nightingale ("Do you think you can bring them so easily to the kingdom of God, just by singing? No indeed, they'll clearly learn that they have to beg remission for their sins with much weeping, before they can ever enter there") comes close at least to the Old Man's initial emphasis on the urgency of repentance ("If you want to be wise, think about this—and give up your silliness and your folly!").[152] Both poems explicitly consider marriage and married life, but whereas the English poem tends to take a distinctly "feminine" point of view, concentrating particularly on the sufferings of jilted girls and abused wives, the French seems to be much more exclusively concerned with men's perspectives on marriage, balancing the Young Man's chauvinistic account of nagging, grasping wives with the Old Man's celebration of his wife's loyalty and "good upbringing."[153] The two poems are also very sensitive to the idea of defamation. In the *Little Debate*, we find the Young Man explaining that it is characteristic of wicked people to slander their neighbours. However, as he goes on to explain:

---

[148] *Seven Sleepers*, vv. 1857–80; The *Owl and the Nightingale*, 1759–78.

[149] Here I develop arguments made in Cartlidge, *O&N* (at xxxi) and "Composition" (256–57).

[150] *Little Debate*, vv. 181–86; *The Owl and the Nightingale*, vv. 71–76; *Little Debate*, vv. 1175–1204, 1415–24; *The Owl and the Nightingale*, vv. 1433–54.

[151] *Little Debate*, v. 194; *The Owl and the Nightingale*, v. 728.

[152] *The Owl and the Nightingale*, vv. 854–59: "Wenest þu hi bringe so li3tliche / To Godes riche al singinge? / Nai, nai, hi shulle wel auinde / Þat hi mid longe wope mote / Of hore sunnen bidde bote / Ar hi mote euer kume þare"; *Little Debate*, vv. 179–80.

[153] *The Owl and the Nightingale*, vv. 1423–44, and 1519–1603; *Little Debate*, vv. 1463–1520, and 1311–38.

Prudent people find it easy to recognise their malice, for they're incapable of saying anything positive: that's not their habit. Now leave them be, good father, whatever they've done in the past, since you'll never make a good hawk out of a kite or a buzzard. Spend your time with prudent people and you won't lose by it, even if you don't gain. As long as you're in the company of a wise person, your mind will be in peace, but if you want to put your trust in fools, then you'll never have any peace on earth.[154]

This at least broadly resembles the justification that the Owl offers for not responding to the abuse she receives from the little birds who attempt to mob her:

I don't want to argue with the rascals, and for that reason I turn as far away from them as I can. It's the opinion of wise men (and they say it often), that there's no point in arguing with an idiot, any more than in trying to yawn wider than an oven. I've heard it said how one of Alfred's sayings once was: 'Watch that you aren't around where there's babbling and brawling at hand! Let fools bicker and you walk away!' I'm wise and that's exactly what I do. Then on the other hand Alfred stated a proverb that is now widely circulated: 'Whosoever has dealings with a fool will never get away untainted.' Do you think that the hawk is any the worse for the fact that the crows cry out against him [. . .]?[155]

In particular, both passages identify malicious slander with "foolish" people, and (conversely) a stoical indifference to such slander with people who are wise. Both suggest that it is essentially futile even to try to persuade "fools" to behave better: that, in the end, the only way to deal with them is to give them a wide berth. It is perhaps a particularly striking coincidence that both of these discussions happen to feature hawks.[156]

This particular comparison is also a convenient illustration of the importance of proverbs and moral commonplaces to the style of the two debate-poems. This aspect of Chardri's writing is particularly prominent in the *Little Debate*, and indeed it is a feature that he himself presents as one of this poem's principal selling-points. As he puts it in his prologue, the *Little Debate* "contains many truthful sayings replete with good sense and eloquence";[157] and it is perhaps no

---

[154] *Little Debate*, vv. 831–44.

[155] *The Owl and the Nightingale*, vv. 287–304: "Ne lust me wit þe screwen chide: / Forþi ich wende from hom wide. / Hit is a wise monne dome, / & hi hit segget wel ilome, / Þat 'me ne chide wit þe gidie' / Ne 'wit þan ofne me ne 3onie'. / At sume siþe herde i telle / Hu Alured sede on his spelle: / 'Loke þat þu ne bo þare, / Þar chauling boþ, & cheste 3are! / Lat sottes chide & uorþ þu go!' / & ich am wis & do also. / & 3et Alured seide anoþer side / A word þat is isprunge wide: / 'Þat wit þe fule haueþ imene / Ne cumeþ he neuer from him cleine.' / Wenestu þat haueck bo þe worse / Þo3 crowe bigrede him . . ."

[156] Cf. also *Little Debate*, vv. 69–72; *The Owl and the Nightingale*, vv. 15–20.

[157] *Little Debate*, vv. 15–16: "Car mult i ad verraiz respiz / De ben assis e de bonz diz."

coincidence that the only author he pretends to quote directly is an author of proverbs, Cato—just as the only author directly cited by the *Owl*-poet is also supposed to be a collector of proverbs, King Alfred.[158] It is never easy to define what exactly is proverbial, but by my count there are at least forty or so expressions in the *Little Debate* that have at least a proverbial aura.[159] This compares with about fifty or so proverbs or proverbial expressions in *The Owl and the Nightingale*, a text that is only slightly longer.[160] This shared penchant for the proverbial clearly has something to do with the fact that both poems describe what we are supposed to imagine as impromptu debates. The proverbial here functions in place of the "authorities" that might govern disputations of a more formal kind (whether legal, patristic, scholastic, or scientific). The two poems also reveal a certain self-consciousness about how oral debates of this kind ought to be conducted, with speakers in both texts emphasising the particular importance of observing due protocol on such occasions. In the *Little Debate*, the Old Man carefully defines the purpose of their discussion (vv. 267–76), and in return the Young Man promises that "You can say what you wish and you won't see me being offended, nor—God willing!—will you be offended either" (vv. 278–80). In *The Owl and the Nightingale*, the birds agree that:

> We should adopt some proper procedure, using fair and peaceable words. Even though we don't agree with each other, we can better plead our cases in decent language with propriety and decorum, than with bickering and fighting. Then each of us can rightfully and reasonably say whatever we might wish.[161]

Both poems also show us their protagonists taking a consciously serious and strategic approach to the business of disputation, thoughtfully organising and adapting their arguments even when they sense that they are under pressure. For example:

---

[158] *Little Debate*, v. 154; *The Owl and the Nightingale*, v. 235 etc.

[159] I would suggest that the following vv. are at least broadly proverbial, either in substance or in form: 115–18, 154–56, 171–72, 173–74, 185–86, 237–40, 301, 315–18, 329–30, 344–45, 362, 587–88, 613–14, 815–18, 837–38, 843–44, 849–50, 887–94, 910, 1107–1110, 1123–24, 1241, 1257, 1298, 1304–06, 1327–28, 1370, 1374, 1419–20, 1517, 1530–31, 1533–34, 1551–52, 1553–54, 1573–74, 1639–40, 1642, 1644, 1649–50. There are also some strikingly proverbial moments in the two saints' lives (e.g. *Josaphaz*, vv. 137, 144).

[160] Cartlidge, *O&N*, xxxv, n. 92.

[161] *The Owl and the Nightingale*, vv. 179–86: "fo we on mid ri3te dome, / Mid faire worde & mid ysome. / Þe3 we ne bo at one acorde, / We mu3e bet mid fayre worde, / Witute cheste & bute fi3te, / Plaidi mid fo3e & mid ri3te; / & mai hure eiþer wat hi wile, / Mid ri3te segge & mid sckile."

The old man stopped and didn't say any more: he held his peace in order to listen carefully. The young man noticed and understood that the old man was now keeping a careful watch on him, in order to be able to trip him up a little bit (whether in word or deed), so as to deny him his happiness, and in this way obstruct his plans.[162]

The Nightingale had well employed her mind on a strategy. Even in difficult and narrow straits, she had considered her tactics thoroughly, and had found a good answer even in these tough circumstances.[163]

In both texts, there is at least a suggestion—though not necessarily an entirely serious suggestion—that the protagonists in each case deserve the reader's attention, not just because of the nature of the issues that they address, but also as models of adroit advocacy.

What all of these points of contact suggest is that the two poems should be seen at least as inhabitants, and perhaps also as products, of a common cultural and intellectual tradition. In other words, the juxtaposition of Chardri's works with *The Owl and the Nightingale* is not necessarily only due to one particular scribe's perception that there happens to be a good fit between them. It is much more likely that these texts survive together because they were designed from the outset for much the same reading public, by authors whose outlooks and assumptions were essentially shared. From this point of view, the fact that two poems were written in different languages is not an indication that they were originally addressed to—and ultimately enjoyed by—completely different sectors of English society. Rather, it suggests that both were current in a society largely defined by its willingness to use both French and English. This in turn means that reading Chardri, or indeed the *Owl*-poet, requires a sense of literary possibility that extends across the linguistic divide.

Editions and Methods of Translation

These translations are intended to be readable as well as accurate, which means that I have tried to do justice to Chardri's characteristic liveliness and complexity of tone. Reported speech is extensive in his work, and he is clearly at pains to make it seem realistically natural and idiomatic, but even as a narrator his style is often rather conversational, even "chatty." More even than most medieval writers, Chardri seems to have cultivated the illusion of immediacy, going out of his

---

[162] *Little Debate*, vv. 479–86.

[163] *The Owl and the Nightingale*, vv. 701–706: "Þe Niȝtingale al hire hoȝe / Mid rede hadde wel bitoȝe. / Among þe harde, among þe toȝte, / Ful wel mid rede hire bitoȝte; / An hadde andsuere gode ifunde, / Among al hire harde stunde." Cf. also vv. 391–410, 1067–74, 1511–14, 1705–16.

way to depict himself as a speaking poet addressing a listening audience. I have tried to capture something of this informality of manner, though not (I hope) at the expense of precision.

The edited texts on which these translations rely are the ANTS editions of the *Seven Sleepers* and the *Little Debate* by Brian S. Merrilees, and John Koch's edition of *Josaphaz*. Merrilees's editions provide a good deal of annotation and analysis, but Koch's edition dates from 1879, and is altogether less helpful, with no glossary and only very sparse annotation. I have checked Koch's text against the more recent (unpublished) edition by T.J.S. Rutledge.[164]

Like most writers in Old French, Chardri regularly shifts between present and past tense in his narrative, but I have regularised this, consistently using the past tense (which is much more natural in modern English). Just occasionally this results in a certain loss of impact, as for example at *Josaphaz*, vv. 2705–706, where Chardri's text says literally that it *is* high time that God helped the saint (rather than *was*), and wishes for his grace to be shown "now." The effect contrived here is that the poet is speaking from within the narrative time of the story, rather than outside it, as if giving voice to Josaphaz's impatience, as much as his own.

Chardri also sometimes blurs speech-boundaries in such a way as to obscure the distinction between the narrator's voice and those of his characters. For example, in *Josaphaz*, v. 496, and *Seven Sleepers*, v. 1270, he apparently switches from reported speech to direct speech in the middle of a sentence, and without any explicit indication that he is doing so. Similarly, it is also not clear how much of *Josaphaz*, vv. 792–818, constitutes reported speech rather than paraphrase (and Koch in fact fails to complete the punctuation here).

Now and then, Chardri's French can be quite elliptical. For example, the syntax in *Seven Sleepers*, vv. 1597–1600, is incomplete, and should perhaps taken to be anacoluthic; in *Josaphaz*, vv. 66–68, it is only implicit that the "other lands" in question are ones in which Christianity was *not* advancing; in *Josaphaz*, v. 1610, when Chardri says that none of Nakor's belief remained, he means (though does not say) his *former* belief (i.e in paganism).[165] In all such cases I have tried to make the implied sense clear.

---

[164] I have made very little use of Rutledge's translation, which is, in places, rather garbled. For example, vv. 1080–83, rendered by Rutledge as "Thereupon the king asked whether he (Josaphat) was angry with him (the king), and whether as a result he (the king) had alienated himself from (the very person) he is trying to comfort." Also, vv. 1551–58, which become: "for he saw that in debate he can do no wrong. For he commanded that he argue forcefully against his (the king's) men. But in truth, he wished him to be defeated for his own advantage. His (Nakor's) eyes often betrayed that he might allow himself to be beaten."

[165] For other examples, see *Josaphaz*, vv. 613–615; *Seven Sleepers*, v. 1056.

I have silently made a number of other small alterations for the sake of readability. For example, where Chardri does not make the referents of pronouns explicit, I have occasionally found it helpful to do so; I have sometimes omitted intensives, toned down asseverations or modified titles of respect, where the translation would otherwise seem awkward or unnatural in modern English;[166] and the conjunctions *si, car* and *e* (which Chardri uses frequently) have not always been translated literally.

In C and J, Chardri's text is divided into sections by large capital letters (*litterae notabiliores*). These occur at exactly the same places in both manuscripts, which suggests that they also existed in the lost common exemplar, X.[167] Their use is by no means arbitrary; in *Josaphaz* and *Seven Sleepers* they coincide with natural breaks in the flow of the narrative, and in the *Little Debate* they only appear where there are changes of speaker.[168] Wherever there are *litterae notabiliores* in the scribes' texts, I have marked this at the corresponding points in my translation with the symbol ¶. Particularly in the two saints' lives, I have found it necessary (for the sake of readability) to create divisions in the text much more often than the scribes do. Paragraphs not prefixed by ¶ are therefore ones that I have introduced at points where there are no section-breaks in the manuscripts.

In the *Little Debate*, the attributions to speakers (in small capitals) follow the marginal ascriptions made in C (to "L'Enfant" and "Le Veillard" respectively): on the relatively few occasions where C omits the relevant ascriptions, I have supplied them in square brackets.

At several points, in all three texts, I have departed from the punctuation suggested by the editors, doing so silently unless this has a substantive impact on the text's sense, in which case I have reported the disagreement in my notes. In a small number of instances, I have proposed emendations to the edited texts, or alternative interpretations to those suggested by the editors, but again I have made this clear in my footnotes.

---

[166] One expression for which I have failed to find any idiomatic modern equivalent is *beau pere*, which the Young Man often uses to address his opponent in the *Little Debate*. In lieu of any more elegant solution to the problem, I have simply translated this quite literally as "good father".

[167] There are no such divisions in V.

[168] On a few occasions in the *Little Debate* there is a change of speaker, but no *littera notabilior*. This occurs at vv. 313, 315, 319, 321, 340, 365, 367, 599, 600, 882, 884, 1159, 1160 and 1161. In both Koch's edition of the two saint's lives and Merrilees's edition of *Seven Sleepers*, the text is presented strictly in accordance with the section-breaks suggested by the scribes.

THE LIFE OF THE SEVEN SLEEPERS

Here begins the Life of the Seven Sleepers.

¶ The power of God, that lasts forever and is forever pure and unerring, should not be left unspoken. No one is surprised when God makes the weather warm or icy, cloudy, clear or windy, whether on land or at sea, because everyone is used to seeing the changes that he brings about with his power.[1] Yet, if only we were able to consider it deeply enough (and if God were willing to help us, for we could never succeed unless he helped us), then we would find it astonishing. For which of us could easily measure the number of the stars in the sky,[2] or the height of the firmament, that shines so clear and bright, or the extent of all the earth or the expanse of the ocean so deep?[3] Anyone who ventured to talk at all about it could only marvel. Yet we think about it very little, for in our foolishness we have planted our affection elsewhere, in wickedness and in treachery; for we have no interest in thinking about anything except the misfortunes that we see occurring in this world. Gentlemen, we delight too much in thinking about such things, since in the end such considerations will bring us nothing but shame and grief. Anyone who wants to love God in his heart and renounce the love of this world, which brings so much trouble, will certainly greatly rejoice to hear of the works of Jesus Christ, the works that he continues to do and has always

---

[1] 1–10 Psalm, 146, 7–8: "Sing ye to the Lord with praise: sing to our God upon the harp who covereth the heaven with clouds, and prepareth rain for the earth. Who maketh grass to grow on the mountains, and herbs for the service of men." The exemplification of God's power by Creation itself is one of Chardri's recurring themes: see e.g. *Josaphaz*, vv. 25–28; *Seven Sleepers*, vv. 385–400; *Little Debate*, vv. 499–506.

[2] 17–18 Psalm 146: 4: "Praise ye the Lord . . . Who telleth the number of the stars"; Isaiah 40: 26: "Lift up your eyes on high, and see who hath created these things: who bringeth out their host by number." Also, Wisdom 7: 17–21: "For he hath given me the true knowledge of the things that are: to know the disposition of the whole world, and the virtues of the elements, the beginning, and ending, and midst of the times, the alterations of their courses, and the changes of seasons, the revolutions of the year, and the dispositions of the stars . . ."

[3] 19–22 Isaiah 40: 12: "Who hath measured the waters in the hollow of his hand, and weighed the heavens with his palm? who hath poised with three fingers the bulk of the earth, and weighed the mountains in scales, and the hills in a balance?"

done. Anyone who abandons his great folly as a result of these considerations will be showing loyalty. In order to foster such intentions and the good that they can bring about, I am going to recount an adventure that is true in every point, concerning a miracle performed by Jesus, who is, and always has been, merciful. Anyone who loves God with a good heart should pay attention now; and in this way he will do what is wise. (1–50)

¶ Gentleman, I do not want to waste my efforts on the fables of Ovid,[4] and I am certainly not going to say anything about Tristram nor Galeron; or waste any attention upon Renart or Hersent.[5] I would rather talk about God and his power, who is, and always was, almighty; and about his saints, the Seven Sleepers, who shone so brightly before the face of Jesus Christ; and so I am going to tell you the truth about them, just as it is written, from beginning to end, exactly as it was. (51–64)

¶ There was once a mighty emperor in the great city of Constantinople, whose name was Decius.[6] He was arrogant and very powerful, but also a pagan in his beliefs, devoting his whole mind to Apollo and Tervagant.[7] Because of this, he had foolishly undertaken to use all of his power to destroy Christianity. And so, in order to give vent to his great fury, he wanted to march into every country, making sure that no foreign nation would in any way dare to resist his savage diktats: or else he would have them immediately killed or delivered over to horrible torture. People were very afraid of that. Setting out from Constantinople, and passing through Carthage, Decius thus reached the city of Ephesus,

---

[4] 51 **the fables of Ovid** *fables d'Ovide*. This is presumably a reference to Ovid's *Metamorphoses*. On Ovid's reception in the Middle Ages, see Jeremy Dimmick, "Ovid in the Middle Ages: Authority and Poetry," in *The Cambridge Companion to Ovid*, ed. Philip Hardie (Cambridge: Cambridge University Press, 2002, repr. 2006), 264–87.

[5] 54–55 **Tristram** and **Galeron** are heroes in medieval romance. **Renart** (the fox) and **Hersent** (the she-wolf) are characters in medieval beast-epics such as the *Roman de Renart*. For the Tristan-tradition, see *Early French Tristan Poems*, ed. and trans. Norris J. Lacy et al., 2 vols. (Cambridge: Brewer, 1998). For Galeron, see *Galeran de Bretagne*, ed. Lucien Foulet (Paris: Champion, 1975) and Gautier d'Arras, *Ille et Galéron*, ed. Yves Lefèvre (Paris: Champion, 1999). (To my knowledge, neither of these romances has been translated into English.) For Renart and Hersente, see, e.g., *The Romance of Reynard the Fox*, trans. D.D.R. Owen (Oxford: Oxford University Press, 1994); and on medieval animal-fiction more generally, see the recent study by Jill Mann, *From Aesop to Reynard: Beast Literature in Medieval Britain* (Oxford: Oxford University Press, 2009).

[6] 67 **Decius** was Roman Emperor from 249 to 251. He instituted persecutory measures against Christians, but the reference to Constantinople is anachronistic because the city was only named as such in 330, long after his death. It is only at this point that Chardri starts following L_1: the material in vv. 1–64 is an addition to his source.

[7] 70 **Tervagant**. Tervagant is "an imaginary deity held in mediæval Christendom to be worshipped by Muslims" (*OED*, s.v. 'termagant'), and often linked in medieval romance with Apollo and Muhammad.

where St. Paul had lived and expounded sacred doctrine, which had thwarted the wicked ways of that perfidious and cruel people.[8] Yet at the approach of the emperor that whorish people, those villains, all emerged. The sons of God, the Christians (but there were few of that disposition) fled into hiding because of those evil, savage people, in fear of the cruelty that they might perpetrate in the city. As soon as the emperor arrived there, he straightaway commanded that a splendid temple should be constructed in the middle of the city, out of grey marble, out of hard stone, where he intended to commit an evil deed: that is, the crime of sacrificing to the devils of hell. There he had idols made out of iron or out of wood or out of stone, in many different designs.[9] Each of them had whatever shape was given them by the invention and intention of the craftsmen who worked on them. There were some that bore the head of an ape or of a cat or of a dog or of a rat; another resembled an owl; others portrayed the months of the year; some were bulls; others sheep; and some looked like bats. Each of them created the image of what he wished to be remembered. Such were the gods that were made, such were the gods they loved and lavishly decorated with silver, with gems and with beaten gold.[10] Never had so much treasure been seen. To these things they made their sacrifice; because of them they imposed cruel punishment on those who refused to worship or to honour their false gods. Every day, from all the cities of the country all around, came both the rich and the poor among that wicked pagan people, the great as well as the not so great; and the town was completely filled every day of the week with blood, billowing smoke,[11] and the stench of the entrails produced by this slaughter. There was vileness everywhere. The Christians were very alarmed when they saw such insanity. All of them got ready to flee — and no wonder! (65–142)

¶ Against this backdrop, the emperor, in his pride and cruelty of spirit, ordered that the land be combed for Christians. He wanted to subject them to great torture if they refused to do what he commanded. You could have seen the people arming themselves and the pagans setting out in aggressive gangs, here, there, and everywhere. They were very happy and eager to shame Christianity. Why

---

[8] 85–87 Acts 19: 1–20. The reference to St. Paul is not in L_1.

[9] 106–108 The Bible's injunctions against idol-worship tend to involve a reminder that they are made out of materials like wood and stone. See e.g. Deut. 29: 17: "You have seen their abominations and filth, that is to say, their idols, wood and stone, silver and gold, which they worshipped"; also Isa. 37: 19; Dan. 5: 23; Sap. 13: 10 etc. The same point is also made in *Josaphaz*, vv. 1524–26, 2195–2200.

[10] 112–123 This description of the idols' different shapes is not found in L_1, so in this context it is presumably "Chardri's own invention", as Merrilees puts it (76).

[11] 135 **billowing smoke** *fumee ki estencele*. Cf. L_1: "fumus hostiarum tanquam nebula" (I, 40: "the smoke of sacrifices like a cloud"). This detail can be traced all the way back to the Syriac version of the legend, which refers to "rauchiger Opferdunst" (Allgeier, 6 [1916], 3).

should I make a long story of it?[12] The faint-hearted fled into hiding;[13] but the faithful, God's friends, confidently and constantly maintained their belief in God their creator, because they were unafraid. They knew well that this life is nothing but a foolish dream. What they wanted, beyond doubt, was that other life, full of eternal joy. Because of this, they were arrested and delivered to martyrdom for the sake of God, who performs miracles. I can tell you the various ways in which they were martyred: some were hanged, some were drawn, some were flayed and then killed, some were drowned, some were burned, some were tortured in every part by hunger, some succumbed to cold, some were devoured by beasts, some were roasted, some were boiled, some were buried alive, some died from their sufferings, many were torn apart. Some were decapitated and their heads were fixed on the gates and towers,[14] in order to intimidate the Christians.[15] The pagans wanted to boast about devising so many different tortures, those horrible wretches! In order to destroy Christianity completely, they condemned God's saints to martyrdom. Gentlemen, in such conditions sons repudiated their fathers out of fear of torture; brothers repudiated their sisters or their kinsmen; and neighbour denounced neighbour in order to save himself.[16] Such slaughter and suffering has never been seen at any time since. There is no man alive with sufficient ingenuity or learning[17] to reckon up the anguish and distress that God's saints suffered for him as they did, in their bodies and in their hearts. (143–202)

¶ In his palace the emperor maintained good men as well as bad, including seven young men noble in ancestry, but all the more noble in spirit, in that they loved God above all else. I can tell you their names: the first was called Maximianus; then there were Malchus and Martinianus, Dionysius and Seraphion, Johannes and Constantinus. They had dedicated their minds, their faithful hearts and their youth to serving God their creator; and they had great compassion for God's friends, whose enemies so cruelly afflicted them with such sufferings. It grieved them deeply, and yet they showed no sign at all that they loved

---

[12] 154 This line (which is an instance of the rhetorical device of *paralipsis*) replicates *Josaphaz*, vv. 819 and 2773.

[13] 156 This line replicates *Seven Sleepers*, v. 95.

[14] 179–82 L_1: "Et supra muros et pinacula civitatis suspendebant eos et capita eorum iuxta civitatem ante portas infigebant in bicipite ligno" (III, 41: "And they hanged them from the walls and pinnacles of the city and they fixed their heads outside the city before the gates on a wooden fork").

[15] 168–83 Cf. *Josaphaz*, vv. 1287–96, 1621–26, and *Little Debate*, vv. 639–40. I have departed from the punctuation suggested by Merrilees, who places a full stop after v. 182, so that "in order to intimidate the Christians" has to be taken with the following sentence.

[16] 189–92 Cf. L_1: "Parentes abnegabant filios, et filii parentes, et amici abnegabant amicos" (III, 42: "parents denied their sons, and sons their parents, and friends denied their friends").

[17] 197–98 These lines are very similar to *Josaphaz*, vv. 2063–64.

Christianity, since they had family connections in the king's court and were so well liked there that, if they had subscribed to those people's wicked beliefs, there was no one in his empire who would have dared speak against them. Indeed they prayed night and day for the emperor: they belonged to his household, so it was only right that they should love him. Yet they took a great risk: whenever the emperor went to perform sacrifices, the seven withdrew to a secret place by themselves, as brothers in their firm faith, in order to worship God, to love and honour him, and to pray for their family and for the emperor who was so fickle. Yet the envy of the wicked is inexhaustible, for their evil hearts rejoice in betrayal, whether by word or deed or injury. So it was with these courtiers: some who were their close relatives accused them before the emperor of wishing to reject his beliefs; and they spoke out in this way, just as you will now hear: (203–48)

¶ "Lord and emperor, ruler of the whole circumference of the world,[18] of the animals as well as the land, the birds in the air, and the fish swimming in the ocean[19] —be our king, lord, and master! May your empire last forever! We are your loyal friends: we owe you our love at all times. For this reason we would not lessen your honour just to get some favour from you. You have compelled various people to come here from foreign lands in order to offer a celebration to our mighty gods, who are the rulers of everything; and these people all travelled from their homelands in order to increase your prestige. But what good is it if the foreigners obey you without demur, while those who are in your own jurisdiction do not respect your word at all,[20] despising both you and your greatness? And what good is your wealth, if in your court you've nurtured, greatly loved, and cherished your enemies, when they despise you and dishonour you more than anyone in this land? Maximianus, the mayor's son,[21] thinks he can protect his six companions in spite of you. We can tell you their names: they are Malchus and Martinianus, Seraphion and Johannes, Dionysius and Constantinus. These seven young men are among the most nobly born, among the best of your barons; but they are all Christians, without doubt. They don't value you more than a dime,[22] nor your gods, nor your sacrifices. Not one of them thinks any of this is worth anything at all. They worship 'omnipotent God'[23] in defiance of your authority."(249–90)

---

[18] 250 **the whole circumference** *trestut a la runde*. The phrase *a la runde* is also used geographically in *Josaphaz*, v. 26.

[19] 249–52 These claims on behalf of Decius's gods are an ironic echo of the celebration of God's power in the first 10 lines of this poem. There is no precedent for them in L_1.

[20] 268 **at all** *une alie*: literally, "[any more than] a sorb-apple."

[21] 275 **the son of the mayor** *le fiz le maire*: in L_1, "filius praefecti."

[22] 286 **dime** *maille*: literally, "a half-penny." Cf. *Josaphaz*, v. 2538; *Little Debate*, vv. 498, 1318, 1500.

[23] 289 The pagan courtiers' use of this epithet is presumably sarcastic.

¶ When the emperor had heard this, you can be sure that he was hardly overjoyed. Straightaway he had the young men summoned; and he spoke to them in this way:

"Young men," he said, "I understand that, out of silliness, you've gone astray—thus disparaging your lineage and demeaning your nobility, just as if you'd been born and brought into the world by a peasant-woman, and educated at her knees. And this is now the doctrine that your frivolousness has taught you, that you should knowingly despise my greatness and my power! Because I am your liege-lord, I am your king and your emperor. If you commit any further folly, your apostasy will cost you your lives in this world. You've rejected our gods, who are so powerful, and instead attached yourself to a foreigner, some man who was hanged, called 'Jesus' by the Christians, some fool who wanted to be called 'God' and yet was incapable of helping himself.[24] And you who should have been wise, have become so spiritually corrupted that in your folly you have renounced those gods to whom the whole world bows, who rule and sustain everything and from whom all benefits derive. By peerless Apollo, I swear, if you do not agree to worship them, then I'll tell you a different story—i.e. that you'll live in enormous shame, pain and suffering for as long as I am emperor, and then you'll die a terrible death. You'll have no other consolation but that. I don't want to put you under any misapprehension. So go and sacrifice straightaway, in order that worse does not befall you, and so that I don't feel the need to do anything more severe."

Maximianus replied:[25] "My lord emperor, I'll tell you the truth: I and all my companions despise your idols more than mongrels, because they're worthless and can do no good for those who have honoured them. They would take no more notice if they were lying in some great latrine than if they were clothed in gold and silver in the most beautiful temple in Spain, for they are deaf and dumb, and incapable of existing by themselves. They're made of oak, or pearwood, or some other wood—of whatever kind it may be—so that they neither feel nor see a thing.[26] They're good for only one thing, and that's as fuel in the furnace. They'll betray you in the end, because you'll be boiled in hell. You'll pass from

---

[24] 315–16 Cf. Luke 23: 37–36: "And the soldiers also mocked him, coming to him, and offering him vinegar, and saying: If thou be the king of the Jews, save thyself"; also Mark 15: 31.

[25] 336–414. Chardri's version of this speech is considerably longer and more pugnacious than in L_1 (IV, 45–46).

[26] 346–50 Emphasis on the inanimateness of pagan idols is a recurrent biblical topos. See e.g. Deut. 4: 28, which refers to "gods, that were framed with men's hands: wood and stone, that neither see, nor hear, nor eat, nor smell"; and Wisdom 15: 13–17, which refers to "the idols of the heathens for gods, which neither have the use of eyes to see, nor noses to draw breath, nor ears to hear, nor fingers of hands to handle, and as for their feet, they are slow to walk. For man made them: and he that borroweth his own breath, fashioned them."

the fire to the cold;[27] and that's where you'll stay forever. But our God who created all things, both heaven and earth and all that they contain, and who resides in the holy Trinity, delivered us from death to life; and he will grant eternal joy to anyone who bows before him. God grant that I might be one such! (291–364)

¶ "The King of Heaven who created us sent his son to earth on account of the trespass that Adam committed and in order to seek and save his people. He was born of the sweet maiden who was and will always be pure and immaculate, and in this way he offered himself as our ransom, undertaking both pain and suffering in order to deliver his creatures from the eternal fires of hell. Like a valiant and powerful man, he led them away to the joy and happiness of heaven that has no end. This joy he will give to those who are his own. In exchange for this joy and this life, we have rejected great folly. We believe in him, we will honour him, and we will dedicate both body and soul to him. He is God and he is king. He is the founder of our faith. He made the sea and he made the wind. He made the whole of the firmament. He made the sun and he made the moon, and there isn't a single star that he didn't make. And how did he do so? He did it all by means of his command. And he governs everything that exists, because he is God, lord and master. He who is without peer makes both heaven and earth tremble, whenever he wants to. There isn't a bird flying in the air nor a fish in the sea nor an animal alive that doesn't live and move because of him, the one who founded the whole world: that is, our Lord Jesus Christ who rules everything and created all this.[28] But the gods that you have made mean nothing to us, you may be sure. They will rot and you will die, no matter how you succour them. The gold that's fastened on them now will be pulled off with pincers. Those who want to take the gold of your gods will smash their faces with hammers. And that will be a very great shame, for people won't care about them anymore. No one can take away our treasure, no matter what they might contrive, for we've placed it in heaven, where no one can be a beggar." With that he fell silent and spoke no more. The king had been abashed by the boy, because of how eloquently he spoke, but now he looked up.[29] (365–418)

¶ "Young man," he said, "I am deeply displeased both by your words and your conduct, for you all come of a noble lineage. For this reason it would seem to me a great pity if I were compelled to set my mind on disgracing such very fine

---

[27] 355 Merrilees compares Judas's account of hell in *St Brendan* (*Benedeit: The Anglo-Norman Voyage of St Brendan*, ed. Ian Short and Brian Merrilees [Manchester: Manchester University Press, 1979], vv. 1323–1438. However, cold and fire appear together among the torments of hell described elsewhere in medieval literature: see, example, the *Visio Pauli*, caps. 31–42, trans. Elliott, 633–38.

[28] 385–400 Cf. *Seven Sleepers*, vv. 1–24; *Josaphaz*, vv. 25–28; *Little Debate*, vv. 499–506.

[29] 416–18 More literally: "The king lifted his head, which he had lowered on account of the boy."

young men. It would be a serious blemish on my court if ever your lives were lost. Go away like prudent fellows and think about living long lives of great dignity and comfort, and abandon this foolishness, for I know very well that it's out of thoughtlessness that you've entered upon such madness. I'll grant you a generous reprieve in which you can reconsider for a bit and take such counsel as will bring you to show prudence." (418–36)

¶ With these words he allowed them to depart and set them at liberty to do the sensible thing, and not abandon their faith. Then he set out from the city. He had enlisted more than five thousand pagans, and with that band of whorish, hated people, he went off into the country in order to complete what he had set out to do: to cleanse the whole land of Christians and their activities. He caused terrible harm everywhere throughout the land. (437–50)

¶ The youths I told you about went away in fear, when this reprieve was granted, but they behaved like good men. They took all their wealth from their friends and relatives and they secretly distributed it to the needy. They gathered together clothes and food, gold and silver—everything they could procure—because they wanted to give it all to poor folk. Then they took counsel together and committed themselves to doing all this, on the grounds that waiting for the emperor would do nothing but increase their suffering. They were going to have to leave the city out of sheer necessity.

"Gentlemen," said one, "let's leave the country together. If the emperor is able to catch us, he'll hang all seven of us from the gallows, [in this land] where it is obligatory to sacrifice. He's warned us that he's certainly prepared to do it. Time is short and waiting will bring us grief. There is a mountain near here called Celion, uncultivated and far from any habitation, where in a hidden spot there's a wide, deep cave. As long as we've got food, we'll be able to stay there for a long time without anyone's knowledge."[30]

"This is an attractive plan," they said, "since there's nothing else we can do." (451–86)

---

[30] 469–84 In L_1 (VI, 47) the young men retreat to the cave not as a means of avoiding persecution, but in order to give themselves time to prepare for it: "eamus in speluncam grandem in monte Celio et ibi deprecemur Deum incessanter et erimus sine timore abominationis [Hüber reads "ab omnibus", which makes no sense], usquequo revertatur imperator et iudicemur ante ipsum, et non impediamur ad gloriam Dei; sed secundum voluntatem suam Deus faciat nobiscum, ut perficiamus in conspectu imperatoris martyrium et recipiamus immarcescibilem coronam fidelium" ("let us go into the large cavern in Mt. Celion and there pray incessantly to God; there we can be without fear of outrage, until the time when the emperor returns and we are judged before him; then we will not be impeded from God's glory, but rather God will do with us what is according to his will, so that we might attain martyrdom and receive the everlasting crown of the faithful").

¶ And so they raised money and from what they had been given they collected enough to support themselves for a long time afterwards. Then all seven set off and hid themselves in the cave that they had previously chosen together. All seven lay there night and day, praying sincerely to the Creator. They were there for a long time without anyone knowing.

After they had been staying there for a while, they unanimously elected one of their group to go into the great city in order to get provisions and to find out some news about their countrymen. He had to go about this very cleverly because he and the others were very well known. He put on old, patched clothes in order to conceal himself adequately; and then he set off straightaway. Pretending that he was a penniless peasant, he kept company with poor men.[31] By these means he shrewdly asked for news everywhere he went. He listened to whatever he was told about where the emperor had gone and about the young men who had disappeared; and then, when it was late in the evening, looking rather cowardly, he furtively purchased food for his companions. Then he cannily slipped away out of the crowds, and went straight back to the cave. In this way he found food for his companions and kept them informed about the cruel and harsh events that he learned of in the city. He gave them a comprehensive account, for he was very clever, this Malchus (as he was called). As he came and went, he often gave generously to the poor out of the money that he carried. (487–534)

¶ While this was going on, gentlemen, it did not take long for the emperor to complete his tour throughout the whole country. In great pomp he returned to the fine city of Ephesus; and in his fury he ordered that all his barons should be summoned. He also ordered that there should be a summons for Maximianus and his companions. Malchus was in the city to keep watch, as usual, and he saw the Christians fleeing in great fear of being killed, for the emperor had sworn by his evil god that there was no man in his land so noble, so rich or so proud, that, if he were unwilling to sacrifice, he would not be handed over to suffering, torment and sorrow, as an example to everyone else,[32] and then he would die a horrible death, rightly or wrongly.[33] When the Christians heard this, they did not linger in the city, but fled in every direction in order to save themselves by any means they could.[34]

When Malchus heard about the emperor and all the harm that his fury was causing, he was more afraid than he had ever been in his life. The best thing he could think of to do was to buy food quickly, full of heartfelt anxiety about how

---

[31] 507–11 L₁ (VI, 48) says that he disguised himself as a beggar ("induebatur figura mendici").

[32] 556 **as an example to everyone else** *Ke pour avrunt li plusur*: literally, "so that the majority would be afraid."

[33] 557–58 These lines almost completely duplicate *Josaphaz*, vv. 1349–50.

[34] 562 **by any means they could** *par chaut, par freit*: literally, "whether by heat or by cold."

best he could escape without the pagans catching him. Using all his cleverness, he was able to get away, carrying just enough bread with him,[35] and he headed straight for his companions, whom he found at their devotions.[36] In tears he told them everything he had heard, how the emperor had commanded that they should be hunted down both in the city and in the countryside, and all about the emperor's oath: how he had sworn by his religion that not for all the gold in the world would any Christian ever be redeemed from instant death, if he refused to sacrifice. Everywhere people were fleeing because of this: never had the need to do so been so great.

"And we," he said, "are wanted men throughout the country, just as we feared."

Then they all wept together in sorrow; and on account of their great fear, they trembled in every limb, anguished and perspiring.

"Gentlemen," said Malchus, "there's only one thing for it. Since you've been fasting, I advise you to eat a little something, in order to distract you from anxiety. If we're in good heart, we won't be so afraid of falling into the hands of the wicked. Then if the emperor summons us, our words will be more effective, and we'll be more courageous in the face of both his words and his deeds."

With that Malchus stood up and, acting as their steward, served out their bread. They ate the food that he gave them and then they all talked. They almost went mad with grief, discussing how they would resist when they came before the emperor. (535–612)

¶ While they were so intent on their conversation, day gave way to evening. Whether out of distress or out of worry, the seven young men went to sleep—for it often happens, you know, that when people are very sad on account of the weight of their worries, it is natural that they are prompt to slumber.[37] Indeed it was God who loved them, and put them to sleep, just as he pleased. Their faces were like roses that have just opened. In this fashion, these seven youngsters lay next to each other, sleeping on their sides. He who wrought the sea and the earth and heaven, granted them such repose[38] in order to show everybody else a miracle. No one has ever heard the like of it. This miracle God brought about by means of his power: you're about to hear how it happened.

---

[35] 574 just enough bread *assez de pain.* L₁ says "small loaves" ("modicos panes", VII, 49).

[36] 576 at their devotions *en afflictiuns.*

[37] 617–20 Cf. *Josaphaz,* vv. 1943–44; and Eccles. 5, 2: "Dreams follow many cares." L₁ says that "their eyes were heavy from weeping and because of the sadness in their hearts" ("fuerant enim oculi eorum gravati ex lacrimis et ex tristitia cordis eorum" (VII, 50).

[38] 627 repose *repos* Chardri is careful to leave open the question of quite what state the seven are actually in at this point. Earlier versions of the legend tend to make clear that this is only the appearance of sleep and that they have in fact died. L₁ says that God gave them "a quiet and sweet death" ("mortem quietis [. . .] et suavitatis"), so that they were "like people asleep" ("sicut dormientes": L₁, VII, 50). Similar phrasing is used in the Syriac text (Allgeier, 6 [1916], 13).

Next morning when it was daylight, the emperor ordered that the seven be sought. Throughout the country, throughout the land, he had them searched for everywhere—this way and that, up and down, on foot and on horseback. But he couldn't find them, not by any means. This weighed heavily on his heart. Because they were of noble ancestry, the young men were all the more regretted. (613–42)

¶ The king said to his barons, "Gentlemen, it is a very great pity that these young men should go astray like this. In this way their beauty and nobility will be lost to us. My heart is deeply troubled by their sorrow and distress. They thought that I would be angry and that's why they've run away. But you should understand: I wasn't angry, I merely wished to correct their faults by speaking forcefully to them. Apart from that, I wouldn't have done anything to them. We have lost them as a result of misguided intentions. Alas that ever I looked on their youthful beauty!' (643–58)

¶ "Sire," said the barons to the king, "You shouldn't get so upset on account of such very stupid people, since, once they'd flouted your commands, they were never afterwards going to leave off doing dishonour to our religion. We tell you in all honesty that they were rooted in malice, as long as you allowed them to have the upper hand.[39] When you gave them a reprieve, then for the first time you brought out their irrationality. But who cares if they've left the country, when they don't want to do your will? No one can say a word about them, whether they're in your empire, whether they're dead or alive. Those seven wretches have simply disappeared. If you want to proceed any further against them, they have a large number of relatives. Make them come before you and confess in full where those boys might have gone. And if they don't satisfy you, it would be embarrassing for you if you didn't take revenge on them."

"This is good advice," said the emperor, "They should be summoned without delay, to come tomorrow at dawn. I want to investigate this matter."

They did as he wished: all the relatives were summoned. Plenty of dukes, counts, and lesser noblemen[40] arrived before their lord.

The king addressed them in this way: "Gentlemen," he said, "it's my opinion that you ought loyally to guard my honour. You're not doing that, which I regret: rather, you've all betrayed the loyalty that you promised me, because you're supporting my enemies. It's from you that they're getting both advice and encouragement, against my solemn prohibition. I mean these young men, who are so flighty and thoughtless that the other day they ran away. The reason for this was their great fear of the threats that I made against them, regarding matters in which they had done wrong: not wanting to sacrifice to the gods who wish to

---

[39] 668 **allowed them to have the upper hand** *vus les meistes a cheval*. This is Merrilees's interpretation. Perhaps it would also be possible to read "allowed them to sit on their high horse."

[40] 692 **lesser noblemen** *vavasur*: a stratum of lower-ranking noblemen, vassals holding sub-fiefs from greater lords.

rule all things. Instead they have all fled from here. By Muhammad[41] and Lord Tervagant, if you don't make them come forward, you'll be condemned to die a horrible death. I won't spare you for all the treasure in Damascus."[42] (659–716)

¶ "Lord Emperor," said the relatives, "We have submitted to your high authority, and have been loyal towards our liege lord, right up to this day. We are and always will be obedient to you, sire, as long as we live. Why should we die just because these boys are behaving like fools? We will tell you whatever we know about them and whatever we have heard from others. The boys that you demand from us are not at our disposal, but rather they are carefully hidden in a cave — so people are saying — located in that great mountain over there. There they are hidden, there they are concealed. Whether they're alive or dead, we don't know. There's nothing else we can tell you about them. Now it's in your hands,[43] sire," they said. "You can do whatever you want, but there's nothing else you'll ever be able to learn from us." (717–38)

¶ "Noble barons," said the emperor, "since you've told me the truth about how this business has happened, and where they are now in hiding, you may all go free, as wise and worthy men. From now on you'll be all the more favoured by me, since you have demonstrated such loyalty."

With that they withdrew, leaving him complaining at length to his intimates about how he could best avenge himself on the seven, without dishonouring or harming them. He did not want to see the bodies of such very beautiful people subjected to torture.

"There's only one thing I can decree," he said, "in order to confound those fools. I will have the entrance of this cave — broad though it is — stopped up with a wall. In this way they'll be dishonoured.[44] They'll be buried alive and they'll die of hunger and privation, whether they like it or not." (739–60)

¶ The emperor did not want any more delay. He ordered carts and waggons to be filled with lime and hard stone, so as to stop up the entrance to the cave in which they were hiding. The workmen finished their task quickly. But among the many in the king's employ there were two who were Christians. These two drew apart and together resolved to do something. They wanted to make sure somehow that this holy martyrdom would not be concealed from people's knowledge — thinking that one day it might be revealed, in the name of God, to future

---

[41] 712 **Muhammad** *Mahun*. Chardri's anachronistic references to Muhammad, here and in *Josaphaz*, are additions to his sources. It is not unusual in medieval French literature for Muhammad to be cited simply as an example of a "pagan" god, as Merrilees points out (76).

[42] 716 **Damascus** *Damas*. Cf. *Josaphaz*, vv. 478, 1894.

[43] 736 **in your hands** *sur vus*.

[44] Line 757, in which the emperor declares how he intends the seven to be "dishonoured" (*huniz*), seems to contradict v. 750, in which it is said that he did not want to "dishonour" (*hunir*) them.

generations. For this reason they were very keen to put the lives of the seven into writing. And they did as they proposed. Theodorus was the name of one of them; the other was Rufinus, beloved by God. Using a lead plaque,[45] these men wrote down the lives of the seven: the cruelty and fury directed against them by the emperor. Without any noise or fuss they set the lead in the wall in such a way as to be sure that, as long as it stood there, it would never wear away. They did it so cleverly that none of the people saw it. It was customary among the ancients who lived in that time to write the history of anything that they wished to remember on lead, for lead will never decay, as long as it lies in a dry place.[46] With such care and cleverness Theodorus and Rufinus secretly inserted the lead, looking forward to the time when almighty God would, by means of his power, make the story of the seven martyrs public again. When the cave was stopped up, all the people were distressed in their pity for the young men who were dying in such torment. Then they all went away. However, the emperor never on this account repented of his folly. Instead, he grew continually worse afterwards, for as long as he lived. (761–812)

¶ Time passed and eventually the emperor had to die; and all of those who lived at that time departed from this world. As one goes, another comes[47]—gentlemen, that is how it has to be. When one dies, another is born[48]—that is how God arranges it, just as he pleases. So it came about that in those years all the ancients died; and another age passed away, just as all the ages before it had done.

After Decius came many rich and powerful emperors. One of them was particularly renowned: he was called Arcadius.[49] He had a son of great valour, called Theodosius,[50] who was emperor after him, and a protector of Christianity. Before their time there were plenty of Christian kings and emperors, but none of them loved the Christian faith so much nor cherished it so well. Theodosius enforced justice and loved Jesus Christ more than anything. He exalted Christianity and was full of every kind of virtue. Because of this, the Creator loved him and maintained him in great honour. But he wished to test his generosity and his loyal heart in a manner that you are just about to hear me recount—for God increases the reputation of his friends by testing them; and when he finds them

---

[45] 783 **using lead** *en plum* Chardi fails to make it clear how exactly the lead is being used, but L_1 mentions an "inscribed leaden tablet" ("tabulam plumbeam scriptam": 72) and the Syriac text refers to "two tablets made of lead" ("zwei Tafel aus Blei": Allgeier, 6 [1916] 37).

[46] 793–96 These lines are an addition to Chardri's source.

[47] 817 Cf. *Little Debate*, v. 317.

[48] 819 Cf. *Little Debate*, v. 329.

[49] 828 Arcadius, Emperor of the Eastern Empire (395–408).

[50] 831 Theodosius II, the Younger, Emperor of the Eastern Empire (408–50): see Fergus Millar, *A Greek Roman Empire: Power and Belief under Theodosius II (408–450)* (Berkeley: University of California Press, 2006).

truly loyal even in the midst of anguish and suffering, he takes away all their terrible misery, giving them joy and granting them both great glory and [a martyr's] crown.[51] In this way God wanted to test Theodosius, his dear friend. The king had reigned for thirty-eight years when a great and powerful heresy[52] arose in our religion because of false, deluded folk. With foolish intent they said that no man born of a woman will ever be resurrected on Judgment Day if he had previously suffered death.

"It cannot be," they were constantly saying, "that a dead man might ever rise again, nor that any man, no matter how wise [. . .][53] to live, whatever he might do, and whatever grace he might get from God. No one can live more than a hundred years, whatever might be written in books. After that he'll die, nor will he ever be resurrected in the flesh."[54]

Such mad ideas were spread about and also written down by the heretics, which almost brought about the complete destruction of Christianity. (813–76)

¶ They had so charmed the emperor that they nearly led him into error. These mad, stupid people had so sweetened their words,[55] which were poisoned with so much misery, that their doctrines were widely accepted. Their campaign

---

[51] 852 Cf. *Josaphaz*, vv. 2801–804.

[52] 857 **a great and powerful heresy** *une heresie e fort e grant.* Koch suggests that there is no historical basis in this period for any such heresy, which he describes as "apocryphal" (16). However, it could perhaps be taken to reflect both the "Origenist controversy" beginning in the 370s (on which see Elizabeth A. Clark, *The Origenist Controversy: The Cultural Construction of an Early Christian Debate* [Princeton: Princeton University Press, 1992]; Bynum, *Resurrection of the Body*, 86–94) and the "Nestorian" and "Eutychian" disputes that arose in the second half of Theodosius's reign (Millar, *Greek Roman Empire*, 149–67). Centrally at stake in all these arguments was a precise definition of the way in which Christ was embodied at the Incarnation, and of how resurrected bodies might be embodied at the end of time.

[53] 866 A line is missing from both the extant medieval copies of the poem.

[54] 872 **resurrected in the flesh** *en charn . . . relevera sus.* According to St. Augustine, "No Christian should in any way doubt that that the bodies of all men, whether already born or yet to be born, whether dead or still to die, will be resurrected" ("Resurrecturam tamen carnem omnium quicumque nati sunt hominum atque nascentur, et mortui sunt atque morientur, nullo modo dubitare debet christianus": *Enchiridion*, cap. 84, PL 40, col. 272). This statement weighed all the more heavily in medieval culture because it was quoted by Peter Lombard at the beginning of his discussion of Judgment Day in what was to become the most authoritative and widely circulated medieval textbook on theology, the *Sentences* (Book 4, Dist. 43, PL 192, col. 943). However, the context in which St. Augustine makes his assertion that no Christian should have any doubts about the resurrection of the body is an extended consideration of the various philosophical (and logical) difficulties implicit in this doctrine—for example, those raised by aborted fetuses, bodies divided or dismembered, and clippings of nail or hair (cf. also *City of God*, Book 22, caps. 4–5, 11–21). See further Bynum, *Resurrection of the Body*, esp. 94–104, 121–37.

[55] 879 **sweetened their words** *la lange affilee*: literally, "filed their tongues."

caused trouble throughout the whole church. The king almost killed himself because it was during his reign that such a heresy against our faith had grown up. He was so miserable on this account that he was continually overwhelmed by tears, so disheartened had he become; and he urgently beseeched God that in his pity he might consent to make some demonstration of the principles of true belief, for matters had gone so far that all the most important people in the land had been infected with this evil, which was prevalent in equal measure everywhere. Because of this, the king was wretched: he had never been more wretched than he was then. But God who arranges everything that is good and who is full of pity and mercy, did not want his friend to be distressed any more by so much sobbing and sleeplessness, but instead made him very happy, for reasons that you are about to hear. (877–906)

¶ While this madness was going on, God put it into the heart of the prominent man who owned the high mountain of Celion, Dalius by name, to construct sheepfolds all round the mountain with the help of his workmen, just as God instructed him. But the men doing the work found a great quantity of stone blocking up the entrance of the vast cave in which the seven saints whom God loved so much were lying. The workmen were delighted by this, when they saw so much stone, because it would help them speed up their work. They laboured very vigorously to dig out this good stone. They laboured so hard and dug out so much that the entrance became completely exposed, but they paid no attention to this entrance or opening. They completely finished their work without doing anything else to the cave. (907–32)

¶ Just as this was happening, God, by means of his great power, awakened the seven young men who had slept there so long. They all got up together, very shocked and worried, but strong and resolute, since this was the first night that all of them had been asleep simultaneously.[56] As far as they were concerned, they were quite sure that they had gone to sleep in the evening and woken in the morning, each of them faithfully believing that they had slept just one night. Their complexions were as bright and beautiful as roses in first bloom.

"Gentlemen," they said, "it's long past dawn. We ought to be very afraid of the emperor who's threatened us so savagely. May God grant us His grace and protect us as He wishes, so that the devil can have no power over us; and may He grant us the strength and the resolution to resist the tyrannical emperor!"

Maximianus said this to them: "Gentlemen, for the love of Jesus Christ, don't fear the emperor in any way, either his madness or his folly, but let us put our trust in God that he will help us by means of his power. Make sure that your courage doesn't falter in the face of this fierce ordeal! When we suffer for God's sake, we will be earning a great reward from Him. Malchus, my good brother,

---

[56] 940–41 The point, presumably, is that up to this night at least one of the seven has always kept watch.

what was the emperor saying in the city yesterday evening, when you were there? Now tell us what you know about it." (933–70)

¶ Malchus replied: "I told you yesterday evening all the news that I'd learned, how the emperor was having us sought everywhere throughout the land, throughout the country—in order to kill us and disgrace us."

"Certainly," said Maximianus, "that's bad news! May the Creator who perceives everything be our shield and guarantee! But now, Malchus, my good friend, I think you need to go into the city in order to find out some news, just as you did yesterday, and also to buy plenty of bread, as long as you can do so cleverly. The loaves that you brought us yesterday were small: you left behind the big ones that would have been a better buy. My dear brother, now I ask you, bring us some nice big loaves—you've got enough shiny[57] coins. Now spend quite generously—you've got plenty of gold and silver."

"Very willingly, gentlemen," he replied. "Meanwhile pray for me, that God will enable me to come back alive." (970–96)

¶ He took the coins and set off, very fearful, sad and upset. The money had been issued in the time of the notorious Decius. There was an inscription all round the edge, saying that it had been made in the time of Decius the emperor, in the year that he was crowned; and his name had been stamped in the middle. You should know that, from the day that they entered the cave until the day that they woke up, it amounted to 362 years[58]—but they didn't know a thing about it, only that they had gone to sleep one evening.

It was still morning when Malchus, that clever, prudent man, set off to do his errand for the group. But when he reached the exit of the cave, the sight of that great quarry made him tremble throughout his body. Because there was so much stone, he even thought that this was the rubble swept down the mountain by some great flood[59]—but he didn't want to stop and worry about it, since that could easily have happened. He quickly descended from the mountain and travelled across the lowlands, in great fear of being seen or recognised by anybody who might spitefully denounce or accuse him to the emperor. He didn't know that the emperor's very corpse had already rotted away. He went on nervously,

---

[57] 990 **shiny** *blancs*: literally, "white."

[58] 1005–1008 **362 years**. In L₁, the number given is 372. However, there are fewer than 200 years between the reigns of Decius (249–251) and Theodosius II (408–450). Koch suggests (*Siebenschläferlegende*, 70–71) that the explanation for this discrepancy lies in confusion between Decius and another notorious persecutor of Christians, the emperor Nero (who died in 68 A.D.). The difficulty was also noticed in the Middle Ages: as *The Golden Legend* puts it, "there is reason to doubt that these saints slept for 372 years, because they arose in the year of the Lord 448. Decius reigned in 252 [*sic*] and his reign lasted only fifteen months, so the saints must have slept only 195 years" (trans. Ryan, 2: 18).

[59] 1020 **flood** *cretine*. In the Latin, Malchus is amazed ("miratus": XIV, 61), but does not speculate about a flood.

afraid of everybody, until he reached the city. Anyone who had been there would have taken pity on him if they had seen the way he looked, in his nervousness and trepidation. (997–1036)

¶ He went straight to the gate of the city, where, glancing upwards, he saw in front of him a beautiful and impressively big cross standing above the gate. He stopped dead, he was so amazed—he was so shocked that he almost fell over.

But then he recovered and said to himself: "Is this the Cross that I see here? Yes, it is! No, it can't be. On the contrary, it's either a dream or a blatant deception."

And with that he set off and went towards another gate. There he saw another cross firmly fixed above the gate.

"Now, I know very well that this can't be the truth," he said, "But I must be asleep, for I'm sure that there is a cross up there. For if it were the truth that this was the situation[60] in the city, and Decius was willing to bring it about, then that would be a joyous event. I'll keep going. If it's a dream, I'll have a good story to tell tomorrow."

He went to the third gate and he found a third cross there. He checked every gate and at each one he found a cross.

"Oh God!" he cried. "What can this mean? I'm sure that, whichever way I look, there's a cross staring me in the face. I've been driven mad by heathendom,[61] because this is certainly no dream. I can both touch and feel my head and my limbs in every part.[62] And I could eat bread, if I had any, because I'm hungry. So this can't be a hallucination? I could say either yes or no. (1037–76)

¶ "By my Lord Jesus Christ who designed and made the whole world, I want to know for sure whether what I say is true or false."

With that, he entered the city. Whatever he saw seemed topsy-turvy. He didn't recognise anything that he saw. Because of this he thought he had gone daft and that this was a dream. Then he heard people calling on St. Mary and confidently swearing by the Holy Cross in loud voices.

"God, what should I do?" he said. "Yesterday evening there was no one in the land so great that he would have dared say such a thing, since the emperor would have had him killed. Yesterday evening the Cross was everywhere hidden—or else it would have been burned or broken apart: but now the Holy Cross is everywhere invoked and venerated, together with Jesus and his sweet mother. So what's the emperor up to now? I've gone mad, I'm sure of that—nor can I be sure

---

[60] 1056 **this was the situation** *issi fust*: literally, "if it were like this" (i.e. that the city had become Christian). Chardri is at this point particularly elliptical.

[61] 1069 **heathendom** *reneerye* (as in J). Merrilees follows C to read *revesrie*, which he translates as "dreaming", but this would directly contradict the sense of the following line.

[62] 1072 **in every part** *planier*. This is not the verb 'to touch' (as according to Merrilees's glossary; *AND* s.v. *planer*), but the adjective 'plenier', used quasi-adverbially in the sense of "in full force" (cf. *AND* s.v. *plener*[1]).

of anything else. God save me!" he added, "This is never Ephesus, but some other city! Perhaps I could find out who's entitled to rule this country."

At that moment he met a young man coming towards him.

"God help you, lad," he said, 'Stop a moment and tell me, without any deceit, what is this city is called?"

"Don't you know, man?" he replied. "By God, the Son of Mary, it's called Ephesus the great, and the whole world has heard of it." (1077–1114)

¶ When Malchus heard this, you can imagine, he was hardly overjoyed. Now he knew for sure that he had lost all sense and understanding. He called himself a hopeless wretch, saying unhappily, "Alas that I was born! I've run into some fairies, I'm sure, and they've enchanted me in this way![63] But if God in his wisdom[64] wants me to lose my mind, I'd rather go outside the city, where's there no need for me to go any madder. I might wander about so much that I wouldn't know how to get back, for I don't recognise these streets or any of these houses that are so splendid. I hope I can come across my companions, so that I can hold onto them[65] and tell them about this strange experience, which has been so difficult and distressing for me. But before I can get away from here, I need to buy some provisions for them." (1115–36)

¶ With that he set off grieving and sorrowing. Carrying his money in his hand, he went into the bakery where the bakers were selling bread. The bread was very appetising: he threw his money on the counter. The baker looked up and came to check the coins. He took one of them and bit it.[66]

"God," he said, "what kind of money is this? It's money of a very different stamp from what we use in this country."

The baker showed it to his neighbour, who marvelled at it endlessly, since they had never seen money like that in their land. On every side people were discussing it, both the clever and the slow-witted, and they all agreed, "The truth is that this lad has found a treasure-trove."[67]

---

[63] 1121–22 Malchus is perhaps implicitly referring to otherworldly encounters like the mysterious city in *Yonec*, vv. 360–76, ed. Alfred Ewert (Oxford: Blackwell, 1952), 91, trans. Glyn S. Burgess and Keith Busby, *The Lais of Marie de France* (Harmondsworth: Penguin, 1986; repr. 1988), 90–91. There is no reference to fairies in L_1, in which Malchus is worried only about his "excessus mentis" ("going out of his mind": XIV–XV, 64).

[64] 1123 **in his wisdom** *en sa uertu*. Both manuscripts (and both editors) read *e*.

[65] 1132 **so that I can hold onto them** *ke jeo les tenisse*. Merrilees prints the **C** reading *truisse*, which, as he rightly says (84), seems "pleonastic" (because it means that this line essentially adds nothing to the sense of the previous one). I have preferred **J**'s *tenisse*.

[66] 1145 **bit it** *mania*. Merrilees says that this word is from *manier* ('to handle'), but it is much more likely to be from *manger* ('to take a bite'). The baker is putting his teeth to the coin in order to test its genuineness.

[67] 1156 It is perhaps implicit that Malchus's silver coins have a higher bullion-content than the bakers are used to, since medieval currency tended to be debased over time.

Malchus saw all this and was dismayed at the way they all looked at him; and he said to himself, "Now they've seen me, now they've noticed me, now they suspect me, these bakers—these treacherous rogues. Now please God they all had their eyes poked out—and let me be a league away on horseback![68] Never again will I have any dealings with these vile people! But now it's all turned out differently:[69] they're going to make a present of me to the emperor, who hates me so much and who is capable of doing the seven of us so much harm. That's why the rogues are consulting among themselves in twos and threes. I can clearly tell from their faces that they don't like me very much at all. And I—what am I going to do now, unhappy and unlucky as I have always been? I'd rather lose my money than let these people detain me." (1137–80)

¶ "Gentlemen," he said, 'Don't worry, and, if you please, don't denounce me! By God and his apostles, this money is all yours. And the bread, gentlemen, you can keep it. In this way you're very well paid, for I'm neither miserly nor stingy [. . .].[70] But rather, you'll have so much of my money, gentlemen, that you'll all be very well paid. If you don't want this reward, you can do with it what you like. And if you give me my money back, you don't have to give me anything of yours, and I'll just go away—with your permission—thanking you for your kindness."

"By St. Clement," they said, "these aren't the terms we should be talking in, lad, for you've found some treasure, and you'll be exposed as a thief if you don't do what we say. We'll cooperate with you in hiding the hoard, as long as you tell us, in secret, where you found it—for these are antique coins that you've just given us. Show us the treasure straightaway," they said, "if you know what's good for you!" (1181–1208)

¶ "Gentlemen," he replied, "not me! I don't know about any treasure, nor have I found any. I'm giving you the money voluntarily: now accept it in good faith as a token of peace and goodwill. With your permission, I'd like to go now."

"In faith," they said, "That's being silly! By the faith that we owe St. Mary, this boy takes us for right idiots!"

So now they grabbed him from every side, bound him tightly, shoved and beat him, listening very carefully to everything he said[71]—for city-folk are by

---

[68] 1166 **on horseback** *U sur chevail u desure uve*: literally, "on a horse or on a mare." L₁ says only that Malchus "was afraid and trembled all over" ("formidabat et omne corpus tremebat": XV, 64).

[69] 1169 **turned out differently** *avenu autrement*. In the context, the meaning of this is not entirely clear. Perhaps Malchus means simply "differently from what I expected"; or possibly the manuscripts here preserve a faulty reading: *avenu austerement* ("turned out harshly") would make more sense.

[70] 1188 A line has been lost from both the extant medieval copies of the text.

[71] 1220 "Presumably they are trying to extract information about the treasure," as Merrilees suggests (85).

nature more stupid than animals in a herd.[72] Whenever they get themselves into
a position of power, they know neither moderation nor courtesy. (1209–24)

¶ When Malchus found himself being treated so badly by these people, he
sighed, groaned, and cried profusely, for his denials achieved nothing. These men
led him into the city-centre where people assembled from ten miles around to
hear what the bakers were saying about the youngster they were leading about
so roughly. The news spread throughout the city of the capture of a young man
who had discovered a huge and astounding treasure, but who refused to confess
it. People gathered from all around on account of this boy—who was trembling
with fear. They all looked at him, but no one knew him: no one knew where he
came from or where he belonged. Meanwhile he looked all about him, to see if he
could see a brother or a sister, father or mother, relative or friend,[73] who might be
able to vouch for him. The more he looked and listened, the more he saw strangers. He could not see anyone he knew and at heart he was in terrible uncertainty.
The evening before he had known everybody, but now a day later he recognised
nobody. To him, it seemed that this had to be so, or else he had lost his mind.
Like a halfwit he stood astonished in the middle of the crowd.[74] (1225–54)

¶ Gentlemen, just at the same time as the people were in this state of excite-
ment, the bishop, Marinus (who was a good pastor to them), had gathered together all the clergy in order to conduct a disputation with the heretics, concerning some of the theological propositions that they had put forward. Antipater,
who was the viscount and had authority over the city, was then in attendance
like a prudent lord, together with many very important people. The assembly was
large and impressive.

Then someone turned up with the news that a mysterious young man had
been accused in the city of having found a treasure-trove—"And yet the charge
can't be proved against him by anyone here, because he continues to deny it, even
though no one believes him, since he was caught red-handed with the coins. And
so he awaits your verdict."

When the bishop and the viscount heard this, they commanded that the
young man should straightaway be brought before them. The messenger set off
and Malchus was quickly produced. Great efforts were made to keep him under
guard until he could be brought before the bishop sitting in council in the middle
of the city. Now Malchus was certainly thinking that he was going to be brought
before the emperor Decius, who hated him so much. He was completely and utterly stunned, but those ignorant people didn't leave him alone. They dragged

[72] 1222 **animals in a herd** *bestes en pasture*: literally, "beasts in pasture." L₁ offers no
precedent for Chardri's derogatory remarks about city-folk.

[73] 1241–43 At this point Chardri is closely following L₁, which reads: "Et
prospiciebat in populum, volens cognoscere aut fratrem aut aliquem de consanguinibus
suis aut notum suum" (XVI, 66).

[74] 1253–54 Cf. L₁: "insanus stabat in medio populi civitatis" (XVI, 67).

him forwards in front of the great assembly, just as if he were guilty of some great theft. All his "antique" coins were brought along with him and were committed to the hands of the viscount. Malchus was greatly ashamed at being treated like a thief in this way, but he did not know how to reply, or what to say, or how he might defend himself. The viscount was amazed when he examined the money — and the bishop was just as amazed, you can be sure of that. (1255–1302)

¶ The viscount then addressed Malchus, who remained speechless: "Young man," he said, "it's clearly proven that you've found some great treasure by the fact that you were caught with this money in your hands; and, in this, you've committed a serious fault: you didn't come to me before in order to report the treasure to the king. By my lord St. Peter the Apostle, you wanted all of it to be yours! That's why you've kept it so quiet that you haven't informed either me or anybody else about it! You should know that it will turn out very differently and I can easily tell you just how: you're going to tell me how these coins came into your hands, whether you like it or not. Tell me about the treasure, my friend, and then you can leave here scot-free." (1305–20)

¶ Malchus replied: "By the faith I owe you, my good lord, I've never in my life found any treasure, not even a sliver of either gold or silver. But these coins that you're holding — and because of which you've accused me in this way — I didn't take them like a thief. In fact they're coins from my father, who lives in this city. Now please God I hope I'm never charged with larceny or robbery as long as I live. But I don't know how this very terrible misfortune has happened to me."

The viscount replied: "Now tell us, young man, which city are you from?" "My lord," he replied, "I won't hide it from you, because nothing in my life matters to me much now. If this is the city of Ephesus, then I was born in this city. I'm absolutely amazed that I don't see any of my friends here now. They'd be willing to vouch for me that I'm not trying to deceive you in this."

"Now don't be afraid or ashamed," said the viscount. "Just tell me what it's called, this family that you're boasting about."

"My lord," Malchus replied, "I'll tell you: my father and mother are named such-and-such[75] and so too are my brothers and sisters: there's no doubt about that, gentlemen. My uncles and all my relations are well-known throughout the city." When he had listed all their names, the lords were all astounded. (1321–56)

¶ The viscount then told him, "You're resorting to arguments that are utterly foolish, to lie so blatantly before this discerning audience. You're putting on false pretences: that we can clearly see. Nothing that you say is true. But do you think this deceit will enable you to escape justice unscathed? No, by almighty God, you're going to sing a different tune! No, you wicked, silly, evil wretch, you're clearly of a malicious disposition, to think that you might in this way trick such a

---

[75] 1352 **such-and-such** None of the sources actually name Malchus's family; and Chardri simply uses *issi* ("thus, in this way"). The inexplicitness resides in his report of the speech, not (we should imagine) in the speech itself.

wise and respectable group of people. You're making fools of us at the instigation of the devil who goads you on,[76] when you try to tell us in this way that this money was taken from your father's purse and that your father gave it to you. We've noticed that the stamped inscription clearly says this coin was minted in the time of the Emperor Decius, at the beginning of his reign. You wicked, good-for-nothing rogue, more than 362 years have passed since those days—that's the opinion of everyone who's looked at the coin. As to the relatives you named, more than three hundred years have gone by since they died. They were rich and important people, and you're just a boy: did you think to trick us all?[77] This coin and your youthfulness prove you to be dishonest and not very clever. There's no man now alive who knows enough about antiquity to have any understanding of events at the time when this coin was current in the world. But you're a criminal and a scoundrel and that's why you thought to dissemble. That's definitely not going to do you any good: all your trickery has failed you. If you don't tell me about the treasure, I'll make sure you're cruelly discomfited. You won't be sleeping on soft feathers: you'll be lying in a filthy gaol until you admit the truth about the emperor Decius's treasure, which there's no doubt you've discovered. Now confess it, with God's blessing, and by this admission you'll be saved from a great deal of trouble." (1357–1412)

¶ Malchus then turned his face towards him deep in thought and sorrow. It is no wonder that he was sad and miserable! Once he had heard all that, he threw himself at full length on the ground, saying, "Lords, have mercy on me, for I'm completely dumbfounded. You're even lessening the great anger that I've so long had in my heart towards Decius, the rich emperor, who has upheld heathenism all this time. I call on the emperor Decius. Just the other day he gave us a reprieve, so that we could prepare our answers for the time when he would summon us; and yesterday he entered the city. I'll be soon vindicated. Is he in the city now? And is he coming to this council?"[78] (1413–32)

¶ The archbishop Marinus replied to him in this way: "Young man, it seems to me you're being very silly. There's no man now alive who could summon Decius. This Decius of whom you speak—it's now nearly four hundred years since he rotted in the earth. So what can we tell [him] about your case?"

"My lord," Malchus replied, "I ask you mercy: I'm shocked, miserable, and sad at heart that you don't believe me, gentlemen. By God, and all his names, come and see my companions, and them you'll be very well able to believe that

---

[76] 1372 **who goads you on** *ki vus corne*: literally, "who trumpets you on."

[77] 1391–92 Cf. L₁: "Tu vero, iuvenis constitutus, vis decipere senes et sapientes Ephesi" ("Truly, you who are just a young man are trying to deceive the wise elders of Ephesus": XVI, 69–70).

[78] 1421–32 Malchus's fear of Decius is presumably diminished by the fact that, from his point of view, the viscount is also threatening to punish him. In L₁ Malchus simply asks where the emperor is (XVI, 70).

I haven't lied about anything! I'll lead you there and then you'll see them, where they've gone to earth[79] in a cave, on account of their fear of the savagery of the cruel emperor, Decius. We fled from him and have hidden ourselves, me and six other lads. And I know very well that yesterday at daybreak the emperor entered this city — if this city is Ephesus the great, for I'm very surprised that I don't recognise anything that I see. Lords, have mercy upon me!" (1433–60)

¶ The bishop was wise and perceptive, and so he had great pity for the boy. There seemed to him no doubt that this was some kind of vision that the lad had seen, as a result of which he been so greatly disturbed, or else that God had secretly revealed to him some remarkable happening, making use of the boy in the service of his infinite pity.

"My lord," he said to the viscount, "This is a very wonderful tale. Let's all get up and go with him: then we'll see whether he's telling the truth or not."

They all set off together, along with a great crowd of people; and Malchus took them straight to the cave that he knew so well. He went inside it, and the bishop followed him, since he was very keen on investigating what events might have occurred. As soon as he looked to his right,[80] he saw the lead on the wall: the lead of which we spoke earlier, on which the story of the seven was completely written out, from beginning to end, just as it has been told. Theodorus and Rufinus, who were Christians all their lives, loyally undertook to arrange things so prudently that, in a later age, Jesus could bring about a revelation by means of his great power. (1461–92)

¶ The bishop took hold of the lead. He did not do with it what an uncourtly person would have done: he did not break the seal[81] or open it until all the people were assembled. When the crowd had gathered, all of them agog, the viscount promptly commanded them all to be silent, in order to hear the bishop tell them what he could read on the lead. The bishop broke the seal and studied it for a long while: nobody there made a sound.

---

[79] 1450 **gone to earth**. The two manuscripts read *enterrez*, which both Koch and Merrilees take this to be a form of *entrez*, on the grounds that this is "the sense demanded by the context" (Merrilees, 86). However, some sense can be made of *enterrez* ("buried, earthed up"): this could be taken to imply "hidden" as well as "buried" (as in the register of hunting-terms from which I have drawn my translation). By comparison, *entrez* seems rather lame — a *facilior lectio*.

[80] 1482 **to his right** *sur destre*. L₁: "in dexteram partem" (XVII, 71).

[81] 1495 In his previous description of how Theodorus and Rufinus arranged for their record of events to be preserved (at vv. 781–804) Chardri does not say anything about a seal. However, L₁'s description of their activities does refer to letters being sealed ("litteras . . . sigillantes": X, 54). What the bishop later discovers in L₁ is actually an "onyx chest sealed with two silver seals" ("nihinum loculum sigillatum duobus sigillis argenteis": XVIII, 71).

When he had read it through he was deeply moved by compassion, crying out in everybody's hearing: "Now listen, all of you, how I've discovered in these writings something that is both very touching and very joyful, something concerning God's saints that has been openly revealed to us in a lovely way. Listen to what the writing says about this marvellous episode: the writing that I'm looking at here says that in the time of Decius the king, seven young men fled away in great fear in order to go into hiding. The first of them was Maximianus, then Malchus and Martinianus, Dionysius and Johannes, Seraphion and Constantinus. Decius condemned these seven young men of his empire to such a martyrdom as this: to be walled up behind a stone wall in this great deep quarry, because they'd hidden here on account of their great fear of him. But Rufinus and Theodorus, who were excellent Christians, placed this writing here which has endured up to now, and still endures, because they did not want these martyrs, who perished here, to be forgotten. Those seven martyrs, those pre-eminently good men, were walled up alive here. Whoever finds this writing, he can be sure that they spoke the truth, those worthy men who witnessed it all and made this memorial of it. Now we should richly honour the seven young men, for they were glorious martyrs." (1493–1544)

¶ When the bishop had read all this and the people had listened to it, all the citizens wept in pity. Then they went into the cave, where they found the seven martyrs,[82] all sitting together. Each of them was trembling in fear; their faces had all gone as pale as the flower of the hawthorn.[83]

When the bishop saw what had happened he immediately threw himself down on the earth, venerating them most tenderly, and the viscount did likewise; and the people tried to outdo each other in venerating the seven saints, lauding almighty God for bringing about such miracles among humankind.

Then there was no end to the praise that the people went about shouting. There wasn't either a young man or an old who didn't say, "Bless you, Jesus! Out of your great nobility, you've not refrained from showing us such generosity, despite our sins and our presumptuous trespasses. All of us have done you harm. In return, you give us all love. You desire that we serve you without recompense as our lord, not for your advantage, but for our own—for there's nothing you need that we can supply. Yet in order to attract us to you, like a mighty lord you show us both great miracles and great love, for it now appears, that, by means of your might, Lord Jesus, you have brought your sweet saints back to life, out

---

[82] 1550 **seven martyrs** *set martirs*. This should in fact be "six", since, as Merrilees points out, Malchus is not in the cave at this point. Nor is it entirely clear that they are in fact "martyrs" (whatever Rufinus and Theodorus say), since by contrast with earlier versions of the legend, Chardri is careful not to identify the Seven's miraculous sleep as a form of death (see above, note to v. 627).

[83] 1553–54 Cf. L$_1$: "Et facies eorum tanquam rosa florens" ("And their faces were like a rose in bloom": XVIII, 73).

of pity—in order to combat the great deception practised by these heretics, who want to seduce souls into hell and destroy all Christianity. Now this malicious enterprise has been utterly confuted, since we can all now truly perceive that here are dead men who have been brought back to life, and thus we can be sure that every one of us will rise again on Judgment Day, in just the forms that we now have.[84] Shame on those who are so infantile as to attempt to make us believe anything else!"[85] (1545–96)

¶ When the bishop heard this outcry[86]—he had heard many like it, but never in all his life one that had touched his heart so much. . .[87] But Malchus immediately led him straight on, together with[88] the viscount and the citizens following as fast as they could, right up to his companions; and the saints stood up to meet them, thinking that they were about to have a very unpleasant meeting. But the bishop told them kindly that they were not to be afraid and made them feel reassured. And when they had stopped being frightened, they all described the foolishness committed in the time of the emperor Decius, how he had almost completely destroyed Christianity and the pain and suffering to which Christians had been subjected by this emperor. They recounted for the bishop the events of that ancient time in which they lived. The people were amazed to hear such a strange story and they were wholly intent on listening to the young men, thinking it a very wonderful thing that they had been alive at such a time. (1597–1624)

¶ The bishop instructed that this event should be set down, from beginning to end, in a letter, which he sent without delay to Theodosius, the good emperor. All of the messengers together told him everything, just as you have previously heard, and they asked him very politely to come quickly in order to witness the power of Jesus Christ, which he had allowed them to see with their own eyes. As

---

[84] 1593 **in just the forms that we now have** *en cest guise*. Cf. Canon 1 of the Fourth Lateran Council of 1215: "all of [the dead] will rise with their own bodies, which they now wear, so as to receive according to their deserts, whether these be good or bad; for the latter perpetual punishment with the devil, for the former eternal glory with Christ" (*Decrees of the Ecumenical Councils*, ed. Norman Tanner, 2 vols. [London: Sheed & Ward, 1990] 1: 230–31).

[85] 1595–96 The people's reasoning is in fact rather dubious, since it is not at all clear that the Seven Sleepers have actually died. In any case, their apparent "resurrection" is clearly so exceptional that it hardly supports any general deductions about the fate of humanity on Judgment Day.

[86] 1597 **outcry** *plainte*: literally "lamentation, legal action, complaint." Here the term perhaps implies a religious discourse of both emotional and philosophical force (which is what the related Latin word *planctus* can imply).

[87] 1597–1600 The syntax is incomplete in Chardri's text, as it stands in the manuscripts, which may be explained either in terms of textual corruption, or as deliberately anacoluthic.

[88] 1602 **together with** *o tot*. This I take as equivalent to *atut*.

soon as the emperor heard and understood this message, he was overjoyed. He
straightaway ordered that Ephesus should be next on his itinerary, without any
delay; and he set off from Constantinople, impatient to get there.

When the citizens heard that the emperor was coming they rejoiced at the
prospect; and they all went out to meet him, carrying palm-branches and can-
dles—but not like a procession of prisoners: rather, they went out tripping to
dance-music, singing and laughing as they talked. This one played a harp, that
one a viol; this one danced, that one played the pipes; this one carried a fiddle,
that one a hurdy-gurdy. So much joy as the citizens of Ephesus expressed at seeing their emperor had never been heard before. They led their sovereign to the
cave in the mountain where God's saints still were, for they had never left it.
(1597–1658)

¶ When they saw the emperor coming, all of them straightaway went out
of the cave in order to meet him, joyful, happy, and at ease. As soon as he saw
the young men, he immediately threw himself to the ground, so as to venerate
them very humbly, for their faces were shining and glowing like the sun when it
is warm in the middle of a May day.[89]

By means of sighing and weeping the emperor gently greeted them without
even opening his mouth; and then he said, "Gentlemen, may Lord Jesus keep
and protect you, through the power of his holy name! This is all his doing, of that
we are sure. Gentlemen," he added, "It seems to me that I when look you in the
face, I see Jesus who showed pity and brought Lazarus back to life;[90] and how in
his own most holy name he preached the resurrection of the dead on earth for
all the people who will rise on Judgment Day. Belief in the truth of this has been
sapped by the wickedness of the heresy that has recently spread, which has dam-
aged the faith. Now, thank God, it has been restored by your blessed arrival. We
can no longer doubt in any way that everyone of us will be present on Judgment
Day." (1659–90)

¶ To this Maximian replied: "Lord Emperor, what you say is true. By means
of his glorious power God has made us into a demonstration for your benefit, so
that the heresy might be exposed, and so that you might be more certain in your
belief that all will rise on the Last Day before God the Creator, each of us to be
allotted his just deserts, whether for good or ill, whichever it might be.[91] And
in order to affirm this truth God has brought us back to life. You should know
that, just like an infant in the womb of its mother,[92] without anxiety, seeing

---

[89] 1666–68 Cf. L₁: "splenduerunt facies eorum tamquam sol" ("their faces shone like
the sun": XVIII, 75).

[90] 1678 The reference to Lazarus follows L₁ (XVIII, 75).

[91] 1697–1700 Cf. 2 Cor. 5: 10: "For we must all be manifested before the judgement
seat of Christ, that every one may receive the proper things of the body, according as he
hath done, whether it be good or evil."

[92] 1704 This comparison is also made in L₁ (XVIII, 76).

nothing, feeling nothing, knowing no discomfort, understanding neither good nor evil, life or death, pain, sense or folly, so it was with us the whole time. We suffered neither discomfort nor unhappiness. It seemed to us all along as if we were asleep. (1691–1712)

¶ "But now, sir, rightful Emperor, we pray to our Lord, that just as truly as he was born into this life of the virgin Mary and suffered both pain and suffering and was then brought back to life, so may he give you grace and keep you in peace for ever more, on account of our prayers; and may he in his pity protect your empire from wickedness and adversity, so that never again in this life will you be disturbed by the sorrow of another heresy; and may he be kind to all of us and grant us eternal joy. To that, let everyone say 'Amen, amen!'"

When he had finished this speech, in the hearing of all the nobles and of the emperor (who was so wise), all seven sat down, and without any pain or any other discomfort, straightaway rendered their souls to God, the omnipotent, who placed them all in an exalted position in his holiest paradise, where there was no end to their great joy, nor could they ever be troubled by either heat or cold.[93]

Whoever saw that worthy emperor relieving his sorrow with tears and lamentation at this event (letting many tears fall), he would certainly say that there is no one in all our faith who possesses so noble a heart as did that emperor. Weeping, he straightaway kissed each one of the seven in turn, both their hands and their feet. He valued the long silk cloak that he was wearing no more than a straw, unless he could use it to cover their holy remains; and he ordered that his treasury be fetched so that reliquaries could be made for them, for he did not want their remains to be placed in the earth, but in vessels of gold and silver. For the sake of God he had all of his gold gathered there (for he had a lot of treasure); and he continued to think how he might do them greater honour. And while he was in this frame of mind, the saints had no intention of forgetting him, but rather they appeared to him in a dream—you can be sure that this is no lie—and in this way all seven spoke to this king, who so greatly loved both God and his faith.

"Why," they said, "have you gathered so much treasure for the translation of our relics? That seems like a temptation. We give you thanks for your goodwill, [but] because we were in the cave, we beg you to put us back there. No other place should receive our bodies but this great wide cave, where we found joy, and where we seven slept 362 years: where our Lord (who created us) brought us back to life, and where we will surely rise again along with everybody else on Judgment Day." (1713–80)

---

[93] 1737–38 Cf. Rev. 7: 16 ("They shall no more hunger nor thirst, neither shall the sun fall on them, nor any heat"), and the description of paradise in the Middle English *Seinte Katerine*, ed. S.R.T.O. d'Ardenne and E.J. Dobson, EETS SS 7 (Oxford: Oxford University Press, 1981), 88: "ne eileð þer na mon nowðer sorhe ne sar, nowðer heate ne chele" ("no one suffers there from pain or sorrow, nor from heat or cold").

¶ When the emperor had woken up, you can be certain he was happy and delighted that, in their kindness, the seven had deigned to reveal their intention to him. Straightaway, without any long delays, he made a generous distribution of his wealth (which was very great) among the officers who were with him; and they busily set about putting the emperor's wishes into action. They managed to get the huge cave gilded all over; it was enclosed not with beams of wood, but with marble and limestone, and walled all around with great care and labour. And then the emperor had the saints carried into the cave where they had once lain: the translation took place along with a great festival and procession. To tell the truth, all the most important people in the empire were there. The bishops and the clergy, along with the emperor who governed them so well, established a great feast in honour of the Seven Sleepers and their deeds. In this way a beautiful church was made, all bright and new, which was called the Hospital,[94] since anyone who was afflicted with a sickness was received there and God worked miracles there in honour of his glorious saints. Anyone who went there crippled or sick, left happy and healthy. But the wonders that God works there are, of course, known throughout the world, so much does the grace of God abound in that place.

Those who were heretics renounced their great error when they heard these tidings; they believed in God the son of Mary; and everywhere they readily preached the holy resurrection, saying that their previous teaching was false, misleading, unjustified, and wholly composed of fabrications. This blessed event had proved the certain truth that the dead will rise again. The heretics were so repentant that they eagerly followed the emperor about in the great city of Constantinople, losing no opportunity to give thanks to Jesus Christ for having performed the miracle that he did.

May he who dwells in the sacred Trinity preserve us in unity! May he grant us that, by means of his saints, we may come to be near to him in the joy [of heaven]! May he grant, on account of their prayers, that there be peace throughout the world — and that neither heathenism nor heresy impose their madness and folly! Instead, may we be allowed to enjoy happiness and contentment throughout our lives; and may we be delivered from the stinking misery of hell, which is so utterly wicked and venomous! It is the devil who goes to such trouble to make us swap joy for pain. It certainly seems that every day, without letting up at all, he works especially to seduce princes to his cause, so as to do more dishonour to our religion — for once he has got hold of a prince, the poor people will fall into his hands soon enough. Where could anyone find greater treason or treachery, or a greater determination to do evil, than among the world's leaders?[95] Some

---

[94] 1809 the Hospital *l'ospital*. This detail is not paralleled in L₁. See "Seven Sleepers" in *Oxford Dictionary of Byzantium*, 3 vols. (New York: Oxford University Press, 1991), 3: 1883.

[95] 1860 leaders *prelaz*. Chardri's word could possibly be taken to mean just "prelates" in the modern sense of the word — i.e. ecclesiastical dignitaries; but it could also be used more widely in Old French, to imply "persons of high degree."

of them are greedy for gain, others are murderers; some of them go about lying, and afterwards denying it; some of them are traitors; some of them are usurers. I would dare go so far as to swear that there are not many people alive today, either in the courts of the nobility or among the clergy, who are neither simonists,[96] cheats, misers,[97] usurers, nor lechers. It is the devil who entices each one of them into their various sins. There are not many sitting on thrones[98] who are untarred by that brush;[99] and there are very few among these important people[100] who do not know how tarnished they are. It is no great marvel that when people's leaders go astray, they follow those who are supposed to guide them. It is the devil who tricks them into being partners in the crimes that he knows how to devise. May God grant them his grace to be able to abandon that course so satisfying to the devil, whenever he can checkmate and capture them. May God put the rulers of the earth in such a frame of mind that they choose to defend equity and justice without pretence or deceit! And may he bring us out of our stupidity and grant us eternal life, where there can be neither wickedness nor shame!

This is where Chardri ends his tale, saying: May God give to treachery (and all those who love it) a short life and little honour—and so too to those who blame me for saying so! Amen, amen—say it loudly and I'll join in—God be my salvation, Amen! (1781–1898)

The End.

---

[96] 1867 **simonists** *symoniaus* This terms refers to the crime of "simony": i.e. selling church offices, benefices, or preferments. Merrilees suggests that "here the sense seems broader, perhaps 'hypocritical'" (89).

[97] 1868 **misers** *merde*. In his glossary, Merrilees suggests "mean, miserly, grasping." Cf. also *Josaphaz*, v. 2186.

[98] 1871 **on thrones** *en sege*. Merrilees interprets *en sege* as "in priestly function." He is presumably thinking in terms of an analogy with the ecclesiastical connotations of Latin *sedes* (modern English *see*, in the sense of a bishop's see). But the phrase could, in the context, refer to secular authority as well.

[99] 1872 **who are untarred by that brush** *Ki n'unt le pé en icest pege*. Literally: "Who do not have their foot in this pitch [i.e. tar]." I take *pege* here to be a form of "pitch" (Latin *pix*), even though the only meaning that *AND* records for *pege* is "trap." If the *pege* is interpreted as "trap", then the line could be translated "who do not have their foot in this trap," but this makes less sense in this context. Chardri's point is clearly that the great are all corrupt, not that they necessarily fall into any kind of trap because of it; and the structure of vv. 1871–74 suggests that v. 1872 should be parallel in sense to v. 1874.

[100] 1873 **among these important people** *de cel haute gent*; *de cel autre gent* CJ. Merrilees translates *cel autre gent* as "the flock" (i.e. the congregations of the churchmen that he reads as sitting *en sege*). Even if he is right that *en sege* must refer to the clergy, it is a large leap to assume that "these other people" (*cel autre gent*) must be their flocks. It seems to me more likely that *autre* is an error and that the correct reading is *cel haute gent* (cf. *les hauz*, in v. 1852).

THE LIFE OF ST. JOSAPHAZ

Here begins the Life of St. Josaphaz.

¶ Anyone who intends to do good can learn much[1] from an exemplum[2] about the right road to salvation. It has frequently been seen that people are improved much more by a moral tale than by the writings of St. Augustine or St. Gregory.[3] For this reason I want to record the pleasing life-story of a fine young man, as a means of putting a stop to the immense folly in which we delight night and day. I trust in God that my enterprise will not go entirely to waste; for it is often the case that one man loves a story from which someone else gets no pleasure at all. It can sometimes happen that if one person refuses to pay heed to a story, somebody else may think deeply about it. He might love it so passionately that it leads him to amend his foolish way of life. Whether what I have to say is good or bad, it is only for the sake of God that I undertake it, and no other reason. (1–24)

¶ Since God, who made the whole world, the sky, the globe of the earth, and all the things that exist, whether in the [infernal] fire, in the air, or in the deep sea,[4] was unwilling to lose what he had created, he was born (entirely without the help of Nature) to that glorious woman who was simultaneously his daughter, his mother, and his bride.[5] He suffered no little pain and sorrow, as the scriptures tell us, because the creatures he valued most were behaving shamefully: that is, human beings, on whose account he suffered so cruelly. Then he gave us the new Law, and I will tell you exactly why. He did not want to give up on anyone who might one day chose to take his side (whether it happened to be sooner or later, just as it later became apparent). These good and glad tidings[6] circulated

---

[1] 2 **much** *mult* C; *mut* Koch; om. J. Rutledge follows J, insisting that C's reading is only acceptable if "the construction *aprendre a* plus direct object must be allowed", but this is not, in fact, the construction that C uses here.

[2] 2 **exemplum** *essample*. Koch draws a parallel with *Distiches of Cato*, 3. 13: "From men's behaviour learn what to pursue or shun" ("Multorum disce exemplis, quae facta sequaris, / quae fugias").

[3] 7 St. Augustine and St. Gregory also are cited together as representatives of patristic authority in the *Little Debate*, v. 799.

[4] 25–28 Cf. *Seven Sleepers*, vv. 1–24, 385–400; *Little Debate*, vv. 499–506.

[5] 32 **his daughter, his mother and his bride** *fille, mere e espuse*: i.e the Virgin Mary.

[6] 45 **these tidings** *la novele*: i.e. the Gospels.

throughout the world, and everyone who was wise believed in them, thereby coming into the heritage from which they had first been exiled, and then thrown into the abyss. Many people in various countries renounced folly in favour of this life, because Jesus Christ had shown them the Way[7] and because (to tell the truth) he so much wanted them to follow this Way direct to eternal life.[8] Faith increased continually throughout Lombardy and France, England and Normandy, Brittany and Hungary, Burgundy and Germany, Russia and Spain, Lorraine and Poitou, Flanders and Anjou, Ireland and the Auvergne. Anyone who asks about any other lands can certainly go and look for them, but he will find very few or none at all to add.[9] Christianity spread so far that it reached the continent of India.[10] As a result, the inhabitants of India were prepared to renounce their follies for the sake of the faith that pleased them so much; and there were some who publicly relinquished all their property and wealth, so that they could go off into the desert in order to serve God, who had created them and given them so much of his grace. (25–78)

¶ In India at that time there was a king who had a great deal of intelligence.[11] His name was Arvennir. Rich and powerful, he lacked for nothing. He had abundant worldly joy and everything he could possibly want, except that he did not know of the existence of God, and he had no children. He was deeply saddened that he could not have a son or a daughter, and he behaved very strangely. Sorrowful at heart as he was, he nevertheless committed a terrible crime on account of his ignorance of the faith,[12] for he instructed that anyone who preached Christianity anywhere in his realm should be arrested and executed, because he had heard it said that some of his highest-ranking barons were of such a mind that they had become Christians, which dismayed him very much. Some he had arrested and put in prison; some he had savagely beaten; some he left to swing

---

[7] 51 **the way** *la veie*: cf. John 14: 6: "Jesus saith to him: I am the way, and the truth, and the life."

[8] 51–56 This translation contradicts Koch's punctuation of these lines. He places a full stop at the end of v. 54, thus dividing the subordinate clause governed by *Car* (vv. 51–54) from the rest of the sentence to which it is attached.

[9] Lines 1–68 contain material not found in the vulgate Latin version of the legend.

[10] 70 **the continent of India** *Inde la grant*: According to Koch (169), this is an epic formula ("epische formel"), but it also seems to have had quite a precise geographical denotation: "A distinction between 'India Major' and 'India Minor' has been traced back as far as fourth century AD [. . .] 'Nearer' or 'Lesser India' meant roughly the northern part of the subcontinent of India as it is understood today, while 'Further' or 'Greater India' referred to the southern part" (J.R.S. Phillips, *The Medieval Expansion of Europe*, 2nd ed. [Oxford: Oxford University Press, 1998], 192). This is the point at which Chardri starts following the vulgate, which says that the fame of Christian monks "reached all the way to India" ("usque ad Indos peruenerit": **BJL**, 108).

[11] 80 **intelligence** *sens*.

[12] 91 **ignorance of the faith** *mescreance*.

in the wind;[13] and some died while they were being tortured.[14] There were some who renounced God; and others who fled into the desert. They did so in order to serve God and to escape the torments they feared.[15]

Then it happened that one of the king's close friends, a man of very noble rank[16] of whom he had been very fond, and who was highly regarded in the court, wisely fled and adopted the habit of a monk. The king himself regretted this very deeply and had the man sought everywhere. They found him in the wilderness and, with considerable effort, brought him back.

When they led him before the king, this is how the king spoke to him: "My friend, by your loyalty to me, tell me who has seduced you into such folly!"

To this the man replied, "This is no folly. If you want me to tell you about it, I can declare on good evidence that you are currently harbouring your enemies in positions of confidence in your court."

The king replied, "My good, dear friend, give me the names of all these enemies."

"Then listen to my testimony," the man replied. "They are Anger and Covetousness. Anger infringes your legal rights,[17] giving you[18] death in exchange for life. Covetousness does something different: she makes you blind, as you ought to realise. She has succeeded in hoodwinking you,[19] guiding you in this way straight towards hell. This is what you have done,[20] so it seems to me: you have

---

[13] 103 **to swing in the wind** *pendre au vent*: i.e. they were hanged.

[14] 101–104 Cf. *Seven Sleepers*, vv. 169–88. The vulgate text is less specific, referring only to "new kinds of torture" ("nouas . . . species tormentorum": BJL, 110).

[15] 108 Here Chardri departs from the Latin, which says that the Christians fled into the desert "not because they feared torture," but because they were acting according to God's dispensation ("non quod tormenta metuerent, sed dispensatione quadam diuina hoc agebant": BJL, 112).

[16] 111 **of very noble rank** *mut gentil hoem*. In the Latin he is an "arch-satrap" ("archisatrapa dignitate": BJL, 114).

[17] 133 **infringes your legal rights** *fet de dreit le tort*: literally, "perpetrates against you what is legally a tort." Cf. *Little Debate*, vv. 1074, 1220.

[18] 134 **you** *uus* CJ; *nus* Koch. Rutledge notes that this reading was suggested by A. Mussafia in a review of Koch's edition (*Zeitschrift für romanische Philologie* 3 [1879] 599), but is unconvinced by it. "The scribe," he says, "has clearly written *nus*, and such an emendation would change the meaning without clarifying or improving it" (Rutledge, 266). It seems to me that it is actually essential to read *uus* here (i.e. "you" rather than "us", since it is specifically what the king suffers at Anger's hands (not humanity in general) that is at issue here.

[19] 137 **she manages to hoodwink you** *pur lanterne vus vent vessie*: Literally, "she sells you a [fool's] bladder in exchange for a lantern." See N.L. Corbett, "Prendre les vessies pour des lanternes," *Le Français moderne* 3 (1969): 193–97.

[20] 139–140 Koch places a full stop at the end of v. 140, which would prevent the interpretation that I have suggested here, with *cuvetise [e ire]* as the objects of *aserriez*.

installed Covetousness and [Anger][21] in your court, in place of some others who
are called [. . . Wisdom and Justice . . .].[22] Don't do that! Because you can't see
clearly, you're eating leek instead of cabbage.[23] If you give up eternal bliss on account of your wealth, which is just an illusion, you'll possess no joy or happiness
that doesn't pass away like a dream in the night.[24] I've abandoned such misguided
behaviour for the sake of the bliss that lasts forever, and I'm not going to conduct
any quarrel or debate about it."

At this the king grew angry and said, "You're going to pay dearly for having
spoken so impudently!"

He wanted to have him tortured, but there was one thing that made him
hesitate, and that was because he felt so much affection for him that he did not
want to subject him to dishonour. Instead, with great bitterness he ordered him
to go and not return, and never again come before him. That is how the two of
them parted. The courtier went away into the wilderness and he never stopped
serving God. At heart he deeply regretted that he had not been made a martyr.[25]
(79–166)

---

[21] 140 **anger** Both extant manuscripts read *dreiture* ("justice") at this point, which
seems an odd word to collocate with *cuvetise*. It seems simplest to interpret it as an error
for *ire* (cf. "anger and covetousness" in v. 32). This error was perhaps prompted by an eye-
skip (on the part of the scribe of the common exemplar) to the appearance of *dreiture*
in one of the two lines apparently lost after v. 142. Although Chardri's text seems to
have been garbled at this point, its sense can be reconstructed by comparison with the
analogues, as Koch points out: "They all say that Arvennir ought to drive Anger and
Covetousness as enemies out of his court and set Wisdom and Justice in their place"
(Koch, 170, my translation). Rutledge (267–68) argues, unconvincingly, that *dreiture*
makes sense here because the Christian's argument is that "the king is trying to legitimize
slaughter by his *dreiture*."

[22] 142 **in place of two others** *en lu deus autres*: This is Koch's reading, as against that
of both the extant manuscripts, which read *en liu des autres* ("in place of the others"). It
makes good sense, especially if the "two" qualities in question can be taken to be Wisdom
and Justice, as in the Latin ("prudentia et equitas": BJL, 118). Between vv. 142 and 143
at least two lines of text are missing, and they were probably already absent in the C- and
J-scribes' common exemplar. It is presumably in these missing lines that Wisdom and
Justice (*dreiture*) would have been identified. In Gui de Cambrai's version of the story,
they are named as *sens e justiche* (as Koch observes).

[23] 144 **you're eating leek instead of cabbage** *vus mangez poree pur la jute*; *puroec*
Koch: i.e. "you're making a bad choice." Cf. *AND*, s.v. *jute*[1]. The point, presumably, is that
leek is much more pungent than other cooking-greens, and therefore that the difference
between them ought to be obvious?

[24] 145–49 These lines closely resemble *Seven Sleepers*, vv. 161–64, which (in the
context of a similar sentiment) also refer to "joie pardurable," "fable," and "sunge."

[25] 165–66 This is a detail taken directly from the Latin, which describes the man as
"contristatus quidem quod martirium non sustinuit" (BJL, 126).

¶ At this time it came about that there was a happy event for the king. His wife gave him a son, and there was no finer child anywhere. The more he grew, the more handsome he became: he was a particularly graceful young man. The king had him named Josaphaz and celebrated his birth with a splendid feast, abundant with delights of every kind. People from many countries arrived in order to do honour to the occasion, paying tribute to the king's gods with donations of gold and silver. Among all these visitors, there were fifty-five pre-eminent astronomers: you would never find anyone superior to them. Many of them were authors[26] of great acumen and erudition.

The king showed good sense in saying to these astronomers, "Look at the movements of the stars and tell me something of the marvels you understand! Be sure not to conceal from me the destiny of this child!"

One of them said[27] that he would be more powerful than any king or count or marquis then in the entire world, no matter if the whole globe were searched.

Another said, "He'll be strong and sturdy, surpassing every knight in courage."

The third said, "This child will be the most valiant man in the world and, not to mention anything else, the wisest under the heavens."[28]

The fourth said, "This is how he'll be: he'll be fabulously rich."

So one said this, another said that, until an old man with a beard as white as hawthorn stood up.[29] As he surveyed them, his look alone was enough to silence them all. Impressed by his carriage and his venerable old age, they all went quiet, for he seemed very wise.

He said, "Sire, pay no attention to this. I'll tell you straightaway what I can see and what I know about this. I won't tell you one word of a lie. The child you see here will be gloriously crowned in a realm that is different from this one. It's clear to me that he will inevitably become a Christian. My prediction will not

---

[26] 185 **authors** *autres*: here a form of "authors", not "others."

[27] 193–205 In the Latin (**BJL**, 130), the astrologers are asked to state separately ("edicere singulos") what will happen to the child, but it is only Chardri who presents the astrologers coming forward one after the other, each with their own prophecy. It is perhaps possible that Chardri's depiction of this whole scene has been influenced by precedents in medieval romance, such as Laȝamon's account of the "elves" who make similar prophecies or promises at the birth of King Arthur. See Laȝamon, *Brut*, ed. Brook & Lesley, vv. 9608–15. Cf. also the "gifts" given by the fairy godmothers in Perrault's 'Sleeping Beauty in the Wood', trans. Betts, 83–84.

[28] 202 **under the heavens** *suz la chape del cel*: literally, "under the sky's cape." Cf. *Little Debate*, v. 1303.

[29] 207 **as white as hawthorn** *blanche cum flur*: literally, "as white as a flower", but the flower in question is presumably the hawthorn (*flur d'aubespine*), as is conventional in Old French poetry. Chardri himself makes use of this simile in *Seven Sleepers*, vv. 1552–54. The Latin here (**BJL**, 13) makes no reference to the man's old age (or to the white beard which is indicative of it).

deceive. There is no empire so wealthy as the realm whose lord he will become. He will eventually be baptised: there can be no other outcome."[30]

He fell silent and said no more. The king was deeply dismayed, and he began to work out how he could prevent his son from being led amiss. It seemed to him that he ought to go about it in the following way. (167–232)

¶ He immediately ordered that a palace should be built as soon as possible, a beautiful and spacious one. He wanted to have his son enclosed, so that the boy would see no living man apart from those that the king trusted most, and the woman who was his wet-nurse, in the hope that this would prevent someone seducing his son away from him as had been predicted. The king was afraid that, if the boy learned of the Christians' existence, he would want to become one of them. Pleasures and entertainments were arranged for him in the palace night and day. His father made sure that he had everything that gives anyone pleasure: mirth and singing and musical instruments, together with all the luxuries that could be found in the world, everything that he could possibly want, except that he was not allowed to hear any discussion of God. You know why the king did this? Because he was heedless about the next life, which he regarded as a mere fantasy, but if he had actually learned anything about it, he would have had himself baptised straightaway. For this reason no one was allowed to speak even one word about God. If one of the attendants became ill, he was replaced with one in good health. The sick man was sent from the tower, so that the boy would not see any suffering. (233–62)

¶ As a consequence of the old man's prediction that the boy would abandon his faith, the king's savagery greatly increased. He did even more harm to the Christians, immediately issuing a decree that any Christian who was discovered would within three days be burned to ashes, without any hope of reprieve.

An eminent knight in the king's court secretly became a Christian, in such a way that nobody knew of it, since he was very afraid of the king. One day he went with the king and all his huntsmen into a forest. They wanted to do some hunting, for relaxation. By chance, the knight set off on his own into a valley at the bottom of a cliff, where he found a man lying in a sorry plight. A wolf[31] had bitten off his foot at some point during the day, and he had been left on the ground in a terrible state. As soon as the injured man saw the knight coming he began to call out to him beseechingly.

---

[30] 213–226 Hirsh observes that this prophecy ultimately "derives from the prediction of the Brahmins at the birth of Buddha, which was followed by the prediction of the great seer Asita who had learned after looking at the heavens, that the new prince will bring the world to enlightenment, a prediction which brings grief to his father, since Asita insisits that 'he will give up the kingdom in his indifference to worldly pleasures, and, through bitter struggles grasping the final truth, he will shine forth as a sun of knowledge in the world to dispel the darkness of delusion'" (Hirsh, 183–84).

[31] 285 a wolf *un lu*. The Latin says refers only to an animal ("bestia": BJL, 134).

"Lord," he said, "For the sake of God! I'm a poor man that you see here, and I'll tell you what happened to me. It's lucky you've come along, finding me here as you have."

The knight then asked him, "Who are you, my good friend? And what are you doing in this country? Don't conceal any of your story from me."

Then the man replied, "I am an expert therapist.[32] Whatever emotional disturbance anyone might have, I can cure it, whether it is easy or difficult: that is my trade."

The knight had no respect at all for such a trade, but for the sake of God, whom he loved sincerely, he conveyed the man back to his own house and arranged for him to be given what he needed: thus the stranger found himself well lodged.

There were envious people (God curse them!) who were very jealous of the knight. They trenchantly denounced him before the king, and demonstrated with incontrovertible evidence that he was a Christian and that he had been carefully concealing his faith. The king began to consider how he might put him to the test. Alone and without ceremony, he went to the knight's house; and the knight welcomed him and showed great pleasure at seeing the king, thinking that it was something urgent that had brought him all the way there.

The knight said, "Bless your soul that you're prepared to make such a pilgrimage! You do me very great honour, as my feudal lord, to come and see me here."

---

[32] 300 **therapist** *mire de parole*: Chardri's wording is a literal translation of "medicus verborum" ("a physician of words": BJL, 136). This is not a phrase that I have found anywhere in medieval literature, but it seems to mean a doctor who uses words as a form of treatment, in which case "therapist" is perhaps as close an equivalent as can be found, anachronistic though it may sound. In the Georgian text that is the ancestor of all the European versions of the legend, the injured man calls himself a "patcher of words." When he is asked, "how do you patch words?", he replies, "If in speech there be any wounds, I can sew them up, so that no damage results from them" (Lang, *Balavariani*, 61). Western-European writers like Chardri might have made sense this idea of the "medicus verborum" by relating it to the Senecan concept of the wise man or philosopher as being like a physician, attending to vice as a physician attends to disease. See for example, Seneca, *De ira* (*On anger*), 2. 10. 7: "Placidus itaque sapiens et aequus erroribus, non hostis sed corrector peccantium, hoc cottidie procedit animo: 'multi mihi occurrent vino dediti, multi libidinosi, multi ingrati, multi avari, multi furiis ambitionis agitati.' Omnia ista tam propitius aspiciet quam aegros suos medicus" ("And so the wise man is just and kindly toward errors, he is not the foe, but the reprover of sinners, and as he issues forth each day his thought will be: 'I shall meet many who are in bondage to wine, many who are lustful, many ungrateful, many grasping, many who are lashed by the frenzy of ambition.' He will view all these things in as kindly a way as a physician views the sick": ed. and trans. John W. Basore, in *Seneca: Moral Essays*, 3 vols (London: Heinemann, 1928–1935) 1: 106–355, at 188–89). From this perspective, the *mire de parole* could be seen as a role similar to the one adopted by the Young Man in the *Little Debate,* who is Chardri's version of a figure called "Ratio" ("Reason") in this text's Senecan (or pseudo-Senecan) source.

The king craftily replied, "I want to do you honour, certainly, and I love you very much with a pure heart. For this reason I don't want anyone ever to know what's in my mind, apart from you, because I love you so much. This is why I've come to you now, to get advice about my salvation. My behaviour has been very cruel and I've done Christians a great deal of harm. Now I'm sorry about that and I deeply regret so arrogantly declaring war on the being who made both heaven and earth. Now I'm completely resolved to abandon this ambition, and to give up all my foolishness. In order to put it right, I'll follow your advice. Whatever you counsel me to do, I'll do it straightaway."

Listening to what the king said, the knight began to sigh deeply, tears running right down to his chin,[33] and he began to speak in this way: "Blessed is the hour that you were born! And blessings on whoever inspired you with this goal! For now you're on the right road.[34] Although I am a sinner, I'll tell you my advice. Anyone who wants to give it any thought will soon realise that all this glory[35] leads only to shame, and that it's utterly worthless. It doesn't last long, I believe, but the suffering will last forever.[36] For Christians the labour is brief, but their joy and bliss are endless,[37] just as God has ordained."

When the king heard this speech, he almost went out of his mind with grief, for now he realised and understood that what people were saying was true: that the knight was indeed a Christian. Now he would have thought poorly of himself if he had failed to exact vengeance on this man, who had betrayed him like a hardened criminal. Nevertheless he let no sign of his feelings show, not in the slightest. Instead, he departed without saying anything and returned to his palace. But the knight realised that he had been betrayed and was in a nasty predicament. It saddened and depressed him, and he felt it a burden still to be alive. (263–380)

¶ Then he remembered the man he had found in the forest and the claims he had made about being an excellent doctor, a therapist dealing with stress.

He summoned him straightaway, and said, "My good friend, do what you promised me, when I found you some time ago. Now I have need of your skills!"

The man replied, "Sir, I swear, if you have need of me, I may well be able to tell you something that will alleviate your anxiety."

---

[33] 349 Cf. **BJL**, 138: "lacrimis perfusus."

[34] 353 The "right road" referred to here (*dreite veie*) is the way to eternal life (*la veie ... desk'a la vie pardurable*) referred to at vv. 51–54.

[35] 358 **this [worldly] glory** *ceste gloire*: Chardri says simply "this glory," but it is clear from the context that it is specifically worldly glory that he means.

[36] 359–60 Cf. **BJL**, 138: "nam dulcedo horum temporalis; dolores uero perennes";

[37] 361–63 Cf. 2 Machab. 7: 36: "For my brethren, having now undergone a short pain, are under the covenant of eternal life."

The knight recounted what had happened to him, how he had been deceived by the king and how deeply worried he was as a result, to the extent that he could get no peace of mind at all.

To this the poor man replied, "You shouldn't be so distressed on this account. I'll give you some very good advice. I'd be amazed if you found it ineffective. Get yourself tonsured and shaved, cropped so closely that it will look as if you want to become a monk; then get yourself clothed in a long, thick hair-shirt; and tomorrow, first thing in the morning, go straight before the king. He'll ask you, 'Why are you dressed in such a horrible way? And why are you shaved so closely?' And you'll say, without hesitation, 'As a result of the discussion that we had yesterday, here I am now, ever ready to be at your side to suffer pain and sorrow—or to share in the good that God might do you. My heart and my body I give over to you, to do with them whatever you wish, to endure whatever comes, whether good or bad. I have loved you up to now: I'm never going to abandon you.'"

The knight recognised the validity of what the man said. He did not hesitate for a moment to do what he had suggested. He went straight to the king and told him what he had been advised to say. Thus the king clearly perceived that the knight loved him with a pure heart, and he was assuaged of the bitterness and extreme anger that had led him to think of having the man executed. Now he wanted to treat him in completely the opposite way: he wanted the knight to be his teacher in all matters and this was because he understood very clearly that the knight loved him with a wholly pure heart. Anyone who intends to do good[38] can learn from this that counsel is worth much more than ambition. Counsel had got this man out of a deep hole.[39] Counsel had saved this man's life, since in response to it he did what was shrewd. (381–442)

¶ All the time that this was going on, Josaphaz remained in his tower, and nobody was allowed to talk to him or visit him. But then the king sensibly decided that his son should be taught to read and write, under the instruction of good teachers well trained in every academic subject, except that of divinity. He was allowed to learn as much as he liked of the East's scientific knowledge,[40] but there was one thing that irritated him: he had been shut away for so long, without ever being able to see people outside. It unsettled him, both physically and mentally, so that he summoned one of his teachers, and said to him: "I want you to tell me the answer to a question that I'm going to ask right now. Make sure that you don't hide the answer from me! If you tell me the truth, you'll be my trusted companion forever. If you tell me what's going on, it'll be a service for which I'll

---

[38] 438 This line is a repetition of *Josaphaz*, v. 1.

[39] 440 **counsel had got this man out of a deep hole** *Par cunseil est cist de bas munte*: literally, "By means of counsel this man climbed up from a low place."

[40] 451 In the Latin, Josaphaz is "imbued with all the learning of the Ethiopians and the Persians" ("omni Ethiopum et Persarum disciplina imbutus": BJL, 146).

well reward you. Why have I been placed in this tower, never being allowed out? For what fault or slander have I been so long enclosed?"

The teacher was intimidated by the boy, since he realised that he was astute and quite capable of doing him good or ill. Because of this he concealed nothing, but told him the whole story from beginning to end, everything that he knew, whether it was wise or foolish to do so. "Lord," he said, "Take pity on me, for I'm very much your friend. If the king knew that I was doing this, it would take more than all the fine gold in Galatia[41] to save me from being condemned to be executed. Whatever the right or wrong of it, the king would make me die a terrible death. But if you solemnly promise never to reveal it, fear will never prevent me from telling you everything that I know—so great is the love I have for you."

The boy boldly replied: "Tell me everything straight out. I shall never reveal it."

With that he fell silent and the man spoke. He told him everything about the violence that his father had done to the Christians after he had heard the astronomer's prediction "that you will surely become a Christian. This is why he wants to destroy them utterly. To make sure they can't talk to you, he has had you locked in this tower night and day, as you're well aware. The king is having you guarded here so that you won't reject his religion. That's why no one is allowed to come here, unless it's someone that the king trusts." (443–504)

¶ When Josaphaz heard what the man told him, his heart was deeply troubled. By no means could he conceal the turmoil from which he was suffering. In his sorrow he took to his bed; and he did so for so long that the king himself came to visit him, out of growing anxiety for his son. With great tenderness he asked him, "My dear son, if you love me, be sure not to hide from me whatever it is that's troubling you!"

To this the boy replied: "I won't hide it: it's because you're treating me as if you despise me, not allowing me to mix with other people. You've driven me nearly mad by depriving me of companionship. You clearly don't love me very much, if you won't let me share in the pleasures of all those who have lots of fun outside. You're upsetting my health, both mental and physical."

The king hastily answered: "My dear son, that's not the reason for it at all. I've put you in this tower so that you never see sorrow. It's so that your heart

---

[41] 478 **Galatia** *Galace*. The reference is probably to Galatia, a Roman province in what is now Anatolia in Turkey, whose Christian communities were the recipients of a biblical letter from St. Paul. Rutledge, however, reads this as a reference to Galicia, which, he says, was "part of Hungary, Poland and Kiev in the Middle Ages [and] important for its fertile soil and commercial connections" (Rutledge, 274). This seems to me highly unconvincing. Koch suggests that the reference to "Galace" should be seen as an "epische phrase", as in *Seven Sleepers*, v. 716 (which mentions Damascus) and *Josaphaz*, v. 1894 (which refers to "Tabarie", which I take to mean Tiberias). What all three place-names have in common is that they appear in the Bible.

remains untroubled that I've provided for you in this way. As long as I can protect you from what's bad, I want you always to be happy."

"Father," he said, "there's one other thing. I have at heart a mortal sorrow, a sorrow that's troubling me very much, and I'll tell you the worry that's causing it. If you want me to be happy, you should understand clearly that I want to see every bit of what people do everywhere outside the tower. Only in this way can my heart really be at peace. And you should also understand that from now on I want to be able to go to and fro, to look at everything just as I please."

The king was grieved to hear this. Nevertheless he gave no sign of his sorrow. Immediately he ordered his servants to assemble in the tower. They were very many, healthy and good-looking men. Then the king ordered them to be ready to obey Josaphaz's wishes, doing whatever he ordered, going wherever he thought fit. They were enjoined to be entirely at his command. But the king also had it announced that no one who had any love or had sincere loyalty for him would, at any cost, allow Josaphaz to see anything that was not joyful. Instead they were to distract him with an abundance of music and singing, and all the pleasures anyone could imagine. He should not be allowed to see any road that had not been cleaned of dirt, dung, and mud, so that as he went about he would not see anything to cause him emotional distress. This is how devoted the king was to his child. There was no one else he loved so much.

The servants did what they were told, and it was not long before the boy preferred going outside to spending his time lying in the tower. No one can blame a youngster for wanting to have fun: this is how it is with everybody when they are young. Unfortunately it often happens that the old reproach the young for doing exactly what they themselves were even more intent on doing, when they were young long ago.[42] They are upset whenever they see a young person having fun, just as young Josaphaz was doing the whole time that he was coming and going, having fun wherever he went.

So Josaphaz carried on in this way, until by chance it happened that he saw a man who was very disfigured from the ravages of leprosy. There was a blind man walking with him: he was his companion, I think.[43] The boy observed the two of them; and you must know that he would have had no respect for himself if he could not find out who these ugly people were and where they were from. He called his own companion and politely asked him: "My good friend, now tell

---

[42] 580–83 Cf. *Petit Plet*, vv. 113–18.

[43] 590–94 Hirsh observes that in Buddhist texts such as the *Buddhacarita* "this is the first of the traditional 'Four Encounters' with old age, sickness, death, and mendicant, which cause Buddha to perceive the essentially transitory nature of human happiness, and prepare the way for his Great Renunciation, when he leaves his kingdom to seek enlightenment" (Hirsh, 184). In the Barlaam narratives, sickness precedes old age ("a change which is to be found in the Arabic and Georgian versions [of the Barlaam legend], as well as the Greek and all subsequent ones", according to Hirsh).

me: those people that I see over there — tell me if they were born that way? Or is there someone who made them like that?"

To this the companion unthinkingly replied, "It was an accident of nature that they become so deformed."

Josaphaz said: "Now you're having me on! Must this happen to everyone?"

"No, it's the truth," the man replied. "Disease afflicted them as a result of infections[44] that arise."

The boy asked: 'Is there anyone who knows how it is that disease affects them or what causes it to happen, and can anyone say why?"

To this his servant replied: "It's our gods who are the cause of all this. It's because of them that disease comes and it's because of them that disease goes." (505–618)

¶ With that he was silent and said no more. They had not gone very much further before they met a very elderly man coming towards them from the opposite direction. He was very old indeed. His face was wrinkled; his hair was all white; his arms hung down like a saddle-cloth; his back was curved like a hunchback's; his head drooped forwards; there were no teeth in his mouth; he had a dreadful stammer; there was mucus hanging from his nose; his eyes were full of tears; and he never had any relief from any of this. He tottered along like a drunkard. The boy looked at this wizened old man[45] and you can be sure that he really did not like seeing anyone in such a wretched condition.[46] He called over one of his companions and demanded to know what it meant, that this man should be in such a state.

The companion sensibly replied: "This is a man who is very, very old. It's a hundred years, perhaps even a hundred and fifty years, since he was a newborn child. It's because of the limitations set by nature that he's ended up in such wretchedness. Before his life gets much longer, he'll have to die. Nobody can escape that.[47] No one has any guarantee against death, whether they're old or young."[48]

The boy replied: "This life is a very bitter thing,[49] whatever anyone says, when we all face death and no one can escape it."

With that he fell silent and said no more. He felt deeply troubled at heart. When he thought about death, there was no acceptable comfort for it. Whenever

---

[44] 611 **infections** *corrupciuns*. The Latin refers to the "abundance of bad humours" ("humorum malorum abundancia": **BJL**, 150).

[45] 635 **wizened old man** *rokerel*: this word is apparently a *hapax legomenon*. Koch suggests a derivation from Irish *rocan* and Gaelic *roc*, and draws comparison with the Latin *ruga*, all of which mean "wrinkle" (Koch, 173).

[46] 636–37 The old man could perhaps be seen as an example of the "old greybeard" who ends his life in misery imagined by the Young Man in *Little Debate*, vv. 195–96.

[47] 647–48 Cf. *Little Debate*, vv. 330, 339.

[48] 649–50 Cf. *Little Debate*, vv. 171–74.

[49] 652 Cf. **BJL**, 154: "Amara est uita ista."

he was reminded of death, there was a heaviness in his heart, and in his mind he began to wonder (as someone who was very wise) whether there was not perhaps some other life. These thoughts gave him a great deal of pain, and he was often depressed and sorrowful, but he made no semblance of it in public. In front of his father he was always cheerful, whatever he might be thinking in his heart. (619–68)

¶ Let us now leave the boy here, as I carry on with the story. There was an old man who was a monk. He loved and cherished God; and for the sake of God, he fled, very secretly, into a foreign country. He settled in Sennaar,[50] a very spacious land, in order to live a better life. This man was called Barlaam. He was an excellent scholar, highly literate, and gifted above all else with eloquence. No one in the world was more eloquent. God sent an angel to Barlaam, who clearly explained to him how Josaphaz was living, about his good sense and his upbringing, and about the distress the king was causing him by attempting to prevent his conversion to Christianity. God commanded Barlaam to take the boy into his care, if he could manage it.[51] God had given him his grace: now it was up to him to perform the task.

Barlaam had no intention of hesitating, once he understood what his task was; and he praised God for the news, which seemed to him so excellent that he immediately set about changing his clothes almost entirely, adopting the disguise of a merchant. Dressed like this he set off directly for the king's court. He carried a pack with him, as if it contained his wares. He took the direct road that led him most quickly there; thus he set off towards Josaphaz's tower. There he met the child's most trusted tutor,[52] who was passing time at the gate. This man asked him his business, who he was, where he was from, and what he was seeking in this country.

Barlaam promptly replied: "My good lord, I am a merchant and I come from a very distant land. I'll tell you what I'm seeking here. I'm here in order to be better able to sell my wares. Now you know the whole plan. I'll tell you what I have to sell. From Paris to Alexandria, you won't find a gem[53] better than the one I have here: if it were properly assayed, none would be more valuable, more beautiful or more powerful. I think it's very precious indeed. It's a panacea for every

---

[50] 675 **Sennaar**: mentioned several times in the Bible (see e.g. Gen. 10: 10).

[51] 688 **manage it**. The manuscripts have *entendre* ('to understand, listen'), but this would make less sense in the context than *atteindre* ('to be effective, successful': *AND*, v.n. sense 2).

[52] 705 **tutor** *mestre*: literally "master" (as in "schoolmaster").

[53] 717 Cf. Wisdom 7: 9: "Neither did I compare unto her [the spirit of wisdom] any precious stone: for all gold in comparison of her, is as a little sand, and silver in respect to her shall be counted as clay."

illness. There's no fool between here and Pavia[54] that it won't straightaway make wise. Even the Devil couldn't prevent the stone's power from being revealed. I value it so much that I don't like to show it to anybody."

"Go on, show it to me!" said the man.

"I won't do so, and I'll tell you why. Nobody can look at it unless his eyes are unclouded by sin or any other kind of folly and unless he leads a chaste life."

"No way! Don't show it to me then, good brother, for I'm a dirty sinner, and I've been so my whole life!" (669–738)

Barlaam said: "My good sir, you seem like a fine fellow. If you could arrange for me to enter the tower, I'd certainly show the stone to the king's son, as long as I didn't lose anything by it. Indeed, sir, this might well be to you own advantage!"

To this the man replied: "You've no need to worry! A curse on the head[55] of anyone who causes you any loss! Of course I'll carry your message, if you don't mind waiting here. It won't take a moment to tell Josaphaz what you want."

With that he headed off straight upstairs and immediately appeared before the prince, saying: "Sir, by Tervagant, I've got something amazing to tell you. You've never heard anything to match it. There's a merchant outside whose like has never been seen. He's carrying a treasure so valuable that it's worth more than silver or gold! It's a marvellous gem: never have I heard of one so precious. It can completely cure even the gravest of maladies that might afflict anyone, either bodily or at heart. And it can do something else as well. The Devil is powerless wherever the stone holds[56] sway. Of all the precious stones in the world that anyone could ever seek, this one surpasses all others, it seems to me, on account of its beauty."

Josaphaz said: "Off you go then, and bring me this merchant right away. If that's how it is, he'll be welcome, and I'll give him a good reception."

The attendant went out and fetched him: he hardly needed to go to much trouble. When the merchant entered the room, he greeted the prince politely: his words were elegant and courtly. Josaphaz saw that his guest was uncomfortable with others in the room, so he asked them to leave. (739–83)

Barlaam, who knew about manners, kneeled down before him and told him the whole story, how he had left his own country on Josaphaz's behalf, how he had undertaken hardship for his sake, because God had sent him there. This

---

[54] 722 Rutledge (106–9) suggests that this refers to a particular event in 1212, in which a contingent of Pavia's citizens was massacred by Otto, duke of Brunswick. This seems unlikely. "Between here and Pavia" is simply a circumlocution for "anywhere"; and Pavia has been chosen (rather than any city) because it rhymes.

[55] 746 **the head**: *la barbe tute*: literally, "the whole beard."

[56] 768 **holds sway**: reading *n'eist la mestrie* (as in C) instead of *meist la mestrie* (as according to Koch's emendation). Rutledge also follows C at this point; J is not running due to the loss of a leaf after fol. 228.

was the gem[57] that he had brought, and it was the very best in the world.[58] "He made the sky and the deep sea, human beings and animals of every kind, giving shape to them by means of his power. There is nothing that anyone could think of, either in heaven, in the air, on land or at sea, that he did not create all by himself. Neither in heaven on earth is there any other God but him. He made all things, he redeemed all things, he exerts power over all things, and everything that you see he created. You should understand and believe that he made everything that exists, except that he never brought about sin. Certainly sin was invented by us, and you should recognise the certain fact that all the joy we think we possess will turn into damnation, except for the joy that surpasses all else, which is worth much more than this worldly existence. Whoever loves this world too much will be led by it into wretchedly enduring the torments of hell, to which there is no end: but whoever loves God sincerely will possess endless joy. And this is what you should do, without any doubt, for everyone who dies will receive either good or ill."

Why should I make a long story of it?[59] Barlaam told Josaphaz so much about Jesus Christ and his creed that he put the prince in a dilemma; he wavered now this way, now that. But Barlaam carried on speaking, discreetly rehearsing the principles of our religion as they spoke privately together, until the prince replied: "Ah, my good sir! By God, I thank you! Would that my father knew the truth of everything that you've just told me!"

Barlaam replied: "My dear sweet son, there is no man alive who can save him, unless God in his mercy grants him grace; but you should know that if you don't bring salvation to both your father and yourself, that will be a marvel, by my faith, for he will be your father in the flesh, and you will be his father in spirit."

When Barlaam had said all this, the boy then asked if, without any further invitation, he would be prepared to show him his monk's habit and his way of life. Barlaam told him how he had borrowed his clothes in order to visit him in disguise. He told him everything that had happened to him. (784–846)

---

[57] 790 Koch (174) thinks that this description of the gem's powers begins so abruptly as to suggest a lacuna in the extant manuscripts' common exemplar; and that it makes sense only in relation to the parable of the Sower that is recounted in most versions of the legend at this point (e.g. **BJL**, 162). He therefore assumes that several lines of Chardri's text have gone missing and that these would have contained Chardri's version of this parable ("eine lücke von mehreren versen. . . in welchen dies gleichnis erzählt wurde"). The text seems to me perfectly comprehensible as it stands.

[58] 792 Koch does not print speech-marks at this point, or indeed anywhere before he closes them at v. 818, but in his notes (174) he suggests that he imagines direct speech to start in v. 802.

[59] 819 This line is a duplicate of *Seven Sleepers*, v. 154, and *Josaphaz*, v. 2773. Far from making a "long story" of it, Chardri here radically truncates his source, completely skipping about 12 chapters (or text equivalent to over 70 pages of de la Cruz's edition).

Josaphaz then said to him: "Now show me your habit so that I can see what you look like."[60]

And Barlaam replied, "By God, I'll show it to you without any more ado."

He began to remove the clothing he had borrowed, so that his own clothing, which he was still wearing underneath, was revealed. It was an old sack roughly sewn together. It was torn, and peeping through it was his flesh, which was thin, and black and burned by heat and cold. He wore a scapular reaching from his neck to his knees, which was made out of some utterly horrible canvas cloth. Josaphaz had such pity for him that tears fell from his beautiful eyes. Then Josaphaz gave Barlaam his right hand and led him into his own private room, where he could learn all about Barlaam's faith in complete privacy and without any distraction. Barlaam taught him about God so effectively that he succeeded in baptising him.[61] The Holy Spirit descended there, bringing about the completion of the sacrament for him. Barlaam went to his lodgings and sang mass as soon as he could, bringing Josaphaz the eucharist[62] so as to administer communion to him straightaway. Then he thoroughly instructed him what he had to do from then on; and Josaphaz quickly understood how he ought to lead his life.

The attendants who looked after the boy were extremely puzzled about why Barlaam visited so often; and it made them very suspicious.[63] One of them in particular, a clever and prudent man by the name of Zardan, was very disturbed by this. He did not conceal what he was thinking, but rather went straight before the boy, saying to him, "Lord, by Muhammad the great, it's very wrong of you to allow this fellow to come so often into this tower. Don't you know that the king is very fearful about you, and we are too. It makes me very anxious; and I'm worried that this man might be a Christian. You'd be putting us all into danger, if your father found out. If you have any pity for me, you'll prevent him from visiting any more. In this way, we'd be reassured. If you won't do that, you should ask the king to give permission for this man to have access to you. If you aren't willing to do this either, then accept the request that I'd like to make: let me leave your service on good terms, so that somebody else can take my place. If I stay here like a proven traitor, I'll be attainted for my lack of loyalty and not guarding in good faith the treasure with which the king entrusted me. By 'treasure' I mean you, since, as you know, he loves you more than anything." (847–914)

---

[60] 848–64 This scene corresponds with **BJL**, 302: "Rogat igitur senem Iosaphat ostendi sibi ab eo consuetum uestimentum . . ." ("Therefore Josaphat asks the old man to show him the clothing that he was accustomed to wear . . .").

[61] 870 At this point, Chardri abridges two chapters of the vulgate (**BJL**, 310–28).

[62] 875 **the eucharist** *le seint cors*: literally, "the sacred body [of Christ]."

[63] 881–84 Cf. **BJL**, 330: "Ministri uero iuuenis et pedagogi frequentem ipsius Barlaam introitum in palacium cernentes mirabantur" ("The young man's attendants and tutors were amazed at seeing Barlaam's frequent visits to the palace").

¶ When Josaphaz had heard him out, he immediately gave him a very polite response. "Zardan," he said, "there's a task I'm going to explain, and I command you to perform it without delay. I'm going to get Barlaam to come here so that you can listen to him. Just as he's about to enter, you must run and hide, there behind that big curtain,[64] so that he never spots you. When you've heard everything he says, and he's left here again, then you must hear what it is that I desire, and then you'll know what you should do."

"Very willingly," said Zardan. "So send for him straightaway and I'll go and hide over there, just as you've said, so that I can listen to him."

Josaphaz did exactly that and sent immediately for Barlaam, who got ready quickly.[65] Once he was in the boy's presence, they greeted each other; and the boy said: "I've summoned you here because I desire you to repeat the teaching that you've already given me, for it's so excellent that I want to memorise it. That will allow us to be in even closer accord."

Barlaam readily granted him all this. From beginning to end he repeated the sermon you have already heard about. He did not leave off until he had gladly and joyfully told the whole truth about God. When he had said all this, he took his leave, and went back to his lodgings. (915–52)

¶ The boy immediately stood up and said, "Zardan, you can come out now!" And Zardan came out, deep in thought.

Josaphaz wanted to test him out, so he said, "Now listen, my good friend. This trickster wants to deceive me with his with his words, which are worthless. Whatever he says, I don't think much of it and I'm not going to take any of it to heart. But if he thinks he can deceive me in this way he's too confident in his own cleverness. Tell me if you think it's true that he could give you God to eat and drink!"

Zardan replied: "It seems to me that you're trying to put me to the test with your words: I'm sure this is what you're doing. For I clearly see and understand that, when this man was coming in here so often, this is what he was teaching you, and I now realise that it's impossible for you not to have taken it greatly to heart and be persuaded by it. If it now happens that the king becomes hostile and demands an explanation, I don't know what I ought to say to him. You've put me in a difficult position, for the service I've given him has been inadequate. It's only right that I should be punished, since I allowed this wretched fellow to get so close to you in here."

Josaphaz replied: "Now listen to me, my dear friend. Because I love you so much,[66] I don't want you to be so lacking in grace that you don't know the right

---

[64] 925 The reference to the curtain comes from the vulgate ("infra cortinam": BJL, 330).

[65] 936 **was quickly ready** *fu tost en grande*: Koch prints "engrande", but the phrase is "estre en grant" (see *AND*, s.v. 'grant'³).

[66] 985 I have here departed from the punctuation suggested by Koch, who prints a full stop at the end of v. 985.

road, the one that leads us to salvation: at last you know how to recognise your creator. It's clear to me that I have been at fault for having neglected my soul. Even if you don't want to be saved, make sure that this is kept carefully hidden. If you say a single word to the king, you'll be acting like a cursed fool, because it will upset him very much without advantaging you in any way. If you've ever loved the king, you must make sure that not a single word is said to him until you see the appropriate time and occasion. It would be very prudent to do this." After they had argued in this way, the young man angrily left the room. (953–1004)

¶ In the morning, when it was daylight, Barlaam headed towards the tower in order to take his leave. He wanted to go back into the desert right away, to serve God as he had done before. At his departure, Josaphaz wept piteously and said, "My good master, for the love of God, take some gold and silver with you so that you can support yourself, and clothes to protect you better from the cold. Whatever you ask for, you'll have it in abundance. And you should know it's true, master, that I am deeply saddened by your departure. But if it can't be otherwise, then I ask you, for the love of almighty God and for the sake of his Creation, that you leave me your rough clothing to remember you by. Wherever you've gone, I'll meditate on it night and day: it will be my solace and my delight."

Then Barlaam replied: "May God who made the world preserve me! I'll do whatever you want, my dear sweet son, to the best of my abilities." He straightaway removed his clothes and handed over his rough, repulsive coat, which the boy took. Both of them cried together on account of the great love and compassion they shared night and day. Barlaam commended Josaphaz to God and repeatedly prayed to see the boy again one day, happy and joyful on account of his Christianity.

And so he set off, leaving Josaphaz in his sorrow, pale and discoloured from weeping. And Barlaam did not stop until he was back in the desert, and he served God night and day with a pure heart just as he had done before. Josaphaz meanwhile never shirked from serving God the son of Mary, however anyone else might feel about it, just as Barlaam had taught him. (1005–1050)

Zardan, of whom you have already heard, was hardly overjoyed to see the boy's great devoutness. Now he thought that he would be a stupid fool simply to remain in his service until punishment came. He knew very well that if the king found out about it, he would have no hesitation in condemning him to the pyre. He carefully deliberated, then suddenly pretended to be sick, and took to his bed. As soon as the king heard that Zardan was ill, he was deeply sad at heart. Profoundly grieved by this, he sent Zardan his own clever physicians, who assiduously took his pulse and inspected his urine at length, but they could not find the cause of the illness. When they could not do anything for him, they made this known promptly to the king, who was amazed and heavy-hearted; and he realised that, whatever Zardan might say, this was no illness, but rather it seemed possible that the servant had committed some fault which had upset his son. With that he sent Zardan a message, saying that if there was anything that had distressed him, anything making him feel disaffected, he would endeavour to mitigate it, and that he would come and speak to him straightaway the following morning, to see what was wrong with him.

When Zardan heard this message, he carefully weighed up in his mind what, ultimately, he should do. The following day, as soon as it was light, he privately got himself dressed and booted, and went before the king. Knowing full well what he was doing, he threw himself onto the ground with his arms outstretched, greeting the king piteously, as if he were in fear of his life.

The king said to him: "My dear sweet friend, it's sheer folly on your part to come all the way here. I'd just this minute been planning to come and visit you. There was no need for you to go to so much trouble."

Zardan straightaway replied: "My dear lord, have mercy on me, by God! It's not my body that is afflicted in any way: it's from my heart that the oppression comes which has caused me so much turmoil. I'll tell you all about it without leaving anything out. I'll put myself at your mercy and tell you the fault that I've committed: my performance in your service has been utterly feeble. Have mercy on me! My repentance is deep and heartfelt. You trusted me to watch over your son—that I know. But I have failed to watch over him properly, for I allowed an infidel (whom I did not recognise as such) to speak to him in the tower so that he successfully converted him to Christianity. This scoundrel has made great difficulties for me. I know that he's called Barlaam—may God bring him bad luck![67] There isn't a worse traitor in the whole continent of India[68] than this man who's led your child astray. I take full responsibility for everything, submitting myself to do whatever you command. If you show no mercy on me and sentence me to death, it would be wholly justified. This is the affliction from which I have been suffering. Whether I live or die rests entirely with you." (1051–1130)

When the king heard this, he was unhappier than he had ever been in his life. Zardan's words were so apologetic that he had no desire to have him tortured, but instead granted him a full pardon because he had told him the truth.[69] It was only with difficulty that the king could still breathe, for he was on the brink of a complete frenzy. There was nothing to which he paid any attention, nothing at all that he cared about, any more than he might have cared about some old glove, now he had lost his son. His grief was extreme, and it seemed as if his heart nearly stopped, because of the sorrow that afflicted him. He summoned one of his senior courtiers, one of the most noble among his barons,[70] and said to

---

[67] 1122 **may God bring him bad luck!** *Deu li doinst entrer en mal an!* Literally, "may God grant that he embarks on a bad year!"

[68] 1123 **the whole continent of India**: *Inde la grant*: see n. to v. 70 above.

[69] 1133–36 This is not stated in the Latin (see **BJL**, 346).

[70] 1147 The vulgate says that Arachis was second only to the king, and first in all his counsels, but also that Arachis excelled in astrology ("astrologice artis scientia nimium pollebat": **BJL**, 346).

him: "Sir, what's happened to me today is a catastrophe. It's the most upsetting thing that's ever happened to me in my life, that I have lost my son, despite his intelligence, to apostasy. And you can be sure that for the rest of my life my heart will never be at peace until my son in entirely recovered from this folly: for right now I regard him as completely lost." (1131–1158)

¶ The nobleman was called Arachis. From what he saw he realised that the king was in a terrible rage.

"My good lord," he said, "Now listen to me: I'll give you some good advice. He'll never leave off this foolishness as long as Barlaam is alive, unless we do this one thing first: if we can take Barlaam captive, he'll make your son reconsider. We'll make Barlaam renounce his beliefs, and then I think your son will do the same. He'll do whatever his master does: nothing will prevent him from that. If it turns out that Barlaam has completely disappeared and can't be found, there's another strategem that we should pursue: there's a man I happen to know, an old and very scholarly man, whom the people call Nakor[71] and who was once my own master. You can be sure that there's no one in this country more deeply versed in our religion or, so I believe, more astute. There's been no man since the time of Adam who resembles Barlaam more closely in his behaviour and his speech, for he has long been a master among disciples. When it's night, I'll visit him at his house and give him my account of what's happened to you and your child, and I'll go about it so persuasively that he'll agree to impersonate Barlaam. As soon as it's daylight, you, meanwhile, should have Barlaam searched for everywhere, both in this country and abroad, until Nakor is found, pretending to be Barlaam. Then we'll have him led before you and get it announced everywhere that Barlaam, that traitor against the king, has been captured, and that he wishes to defend his beliefs in a disputation. He'll use his learning and his reason to argue that Christianity is the best religion there's ever been. Our own scholars will debate with him and uphold their case so well that he'll be overcome, and he'll admit that he's been proved wrong, declaring that true scholarship demonstrates the superiority of our way of life. When the boy has understood that his master has been vanquished, he'll realise that he's been wicked and silly and he'll come back over to our cause. This man called 'Barlaam' will do whatever you wish."

The king said to him, "My lord Arachis, may our almighty gods protect you and your good sense. I don't believe that any other man who can speak who could have provided his friend with better advice. By Muhammad the divine, you're both wise and loyal. Now our strategy is clear. I'll order all my subjects to assemble, and you must go straightaway to talk to Nakor as you've said. And in the morning, at daybreak, you'll lead my people through the countryside. Do this in search of 'Barlaam' until Nakor is found."

---

[71] 1178 **Nakor** *Nakor* C; *Nachor* J, Koch (who prefers J's spelling because it is also that of the Latin, 177).

With that Arachis set off: it seemed to him a long time before he reached Nakor. Very discreetly and in great secret, so that no one in the country would know about it or see him, he told Nakor what was on his mind. Nakor made a pact with him and swore by Tervagant that he would cleverly carry out the whole plan just as Arachis wished. When the arrangements had been thoroughly discussed, Arachis surreptitiously returned to the court, where he spoke in secret to the king: "I've succeeded very well, believe me. I've taken considerable trouble and everything will happen just as I've planned." (1159–1248)

¶ Then they went off to get some rest, but the next day, as soon as it was light, the king lost no time in assembling all his men. He issued instructions for Arachis to lead them out into the country to seek his enemy, Barlaam, in every corner of the land and not to leave off for any reason until they had brought Barlaam before him, without attacking or mistreating him. Under Arachis's competent command, they spread out throughout the land. There was no mountain or valley that they did not thoroughly search in turn, taking no breaks or rests. For a whole twenty days they hunted Barlaam[72] through woods and through fields, until they spotted a large community of virtuous hermits. The abbot wore around his neck some powerful relics in a little bag that was very plain and unadorned.[73] The king's men saw the hermits. With their sharp spurs they urged on their horses, which carried them at a gallop onto a wide expanse of barren ground where they seized and captured all the hermits.

When Arachis arrived there, he was exultant and swore by his white beard that he would make a present of them to the king, if they refused to tell him straightaway where that wretch Barlaam was, and the location of his hiding-place. The men he had captured swore that[74] never by means of them would he find out. This made Arachis angry, so he brought them to the king, who had them subjected to harsh torture. He ordered that some of them should have their feet chopped off and that others should have their eyes gouged out. There were some whose thumbs he cut off and others who lost their tongues, so that they could not speak. Why should I tell you all the details? It was a terrible kind of justice that he meted out. Even when it meant a choice between life and death, they refused to betray Barlaam. When they could escape in no other way, they all died by the sword.[75]

Then Arachis went roaming throughout the whole country with his men, in order to carry out the deception that he had so wickedly planned, until, searching in every direction, he spotted Nakor walking along, just as the two of them

---

[72] 1265 **hunted Barlaam:** *le siwirent.* This could also be taken to mean "followed Arachis."

[73] 1268–70 Cf. **BJL,** 348: "he was wearing a woollen bag containing relics of some of the holy fathers" ("peram portabat laneam plenam reliquiis quorundam sanctorum patrum").

[74] 1284 **that** *Ke* J, Rutledge; *Ne* Koch. In **C,** the letter is not clear to read.

[75] 1287–96 Cf. *Seven Sleepers,* vv. 168–83, *Josaphaz,* vv. 1621–26, and *Little Debate,* vv. 639–40.

had previously agreed. He vigorously spurred on his horse, gaining on Nakor so quickly that he overtook him in the open countryside.[76] Even though he immediately recognised him, he gave no sign that he had ever seen him before. He asked him who he was, brusquely demanding an answer: "Tell me, my friend," he said, "What's your name and where are you going?"

"Barlaam is my name," Nakor replied, "And I'm leaving the country on account of the king who's had me searched for everywhere, in order to kill and humiliate me."

"Believe me," said Arachis, "that's just what I wanted to hear!" He cried out at the top of his voice, "Now seize[77] him, men! May Muhammad protect you! Right here we've found the man that we've been looking for. I can assure you that the king's going to be very grateful to us when this man is brought before him."

"Well said, sir," they replied. "We'll bring him straightaway."

They grabbed Nakor and immediately led him off, for they were very keen to please the king. (1249–1330)

¶ When he appeared before the king, he pretended to be versed in our faith. The king addressed him very fiercely, "You, you scoundrel, the people say that you're Barlaam, the devil!"

"No devil," he replied, "but rather the servant of God.[78] Barlaam is certainly my name, the servant of God almighty, and you ought to thank me for being willing to take so much trouble over your son that he acknowledged his creator and I baptised him here in the tower."

"You wicked wretch," replied the king, "Because you've confessed all this to me, I'm going to do you what I think is a favour. If you renounce your faith, I will pardon you for this misdeed. If you refuse, I'll allow no end to this trial until you've died a cruel death, whether that's right or wrong."[79]

Saying all this was a pretence, because he knew very well who the man was. (1331–52)

¶ When Josaphaz found out that his master had been captured, he prayed piteously for God to help him in all of this. God clearly heard his prayer and spoke to him by means of a vision: "My good son, do not be afraid. From me

---

[76] 1306 in the open countryside *enmi le champ*. The Latin has "deserta circumeunti, apparet uir quidam de ualle quadam egrediens" (**BJL**, 360), which is rendered into Middle English as "And whan he [Arachis] come into deserte þere walkyd a man in þe valey before hem" (Hirsh, 104).

[77] 1321 seize *seez* **CJ** (as also both Koch and Rutledge), but *sesez* would make more sense (cf. the Latin "comprehendentes": **BJL**, 360).

[78] 1335–36 In this exchange Chardri is closely following the Latin: "'Tu es demonis operator, Barlaam?' Respondit ille: 'Dei operator sum et non demonum'" ("'You're Barlaam, the servant of the devil?' He replied: "I am the servant of God, not of devils'": **BJL**, 360).

[79] 1349–50 These lines almost completely duplicate *Seven Sleepers*, vv. 557–58.

you'll receive the best of help, and your master, if it were indeed him, would have no need to fear any peril. I am yours and you are with me.[80] You need never be afraid of the king."

When Josaphaz woke up, he was happier than he had ever been in his life. Now he had no worry about what anyone might do to him, either by word or by any other kind of threat. The king went into the tower every three days, or more often than that, in order to try to convert his son back again by some means or other. He kept on reproaching him and asking why he had abandoned their faith. One moment he threatened him: the next he was flattering him. Neither inducement nor threats made Josaphaz willing to relinquish the grace that God had sent him. Throughout it all he persisted in his righteousness.[81]

When the king saw that he was getting nowhere with his entreaties, and indeed that they had completely failed, he became extremely angry and said to his son, "My good son, I just want to tell you that your master is in my power, whatever anyone might think about it,[82] fettered in iron both night and day. But I'll do this much on account of my love for you: I'll summon to my presence some of the wise men of our religion, and I'll have Barlaam brought before me too. Then we'll hear which of them we should believe. It'll become clear to us from the disputation which of them we should trust, and which of them we should reject. If Barlaam is defeated in the disputation, then you'll clearly see that he's been deceiving you."

The boy replied: "I can only agree to this. May God decide between them — as he very well can!" (1353–98)

¶ The king ordered that the proclamation should be made and sent his servants throughout the country in order to seek out the very wisest men that he knew, there or in any other land, and he also announced that Christians should also be allowed to attend on that day without fear. Many wise and scholarly people did assemble there, but all of them were pagans, who were there mainly to please the king.

The king called Nakor and said to him, "Now we'll see! To begin with, put up a good defence of their faith, but then incline towards my point of view, allowing our side to come out on top and yourself to be proved utterly wrong. In the end you should surrender to me, and then you can be sure I'll make you rich, if with your help I can win back the son I love so much. He's as sure as he is of his own right hand that you are his master Barlaam."

When day came and the assembly was ready, the king had his son summoned. He wanted him to sit at his right hand in a throne of bright, pure gold.

---

[80] Cf. John 14: 20.

[81] 1369–82 These lines summarise what is in the Latin a lengthy exchange (**BJL**, 362–88) between the king and his son.

[82] 1385 **whatever anyone might think about it** *Ki k'en plurge, u ki k'en rie*: literally, "whoever might cry about it, whoever might laugh about it."

"Certainly not," said Josaphaz, "it's impossible for me to sit next to my father nor is there any way in which I'd ever do so. I'll tell you what I'll do instead: I'll sit down here at his feet."

Out of respect for his father the king, he sat down on the floor in front of him. The boy kept on looking hard at the face of Nakor, the traitor, who was supposed to be Barlaam.

"Come here, my good master," he said, "And sit down here right next to me."

He knew very well that this man was not Barlaam. Nakor quickly sat down. (1399–1440)

¶ The king said to them all, "Now listen and understand what I have to say. I've had you all summoned from far and wide in order to help me out of this difficulty. This Barlaam whom you see before you has led my son astray by means of flattery and arguments that are outrageous and stupid, with the result that my son has been baptised by him. You should all know I've sworn that anyone who refutes him, and can fairly prove that our religion is the better one, will have my gratitude. If all of you are defeated by him, I swear by Muhammad, who does the greatest miracles, that not one of you will escape alive, not one of you will be able to take a single step before being condemned to execution."

Josaphaz clearly heard what he said. "Father," he replied, "What you say is nothing but the truth (so help me God!) and you're speaking entirely reasonably."

Then he went back to sit at the right-hand side of the man who was supposed to be his master. It is no joke that he knew perfectly well this was not Barlaam, but he showed not even the slightest sign that he knew.[83]

"Master," he said, "You're well aware of the extent of the honour and privilege that you made me reject, when you brought me to abjure my religion by means of your promises and your teaching, which was certainly neither wicked nor stupid. My enjoyment would have continued intact, had it not been for your wise instruction. If you're victorious over these people, I swear by Jesus, the high king of glory, that in all the days of my life I'll never desist from serving God, the son of Mary! And you'll be my closest friend—you'll never be parted from me! And yet, master, be sure of this: if it's the case that you're just feigning and allowing yourself to be vanquished, then, by God who's saved me, I swear I'll cut out your tongue with my bare hands—have no doubt about that! I'll rip out your heart and I'll never show you any mercy until I can give your heart to the dogs outside, along with the rest of your

---

[83] 1468 **knew**: Koch and Rutledge print *fust*, but *s(e)ust* would make better sense.

body;[84] and you can be certain that I'll treat your corpse as shamefully as I possibly can!'[85]

When Nakor had heard this, he was not very happy, you can be sure of that! Now he realised that the person trying to deceive others was himself being deceived. When someone attempts to betray others, as Nakor had been trying to do, it is only fair that he should himself feel the consequences.[86] Now Nakor looked utterly downcast. He carefully considered the situation and concluded that Josaphaz had the power of life and death over him; and also that it was best for him to commit himself irrevocably to Josaphaz's cause: otherwise he would soon die a terrible death. Whatever anyone might say, he hated death. Because of this he did what was prudent, choosing to side with Josaphaz; and so he made an agreement with him, by which he would not refrain from telling the whole truth, not for anybody alive. (1441–1514)

¶ The philosophers stood up and clearly explained their case. Nakor hesitated no longer: he quickly got up and proved by flawless reasoning[87] that there is only one God, and that he made heaven and earth and sea, and that no other gods existed. He demonstrated by means of unerring scholarship that they had foolishly manufactured their own gods out of iron and wood, which was against nature, for they were making gods out of things that had been created.[88] Some of them worshipped the elements, and some worshipped the clouds and the rain; some of them worshipped boys, and some worshipped girls; and some worshipped tree-stumps together with their roots. They made gods of different kinds out of this spring and that rock, or out of the sun and the moon, and there was hardly a star that someone did not venerate as if it were an omnipotent god. So by this reason and that he proved that there is no other god but the God of

---

[84] 1487–94 These bloodthirsty threats seem oddly incongruous with the gentle innocence otherwise characteristic of the saintly Josaphaz, but they are not original with Chardri. The Latin says: "Si uero superatus seu ueritate seu falsitate confusionis michi hodie auctor extiteris, statim meam contumeliam uindicabo in te: manibus meis cor tuum et linguam extrahens canibusque ad deuorandum ista cum cetero corpore tuo tradam" (BJL, 392). In the Middle English prose *Barlam*, this becomes "And if þou be ouercome, and þe trewþe be shente by þe, Y shal anon be vengyd vpon þe, and with myn owen hondis Y shal drawe out þyn herte out of þi body, and þy tunge oute of þyn heed, and þy body shal be deuowred with wylde beestis" (Hirsh, 119).

[85] 1493–94 Cf. the anxieties dramatised in the *Little Debate*, vv. 621–56.

[86] 1497–1501 This reflects the Latin "uidens semetipsum decidisse in foueam quam fecit" (BJL, 394), which the Middle English prose renders as "he saw wel þat he was falle into þe dych þat he had made hymself" (Hirsh, 119). This is an instance of a recurring theme in medieval literature, that of the "trickster tricked." See, e.g., *Ysengrimus*, I. 69, ed. Jill Mann (Leiden: Brill, 1987), 210, and the discussion at 20–25. Cf. also, Ps. 7: 15.

[87] 1520–42 Chardri's account of Nakor's "flawless reasoning" is a very selective summary of a whole chapter of the Latin (BJL, 398–414, cap. 17).

[88] 1524–26 Cf. *Seven Sleepers*, vv. 106–24, 336–51, 401–10.

Heaven, who had created everything, and that that is the God of the Christian people. "These people are wise, whatever anyone else may say, for their God has everything in his power."[89]

After Nakor had put such a convincing case, all the other scholars were dumbfounded, so that they could not say another word, which is just what Josaphaz had prayed for. Josaphaz was delighted when he saw that Nakor's interpretation was in every way more persuasive, but the king was dejected,[90] for he realised that there was no action he could reasonably take against Nakor since he himself had ordered him to be bold in opposing the other scholars in debate.[91] But you can be sure that he really wanted him to lose, which would be to his own advantage. He kept on winking[92] at Nakor as a signal that he should allow himself to be confounded, but Nakor was reluctant to do this because he feared what Josaphaz had threatened to do to him.

The disputation went on so long that eventually the sun began to set and it was impossible for them to stay there any longer. The king had it announced that they should all depart straightaway, but that they should all come back the following morning, at daybreak, in order to hear the result of the dispute. They all agreed to this without asking for anything more. Josaphaz asked the king if he could be so bold as to bring his master to stay with him that night, in order to make his master comfortable and give him something to eat. The king made no objection at all to that request, granting it very graciously. Josaphaz immediately led Nakor away to stay at his tower, where he welcomed him joyfully. (1515–78)

¶ In the others' presence he cried out loudly, "Nakor, by God the saviour! You're very welcome here indeed! You've done me excellent service today and capably defended our religion. You should know that, as soon as I saw you face-to-face, I swear I saw through you as clearly as anything,[93] realising that you were not Barlaam. May God and St. John bless you for what you've achieved! Today you've clearly expounded the truth of our religion, just as if you'd always been brought up among Christians. You have an excellent intellect: you clearly perceive the truth. I advise you, in the name of God, to continue to believe in it with a pure heart, and in no account to give it up."

---

[89] 1541–42 This is not marked as direct speech by Koch.

[90] 1550 Koch prints a full stop at this point.

[91] 1551–54 Cf. **BJL**, 416: "Rex quidem, quamuis atrociter iratus fuisset Nachor, nichil tamen in eum exercere mali potuit, eo quod coram omnibus iusserat ei ut fiducialiter et sine ullo timore ageret pro Christianis" ("And þau3 þe kyng were neuer so angry with Nachor, 3it he my3t do hym non harme, because he bade hym before al þe peple þat he shold sey for þe Crysten feith withoute eny drede": Hirsh, 129).

[92] 1557 Here Chardri makes a much livelier image out of the Latin's suggestion that the king tried to communicate "per enigmata" ("by means of hints": BJL, 416).

[93] 1585 **as clearly as anything** *au meuz del munt.*

Nakor saw that what he said was true. By the grace of the Holy Spirit, he began to reflect deeply and, in the depths of his heart, to yearn. He decided to renounce folly and commit himself to a Christian way of life. He took his leave of Josaphaz and fled away into the desert, where he found an old priest who baptised him straightaway. The priest took Nakor into the faith and instructed him: he allowed none of his former beliefs to remain.[94] (1579–1610)

¶ When the king heard that Nakor had already made his escape, his grief was extreme, for he clearly recognised and understood that he had failed in his purpose. Now there could be no peace of mind for him. Yet in revenge for his terrible sorrow, he ordered all the remaining philosophers to be led into the tower, for he was intent on humiliating them. Some of them he subjected to cruel beatings. More than a hundred of them had their eyes put out at his command. He ordered that some should have their hands cut off, others their feet, just as he pleased. According to my source, not a single one of them got away from there without dreadful injury.[95] Then he banished[96] them all, one in this direction, one in that. When they had all gone, he was left behind sorrowing for his son, for in his bitterness he had no desire to serve his own gods night and day, nor did he want to become a Christian. Indeed he did not know which of the faiths to believe in, his own or ours, but wavered between them, in a quandary. And Josaphaz was left pining for his master, whom he loved so much—praying to God almighty that he might take pity and grant that the two of them might once again converse for a little while in peace. (1611–42)

¶ At this time there was a great feast-day approaching, which they were in the custom of celebrating lavishly, and which they loved with all their hearts. They clearly felt sure that on no account would the king want to be there; and therefore they sent for a man who was an accomplished master of the seven arts.[97] He was an intimate of the king, who loved and cherished him greatly. This man was called Theodas. When the king asked for his opinion, he could divine whatever he wanted to know. The most important people in the land had a conference with Theodas in the cave where he lived, remotely secluded from the population.

---

[94] 1610 **allowed none of his former beliefs to remain**: *sa creance ren n'i lessa*. Chardri does not make it explicit that the beliefs in question are those that Nakor previously held.

[95] 1621–26 Cf. *Seven Sleepers*, vv. 168–83, *Josaphaz*, vv. 1287–96, and *Little Debate*, vv. 639–40.

[96] 1627 **banished**: Koch prints *en casa*, and Rutledge *encasa* (as in C) but I follow the J reading *enchasa*.

[97] 1651 **the seven arts** *des set arz* Koch; *de set arz* CJ. The seven liberal arts defined the educational curriculum in the Middle Ages: the trivium (grammar, rhetoric, dialectic) and the quadrivium (geometry, arithmetic, astronomy and music). The Latin text identifies Theodas, perhaps more appropriately in this context, as a master of the "magical arts" ("magicis. . . artibus": BJL, 426).

They said, "Master, we have come here for you. We believe that if you don't watch out, we will lose our religion."

They told him the story from beginning to end of how Nakor had fared. They cajoled and flattered him for so long that he agreed to come with them straightaway so as to give them as much help as he could. He knew all about black magic: he had summoned devils from hell; and on every side they promptly appeared in order to aid Theodas. He stood up with all his followers—that is, all the devils he had at his command—and he got himself ready to go straight to the city to talk to the king. He cut an olive-branch, which he carried in his right hand. (1643–80)

¶ As soon as he arrived outside the city, the king was promptly informed that his good friend Theodas had come to talk to him. The king was pleased and delighted. He went out to meet him; he kissed and embraced him, and gave him a joyful welcome. Then he led him into his palace, where he immediately had him placed in a seat of honour next to him.

Theodas then said straightaway: "Your majesty, it's my belief that it's our gods who sustain this world—who sustain your glory, your realm and all your great wealth. From far away in my own country, I have heard that you organised a disputation here against the Christians, and that they were soundly beaten, giving you a splendid victory. In order to commemorate this, I have left my own land, in order to bring honour and praise to our gods who've given you all this, and who've granted you all these blessings."

The king replied, "Theodas, we didn't win the victory at all! By Muhammad and his power, we were utterly and completely defeated! In their impudence they overcame us, and in this way did me a great deal of harm: for with their foolishness they've seduced away my son, whom I love more than my own life."

The king gave him an account of the whole thing, all that he had done from beginning to end, telling him in great detail all about Nakor and the disputation.

"Your majesty," said Theodas, "Don't be downcast by this! Pay no heed to their foolishness, their flattery and their lies! By the faith I owe Muhammad the great, if they say so much as a word to me, I'll lead them such a dance that they'll confess to being silly louts who know no more than a beast. Now let us properly celebrate this feast that's soon to begin here, and let us pray that our gods help us, so that by means of their mighty glory we will have the victory!"

The king agreed to everything he said. He sent proclamations throughout the realm, which said that no one, on pain of losing his head, should stay away from attending the festivities. Intimidated by this proclamation, a great crowd assembled as soon as it was daybreak. The king himself, as was customary, made sure that the sacrifices were prepared right away: he had a hundred and forty bulls killed, and he also had more than five thousand sheep sacrificed throughout the city. How many animals of other kinds were killed I do not know, for the number is too large for me to handle! No one could keep count of the number of birds the king ordered to be sacrificed there! He did it to appease his wicked gods. There has never been a sacrifice to match it! (1681–1750)

¶ When the festival had been celebrated, the people returned home. Then the king summoned Theodas.

"Now let me see," he said, "whether you're going to do what you promised me, and help me to win back my son."

To this Theodas replied: "I've never lied to you, by Apollo! I'll accomplish this for you easily, just as long as we're able to carry out this one course of action. Order the removal of all the servants currently attending him in the tower, so that not one of them is left there, and then we can do something that's really cunning. Arrange for the very prettiest and most beautiful of our girls to be rounded up, and then have them placed in the tower in order to serve him night and day. They should be courtly and lascivious, the loveliest that there are in these lands, and they should be with him constantly so that he can enjoy himself with them. I'll send a spirit to inflame his sexual desire for them, but you must instruct all these girls to do whatever he wishes. Once he's had a bit of fun with one of them, he'll get a liking for it, and soon he'll be so in love with her that, even to save his life, he won't want to give her up. I'm ready to be executed if he won't do what you want."[98]

The king clearly saw the sense of what he was saying. He did not delay at all, but sent orders throughout the country for beautiful girls to be sought out; and soon he had assembled before him all the most beautiful ones that could be found. They were very elegant and graceful, daughters of the nobility. Straightaway the king himself told the servants to leave the tower and instructed all these lovely and alluring girls to concentrate on presenting their youthful selves to his handsome son, who was also his heir, so that he would take his pleasure with them. If they could make him do this, he would make them rich ever afterwards. (1751–1800)

The girls were delighted with what the king was asking them to do. Straightaway they dressed up[99] very seductively, and eagerly entered the tower. There they found the young Josaphaz, the most beautiful man then alive. Their spirits were so inflamed by love that each of them almost went mad with desire for him.[100] Immediately each of them strove to be the first to win his love, so as to be the first to play a match[101] with him. Now they kissed him, now they cuddled him; they

---

[98] 1782 At this point Chardri omits from the Latin a story told by Theodas ('The Boy who saw Women': BJL, 434–36).

[99] 1803 **dressed up** *atirerent*: Koch prints *atiserent*, Rutledge *atifferent*.

[100] 1808 Cf. *The Owl and the Nightingale*, vv. 509–12.

[101] 1812 **a match** *ju parti*. The term *ju parti*, which is the ancestor of the modern English word *jeopardy*, had particular associations in the Middle Ages both with chess-problems and with a distinct type of medieval debate-poetry (see Paul Remy, "De l'expression 'partir un jeu' dans les textes épiques aux origines du jeu parti," *Cahiers de*

were so aroused that it was driving them nearly crazy. Each of them envied the others for being able to kiss him more tenderly than she could, and each of them wanted to be the first to get a kiss from him—or something more.[102]

Eventually Theodas sent a devil of whom he was very fond. "Go!" he said, "And do everything in your power to get the boy so excited that he can't remain in your power without committing lechery!"

The devil was thoroughly wicked. He went off straightaway to do his master's will and set about urging Josaphaz to take pleasure in debauchery. Never in all his life had the young man endured such terrible anguish. Feeling the flames that such temptation inevitably caused to burn, he quickly began to pray, piteously beseeching God for a relief to his suffering. He sighed and wept constantly, calling on Jesus, the son of Mary, that he, as truly as he was born of Mary, might have mercy on him.[103] And this Jesus did, for it seemed that God himself came to his rescue. The heat of passion began to abate and his wicked thoughts were taken away: his flesh was restored to its proper state. In his affliction, he let himself fall prostrate before God. He lay the whole night in prayer and petitioned God with all his might. By this means, the evil spirit was defeated, realising that he had been completely trounced.

Yet he attempted one more deception: he took possession of the body of a girl who was the daughter of a king and a queen, and also astonishingly beautiful. The girl had been captured in the course of war and handed over to King Arvennir who had taken very good care of her. Because her beauty was so resplendent, he had sent her into the tower. As soon as the devil attacked her, she fell on the floor in a fit. Josaphaz saw this and felt great pity for this girl on account of her high lineage. Seeing her in such a terrible state, he grieved for her extraordinarily deeply. The devil so manipulated her that she cried out in a loud voice: (1801–1868)

¶ "Josaphaz, hear what I have to say! In the name of God who endured the Passion, and in the name of his sweet mother Mary, grant me the one thing that I ask of you: protect me in my vulnerable youth! If you make the effort to do so, I'll willingly become Christian. I'll be baptised along with you, if you'd grant me so much as to allow me to possess your love in private. Nature has put a lot of

---

civilisation médiévale 17 [1974]: 327–33; Arthur Långfors, ed., *Recueil général des jeux-partis français*, 2 vols, Société des anciens textes français [Paris: Champion, 1926]; Tony Hunt, ed. *Les Gius Partiz des Eschez: Two Anglo-Norman Chess Treatises*, ANTS Plain Texts 3 [London, 1985]). Here it is clearly a euphemism.

[102] 1801–18 Chardri's description of the girls' initial eagerness, their subsequent frenzy, their kissing and cuddling and their jealousy is more developed than it is in the Latin (**BJL**, 436). It places much more emphasis on the girls' own perspective, and the effect of Josaphaz's beauty on them.

[103] 1837–40 Here Chardri briefly summarises Josaphaz's prayer, rather than quoting him at length, as the Latin does (**BJL**, 438).

effort into making me exquisitely lovely and desirable. My heart and my body I now offer to you,[104] so that you can do with me whatever you want. You ought to consider carefully the gift that I'm making you here. God will be very grateful to you for having brought about the salvation of another soul. In exchange for giving me your love, you'll convey my soul to the Lord on high."

Josaphaz answered, "Whether it's to do with your beauty or your eloquence, you're just being foolish if, in your stupid pride, you think you'll get my virginity in this way. You'll never do it, since I wouldn't want the flower of my chastity to be withered as a result of your trickery, even for all the gold in Tiberias!"[105]

She replied, "Indeed, my lord, I believe it's always been written in your religion that any man who does not wish to be alone is entirely allowed to take a wife;[106] for woman was created to be man's [help-mate].[107] Put an end to your silly objections! All the patriarchs who ever were had lovers and wives. The prophets long ago were married, as you've heard; and the apostles of Jesus Christ, they too were married, or so the scriptures say. You can take advantage of this. But there's just one thing that you've got to do. Let's sleep together tonight, and take pleasure in each other, and tomorrow, as soon as it's light, I'll very willingly be baptised if that's what you want. Let's get on with this now! It's just a little sin that you have to commit, in order to bring yourself a much greater good."

When Josaphaz had heard this, his heart almost burst, so tempted was he by what she said, for she seemed to him so soft and sweet. When the devils saw that he was on the brink of being overcome, they put all their efforts into making him captive to love. Now you should have no doubt about it: he was undergoing a severe test! Very sensibly, he realised that he was being manipulated. He started praying to God, who had so often been able to help him. Crying bitterly, he piteously beseeched God to use his power to deliver him from this predicament that was causing him to lose faith in him. Now it was entirely for God to decide—either to help him in his need or to desert him completely.

So long did his tears and pleas for God's mercy go on that he fainted out of exhaustion. It sometimes happens that on account of sorrow and anxiety people find it easy to fall suddenly asleep, since anyone who is really sad at heart is ex-

---

[104] 1881 Chardri does not make it explicit, as the Latin does, that the girl is asking him to marry her ("Coniungere michi nuptiarum copula": BJL, 440).

[105] 1894 **Tiberias** *Tabarie*. Rutledge (294) suggests that "Tabarie is a Syrian village, the site of a medieval rabbinical school" and that "the saying probably came from an association of Tabarie with Jews and Jews with wealth." It seems to me much more likely that "Tabarie" here refers to the very much more significant city of Tiberias in Galilee (*Tabariyyah*, in Arabic), which, like Galatia (*Josaphaz*, v. 478) and Damascus (*Seven Sleepers*, v. 716), appears in the Bible.

[106] 1899–1900 The Latin text (BJL, 442) here cites Hbr. 13: 4; I Cor. 7: 9; Matt. 19: 6.

[107] 1901 **help-mate** Literally, Chardri says only that "the one [i.e. woman] was made for the other [i.e. man]" (*l'un fu pur l'autre fet*), but the allusion is clearly to Gen. 2: 18.

periencing something acutely tiring.[108] God took pity on Josaphaz for weeping so deeply. Our sweet saviour Jesus allowed him to fall into a very deep sleep and gave him a revelation in the form of a dream that certainly brought him some repose. (1869–1952)

It seemed to him that in his dream, which he regarded as no illusion, a crowd of monstrous beings was leading him, terrifyingly, through a vast tract of land. He had never seen a country that was more beautiful and alluring, for he could see meadows that were, to tell the truth, blooming with an abundance of flowers; and these gave off a powerful perfume. So vivid were the flowers that no one could ever think how to describe their colours; while surrounding the meadows were trees that were the most beautiful in the world. No one could ever find a tree to equal the ones there, so laden were they with fruit.[109] The branches were so dense with foliage that they looked like clouds; and all these leaves danced in the delicate breeze. No spice could ever compete with the fragrance of the trees, herbs and flowers that scented the air: I have never heard of such sweetness. Josaphaz saw some seats placed there made of pure gold and beautifully adorned with precious stones. No one could ever find any like them in India or in any other country,[110] nor could anyone completely appreciate the workmanship manifested there. The couches that had been placed in the meadows were resplendent with crystal. The cloth from which their covers were made was of pure beaten gold. The streams running this way and that were clear. The stones in the tumbling brooks were of such bright whiteness and the hard rocks so rounded and shiny that they looked like crystal. The sound of this bright and beautiful riverbed offered enormous pleasure to anyone who listened to it for a little while.[111]

Looking in front of him, Josaphaz noticed quite a large city: this was the direction in which they were leading him. This city was built in such a way that every wall was made of pure, refined gold and the towers placed high above them were set with precious stones:[112] no mortal man ever saw such a thing. Just as the stars in the sky illuminate the firmament, so in the same way these gems made the walls of burnished gold seem beautiful all over. Not all the beauty that there has ever been amounts to even half of the beauty that was so finely displayed there. In the city were some people celebrating joyfully. In comparison with the sweetness of their singing, no music that anybody ever heard in this life would be worth anything.[113] (1953–2022)

---

[108] 1943–44 Cf. *Seven Sleepers*, vv. 617–20; and Eccles. 5: 2. There is no precedent for this observation in the Latin text (**BJL**, 446).

[109] 1966–70 Cf. the "trees full of fruit" in the *Visio Pauli*, cap. 22, trans. Elliott, 629.

[110] 1982 Cf. Job 28: 16.

[111] 1995–98 Cf. *Little Debate*, vv. 57–62.

[112] 2002–2006 Cf. Rev. 21, 19–21; *Visio Pauli*, cap. 23, trans. Elliott, 630.

[113] 2022 **would be worth anything** *ne vaudreit pas un esperun*: literally, "was not worth even a spur."

¶ Josaphaz was delighted by everything he saw there, until a voice from on high told him: "This is the place where joy never ends for those who live within its walls: this is where virtuous souls find peace." (2023–28)

¶ At the sound of this voice those who were leading Josaphaz turned back, taking him with them. He begged them to take pity on him.

"Gentlemen," he said, "for the love of God, don't take me away from such sweetness! I'd be content to stay here in this country forever, even in just a corner of it."[114]

"My dear friend," they said, "You can't stay here now. If you can endure the sorrow and the suffering that's to come, if you're willing to persist in your virtue, then at last you'll come back here. Now's your chance to lay claim to all of this, whether to win it or to lose it all."

With that they led Josaphaz away, at pains to travel onwards, until they came to a long, wide valley that was stinking and full of filth. Never had he seen a place so dark. There was much sulphur and pitch burning there, and the souls were bathed in lead. Then they saw a furnace. Anyone in it would not have been very comfortable! There were many serpents and toads there, together with frogs and snakes. The furnace burned fiercely. It was arranged in such a way that the black flames carried the worms[115] upwards, and then threw them high up into the sky, down onto the souls that were lying there. They were constantly in pain. There is no man alive today whose learning is so great[116] that he could ever put into writing the sufferings that Josaphaz witnessed there.[117] May God who made heaven and earth keep us from that abode! The boy was absolutely terrified when he saw these horrors. Then came a clear voice: "Josaphaz, this torment is unceasing, night and day. This is where the sinners are placed." (2029–74)

¶ At this great marvel Josaphaz immediately awoke from his dream, in tears because of the suffering his terror created. He was so moved by his vision that he took no notice[118] of any of the girls around him, no matter how pleasing or beautiful they were. For this reason even the maiden who had flattered him so much that he was tempted meant no more to him than if he had never seen her before. So intently did he meditate on what he had seen that he was totally dazed. As a

---

[114] 2035 This sentiment is also expressed by Josaphaz in the Latin ("concedite michi in uno preclare ciuitatis huius angulo conuersari!": BJL, 448). It resembles the well-known words of Heloise, "In whatever corner of heaven God shall place me, I shall be satisfied" (trans. Betty Radice, *The Letters of Abelard and Heloise* [Harmondsworth: Penguin, 1974], 135–36).

[115] 2059 **worms** *verms*. Cf. Mark 9: 42–47; *Visio Pauli*, cap. 42, trans. Elliott, 637.

[116] 2063–64 These lines are very similar to *Seven Sleepers*, vv. 197–98.

[117] 2047–66 Cf. *Visio Pauli*, cap. 31–42, trans. Elliott, 633–38.

[118] 2081 **he took no notice** *Ne presout mie une cenele*: literally, "he valued them no more than a haw" (i.e a hawthorn-berry, a proverbially worthless object). For this comparison, see also *Little Debate*, v. 970.

result of his anxiety and fear he fell ill, for he did not want to think about anything else but what he had seen in his vision.

The king heard about this, and it hardly seemed like good news to him that his dear son whom he loved so much had so rapidly become ill. You can be sure that he wasted no time in going to his son in the tower.

"My dear son," he said, "if you love me, tell me the reason for your sorrow. Where is it that this malady comes from? In which part of your body is it affecting you most? Whenever I see anything upsetting you it's as if my own heart's about to break."

"Father," Josaphaz replied, "I'll tell you. I won't lie to you in any way."

The king fell silent and the boy told him the whole story that you have just heard. He told him all about his vision, without misrepresenting anything that he had seen. He told him all about the joy and the torment, which had caused him such terror, and eventually he concluded by saying, "Father, if you love me, set me free to serve God my creator, who governs all things as lord. If you're so in love with folly that your life means nothing to you and you have no wish to be saved, then I beseech you, for the love of God, don't prevent me from doing what's right, so that I can seek my own salvation. This is now my intention: I want to abandon the things of this world and follow Barlaam, my master, in serving God, the king of heaven. I wish to devote the rest of my life to being a hermit with him. If you're determined to keep me here, you'll see me perish out of sheer sorrow. If I die here in your house, you'll no longer deserve the name of father, for you'll never have any other child. Now you must choose immediately between forcing me to die in front of you, or allowing me to accomplish what I've undertaken." (2075–2138)

¶ The king understood what he was saying and the anguish it caused him made him sweat all over. All of his cunning had failed him and he felt pain in every part of his body. Now he was going to lose his beloved son and he did not know which way to turn. The king begged for a little more time, so that he could consult with his friends, and the boy allowed him this.

It was not long before the king came back to talk to him, having asked Theodas, whom he valued so much, to accompany him so as to support him in what he had to say. The two of them soon arrived and went straight before the boy. The king began the discussion with him, saying, "Tell me, my dear son, why are you abandoning our religion, so as to remove yourself far away from me? I am your father, I brought you into this world, and you ought to remain with me wherever I go. There's no reason anyone could ever discover for you to oppose my wishes and intentions in this way. You ought to try to please me to the best of your ability."

The boy replied: "For the sake of God each of us must abandon father, and mother too, and all our relatives, so that we can serve him night and day.[119] God should be held dearer than anything anyone could imagine."

To this the learned Theodas replied: "My good son, what you're saying is no lie. We should always put much effort into pleasing our gods, who are so mighty. For their sakes we ought ultimately to abandon whatever we possess. That's why I'm so amazed at you that you're not doing exactly this. They've looked after you throughout your life and they've not stopped doing so despite your folly. Your father is a powerful man, and to him they've given a son like you, so beautiful as you are: in their kindness they've shown favour to him and the land he rules[120] —and yet out of sheer perversity you're intent on repaying all their favours by behaving churlishly."[121] (2139–86)

¶ The boy replied, "My lord Theodas, by the God who sees everything on heaven and earth, I find it utterly amazing that, even though people think you're so wise, I see you speaking such great folly despite your great learning. But, you miserable, evil, wretched man, it's a shame that you're still alive, when you don't understand reason, when[122] you want us to renounce God, the holy Trinity, who has made and shaped all things, in favour of iron and wood that you can see, and in which you foolishly choose to believe! The respect that we ought to pay God you want us to pay to the earth. And you want us to believe in these devils of yours that are so special to you, even though God threw them out of heaven because they were so wicked, into the stinking depths of hell, where the winter cold is relentless. This is where they're getting ready a lodging for you, and where you'll find sorrow like no other. Because you've served them so long, you'll get from them just what you've earned. They'll never give you any blessing greater than what they themselves receive in that place. What awaits you there is unending pain and suffering, unless our Saviour has mercy on you. You should pay attention to what I'm telling you!" (2187–2218)

¶ When Josaphaz had said all this,[123] Theodas realised that he had been completely discomfited, and he began to contemplate the boy and everything he had said. He clearly recognised the truth, just as God wished him to do, and so he stood up very straight in front of the king and promptly said to him: "Sire, it's my understanding that this boy is filled with the power of the Holy Spirit, for

---

[119] 2165–70 Cf. Matt. 19: 29: "And every one that hath left house, or brethren, or sisters, or father, or mother, or wife, or children, or lands for my name's sake, shall receive an hundredfold, and shall possess life everlasting"; also Matt. 10: 37.

[120] 2184 **the land he rules** *sun honur.*

[121] 2186 **behaving churlishly** *la merde faire*: Cf. *Seven Sleepers*, v. 1868.

[122] 2195–96 **when. . . when** *quant. . . ke.* For this construction, cf. *Seven Sleepers*, vv. 1545–46. I have departed here from the punctuation adopted by Koch and Rutledge.

[123] Lines 2187–2218 in fact condense a much longer passage in the Latin (BJL, 454–70).

if God weren't with him, he wouldn't be able to say such things! Sire," he said, "now think about it!"

Theodas then turned directly to young Josaphaz. "In the name of God and his Creation, tell me, blessed creature, whether God will have mercy on me if I choose to turn towards him, and forsake all the foolishness I have done in my life?"

"Yes," the boy Josaphaz replied. "Jesus Christ, the almighty, endured terrible pain and suffering in order to bring salvation to the greatest sinners. Through Mary, he took on flesh in order to save the lives of sinners. And when he was among people here on earth he told them very clearly[124] that he had descended from heaven to earth in order to win back sinners."

The noble Josaphaz talked in this way for so long that he succeeded in converting Theodas, who was overcome with repentance by the boy's words. He did not delay any longer, but went straight to his house and without any hesitation threw all his books on the fire and reduced them to ashes. Then he set off into the desert; and he did not stop seeking out Christians until he found the old priest who had baptised his master Nakor. Weeping bitterly and speaking in between sobs, Theodas pitifully begged the priest to give him baptism. The old man took pity on him, when he saw him so distressed. He made him fast for a whole month and then had him baptised, beseeching almighty God to give him the perseverance to serve him right to the end of his life, and to bring[125] him consolation in full. (2219–74)

¶ When the king heard about this business, he did not know what he could do. Disasters were befalling him from every side and causing him much torment. In the end, he started reconsidering, and he summoned all his barons.

When he had assembled them, he addressed them with these words,[126] "Now listen, barons, do you know why I've summoned you? All of you together are my men, and you are obliged to protect my property,[127] as it seems to me. And in order to protect every part of my property, you ought to exert yourselves to the uttermost. You've all clearly understood how, as a result of what I believe to be heresy, I've lost my son, who's supposed to be the heir of all I have, and become your liege-lord. Now I've lost him with no hope of recovery. By the faith you all owe me, you must give me your best advice about this!"

The king was silent and said no more. All the high-ranking men were keen to give him good advice about the son he loved so much.

When each of them had stated his opinion, the noble Arachis stood and said to the king, "Now listen, sire, what you're asking for is a miracle! There's nothing

---

[124] 2248 **clearly** *ducement*: literally, "sweetly, gently." The reference is to Luke 15: 7.

[125] 2274 **bring** *feit*. Koch and Rutledge print *seit*.

[126] 2283–96 This speech is an expansion of the Latin, which says only that "he assiduously enquired from them what remained for him to do about his son" ("diligenter perquirebat ab eis quid de reliquo suo faceret filio": BJL, 474).

[127] 2286 **property** *honur*.

we can do to try and win back your son that we haven't already done to the best of our ability. Now we're supposed to carry on offering you counsel about this! And yet you should know that I cannot think of any advice apart from the advice I've already given, except for just one single suggestion that I'll tell you straightaway: you should order your land to be partitioned and your son to be given possession of half of it, so that he'll be lord and master of it. I tell you, he'll certainly do with it just as he wishes. As soon as he's risen so high and taken on this responsibility, have no doubt that he'll put enormous effort into the business of government. Because of it he'll forget about his wicked beliefs. He won't know how to protect himself without our help. For that reason he'll turn towards you again. If it's the case that out of sheer folly he wants to persist in his madness, at least you'll have the consolation that your son won't die of it."

When all the barons had heard this suggestion, which seemed quite prudent, they said to the king: "By Tervagant! This is apt advice! You should accept it then, and carry it out in full, because you're not going to be offered any better!"

The king told them: "To speak personally, I wouldn't reject your opinion in favour of anyone else's, or my own, since your advice is so good and so fitting." (2275–2338)

¶ The king immediately ordered that Josaphaz be given possession of half of his land, so as to do straightaway what the barons advised. The king held a great celebration on the day that Josaphaz became the new ruler. As soon as the celebration had finished, Josaphaz set off for his land with a large retinue and took possession of all of its strongholds. In all the cities of his country he had beautiful churches built. On all their gates and towers he had beautiful crosses erected.[128] He brought many of his people to believe in God, the son of Mary. He didn't want there to be any interruption to the baptisms that took place day after day; and eventually, by means of his wisdom, he made the whole of his people Christian. The Christians who had hidden came out of their hiding-places because of their confidence in this boy, who loved God so much. He willingly received them and, as it turned out, gave them a great deal of help: he had them bathed and properly clothed, giving them every comfort and luxury. He himself served them night and day, and treated them with great respect. Josaphaz went out to meet the priests and bishops who came there (but there were not many of them in those days) and received them with a procession. He honoured them as if each of them had been his father a hundred times over. Having built a beautiful church there in the name of our Lord Jesus Christ, he appointed as archbishop of the city a holy man, a bishop, who, to cut a long story short, had endured a great deal of pain and suffering for the love of God. Then, next to the church, he constructed a baptismal pool, which was very richly decorated. The wall enclosing it was exquisitely made out of fine marble and limestone. There anyone who converted to

---

[128] Cf. *Seven Sleepers*, vv. 1037–40. The Latin says only that crosses were put on all the towers, without mentioning gates (**BJL**, p 476).

our faith received baptism from the archbishop, together with all the holy oil. [129] A great miracle took place here, I swear: the water in which people's bodies were immersed healed every kind of infirmity. Whatever sickness anyone might have, if he were bathed in this water, then he would emerge from it completely healed, by means of the power of Jesus Christ. The number of people in Josaphaz's territory kept increasing, while those in his father's were ever fewer, because day after day they continued coming to Josaphaz to be baptised, for the love of God, our lord on high. He gave them baptism, and was very happy to do so. From every land, people came to him with a sincere desire for baptism. (2339–2402)

¶ When his father heard about this and realised that his people were turning towards God—when he saw that they were going in great numbers to receive Christianity from his son, and that sensible people were rejecting his own lunacy in order to give themselves to the new Law—then it was clear to him from this that the truth had been proved. He became deeply repentant for having opposed our faith for so long. This was something that God, in his pity, wanted to happen: it was for this reason that the king was inspired in this way, for God loved the child so much that he did not want the father to be lost. The king set all his heart on faith in Jesus Christ, realising that everything his son had preached to him was the truth. He ordered letters to be sent under seal and he had Josaphaz summoned. In what was written he promised to do whatever the boy commanded. [130] When Josaphaz heard about this, he was never so delighted: it immediately transformed his mood completely. Very early the following day, he set off in the direction of the king's court, leading a splendid retinue. High-ranking man that he was, he was well able to do so. (2403–32)

¶ When Josaphaz arrived, the king gave him a warm welcome: he was joyful and happy to see him. The king gave Josaphaz a comprehensive account of his feelings and his thoughts, and told him that he wanted to put an end to his great madness and folly, in order put his faith in God, the son of Mary, as long as Josaphaz would consent to his father doing so.

The boy promptly gave his consent, giving thanks to the Almighty, and this is what he said to the king, his father: "It makes me very happy to see this, that you want to turn towards God. This will redound to your own honour. In the presence of God almighty, you'll be given a crown of great splendour; and then, so I believe, you'll find yourself in a state of joy forever and ever."

Then the boy was able to give his father instruction, patiently teaching him his beliefs, and baptising him, just as it was his duty to do. The son received his father from the font, and, together with the king, he baptised the whole of the king's retinue, in the name of God. As soon as he was baptised, the king did penance very movingly. He immediately transferred to his son the government of his

---

[129] 2386 **the holy oil** *le cresme*: i.e. the chrism.

[130] 2421–24 In the Latin text, the content of the king's letter is reported in full (BJL, 484–86).

realm, making him the lord and owner of it all. He himself remained deep in sorrow for all the sins he had committed, crying out to receive mercy for his crimes. He quickly became so repentant that he did not dare to say God's name: because he had been such a sinner, he felt himself all the more humble before his Creator.

When Josaphaz noticed that his father could not bring himself to use God's name, he said, "Sire, you are certainly allowed to use the name of God almighty. All your sins were pardoned as soon as you were baptised. And you can be sure, I tell you, that God regards you as his friend. Now you should do your best to love him and feel confident about using his holy name, so that by means of it you can protect yourself against wicked evil-doers."

The king could scarcely bring himself to agree to this. After that he passed four whole years in a life of holiness and exceptional virtue, just as befitted a person of such high status. Then, filled with the Holy Spirit, Arvennir, that mighty king, died. The angels took his soul and brought it joyfully before God. (2433–90)

¶ When Josaphaz heard the news, you can be sure that scarcely any time passed before he was overcome by the profound grief that he felt for his father's death. He gave orders for the body to be taken away and buried in the company of other noble people. The shroud that he ordered the body to be put in was not made of brocade or samite, or fastened with either silver or gold, as if he were someone who had a great deal of money: rather, he ordered the saintly body be placed in the earth in a rough hair-shirt. He also arranged for masses to be sung for him and for the generous distribution of alms. And the son who loved his father so much lay eight days at his tomb, weeping and beseeching God to show mercy, so as to bring salvation to his father's soul. For eight days, night and day, he went without eating or drinking. His love for his father was so extraordinary that it is no wonder if he grieved. He was there for eight days in mourning, shedding many tears. Then he returned to his palace and commanded that all his father's castles and all his money should immediately be distributed to the poor, for the sake of God's love. When he had given away all of the wealth that the king had amassed, he ordered all the important men, who constituted the nobility, to be summoned to the palace, so that not one of them was missing. Josaphaz addressed them in this way: (2491–2524)

¶ "Lords, you've seen how very rich my father was. Now he's dead, as you're also well aware. His wealth did him no good at all: now he's no better off than if he'd been the poorest peasant. And you all know very well what my intention is, without me repeating it. It's been my purpose for a long time now to withdraw from the world, which leads only to shame, since it subjects to humiliation and torment those who are most intensely in love with it. You understand very well that all this world is worth no more than a dime.[131] Now the right time and place

---

[131] 2538 **dime** *maille* Cf. *Seven Sleepers*, v. 286; *Little Debate*, vv. 498, 1318, 1500.

have come for me to carry out my purpose and abdicate publicly, so that I can serve almighty God. Now, gentlemen, you should make arrangements for what is to your own advantage as much as mine. You should elect from among yourselves whoever seems to you to be the best person to be your king and your liege-lord, for never more will I be your king."

When all the barons had heard this, their sorrow was extraordinary. They wept and lamented, grieving furiously, and unanimously cried out, "We swear by the one who suffered on the Cross, that we'll never accept anyone else as our lord except you, whom we love so much. We'll be obedient to you for your father's sake and because of your own virtue. You are our lord and our emperor, and we'll serve you willingly. No one else will ever take your place." (2525–62)

¶ Josaphaz realised that nothing he could say would do him any good. As a ruse, he agreed that he would do whatever they wanted. They all departed and he remained behind, sorrowing bitterly that he could not achieve his purpose with their help and approval, until at last he came to a resolution. He summoned one of his men, a noble man whose name was Barachie.

For a long time the boy reasoned with him; he flattered him cleverly, then piteously implored him to accept sovereignty over all the barons and the whole domain, hoping that that he might be willing to become king. Barachie told him, "By our Father on high, there's no way I'd bring it about that the barons lost their liege-lord, whom they love so much! You are their liege-lord: you know that very well. Not for anything would I do that!" Then he ended the conversation, leaving Josaphaz disconsolate.

After a while, Josaphaz came to another decision. In secret, he set about writing a letter that he wished the people to see. In the letter he firstly greeted[132] all of his subjects, urging them to love God with a good heart and not to leave off serving him at any cost, wherever they might be. This was what he wrote in the first paragraph.[133] He wrote another paragraph after that, to the effect that, if they loved him, for his love they would make Barachie their lord: not for anything should they fail to do that. Then he neatly set his seal on the letter and put it on top of his pillow so that everyone would be able to see it.[134] (2563–2606)

¶ As soon as the night was dark, he went out through a secret postern-gate and set off[135] in a random direction.[136] This was how he left the country. In the morning at daybreak, his retinue approached the tower, but they were reluctant

---

[132] 2593–94 **In the letter he firstly greeted** *En li escrit . . . Il salva.* Koch and Rutledge (following the manuscripts) print *Il li escrit . . . E salva.*

[133] 2598 **paragraph** *vers.*

[134] 2604–2606 The Latin texts says simply that Josaphaz "left behind the parchment in which the letter was written" ("cartam in qua epistola erat scripta derelinquens": BJL, 504).

[135] 2608 **set off** *s'enturna.* Koch and Rutledge print *s'en turna.*

[136] 2608 **in a random direction** *par aventure.* The literal sense of this, presumably, is that he went where his feet took him; but there is perhaps a hint of the sense

to enter because they thought he was asleep. When it had reached the third hour of the day,[137] they said, "Now our lord should be woken: it's certainly about time he was getting up!"

Neither the day before nor on the day before that had Josaphaz wanted to oversleep: he was very well capable of rising at dawn. In trepidation they entered his room—and found no living soul there, only the letter that he had written and placed on his bed. Almost driven mad by their grief, they argued about this among themselves, but then the letter was read and it was apparent to them that he had escaped in secret so that his men would not be able to stop him.[138]

They were utterly amazed by this, and they organised a search for him everywhere. There was no one of either high rank or low who did not immediately set off to look for the boy Josaphaz. Through the woods and the plains they went searching for him: there was no hill or valley in the whole land where they did not seek him. They sought him unceasingly for so long that eventually they found him on the slope of a valley above a wide, deep river, where he was on his knees offering his prayers to God. (2607–44)

¶ His barons were utterly delighted at finding him, and they went to great effort to persuade him to let them bring him back to his palace.

When Josaphaz saw this, he was dismayed,[139] and he loudly told his barons, "By God and all his names, gentlemen, you're disturbing my heart very much! In this way you're doing me great harm, for I don't dare spend the rest of my life doing anything but serving God, our Creator. You can be sure that I'll never ever remain in your company! You can even kill me, if you want to, but you'll never take me back alive! Not for any reason could you possibly keep me with you any more!"

When the barons heard him speaking like this, their sorrow became overwhelming: there was not one of them, either young or old, who did not lament bitterly. There is no one on earth who, if they had seen such lamentation, would not be struck with compassion. [. . .][140] Having uttered their prayer, they said "Amen" on every side. Even at that not one of them could stop weeping, wailing or lamenting: they showed such sorrow that no living man has seen any greater.

"adventurously." The Latin says only that "he left the palace in secret from everyone" ("clam omnibus de palacio egreditur": **BJL**, 504).

[137] 2615 **the third hour of the day** *terce del jur*. Terce was three-twelfths of the way through daylight hours, i.e. about 7 am to 8 am in summer or after 9 am in the winter. It was one of the times in the day fixed for prayer in the Divine Office, the extended liturgical programme followed in religious houses (and, increasingly, as the Middle Ages progressed, by devout lay-people too).

[138] 2611–30 There is no precedent for any of this in the Latin (**BJL**, 504).

[139] 2650 **dismayed** *esmeu*. This is Koch's conjecture (followed by Rutledge): the manuscripts read *esmai* C *ennui* J.

[140] 2670 At least one line seems to be missing.

Without saying anything else, Josaphaz commended them all to God in heaven and set off to leave the country, in such a manner that no one knew where to look for him. He took nothing with him except the robes and the clothing that Barlaam had given him. That was an ill-fitting outfit! (2645–84)

¶ The very night that the noble Josaphaz left the country, he found accommodation with a poor man, whom he talked into swapping his clothes with him, there and then giving away his fine robe in exchange for the poor man's wretched one. After that he set off into the desert, where he lived off herbs and roots. He spent two whole years out there before he found Barlaam, meanwhile suffering all sorts of temptations both of the flesh and of the Devil. Not even St. Anthony, the good hermit, suffered more deeply as a consequence of his great virtue than Josaphaz did then. You have never heard of such suffering. So long was he in the desert that at last he prayed to Jesus Christ, the King of Heaven, who is both kind and powerful, that he might be allowed to speak to his master. It was high time for him to do so, and for Jesus to grant him grace! Just as he was meditating in this way, he saw an old man passing by and he piteously enquired of him where the good Barlaam was living; and in a very kindly fashion the old man told him. Josaphaz thanked him profusely, then wasted no time in going to the place the old man had pointed out. This was a wide, deep cave, located far from civilization in another district.

Josaphaz knocked at the door and Barlaam quickly got to his feet, for the Holy Spirit told him that this was his disciple who had arrived there. He opened his door straightaway and beheld Josaphaz looking impoverished in both his clothing and his demeanour: there was not a single day in his life that he had been so happy. He jumped up and embraced Josaphaz, and Josaphaz embraced him in return. They kissed each other very affectionately and wept tenderly for joy. In his happiness, Josaphaz told Barlaam all that had happened to him, and everything he had done after Barlaam had gone away. He told him all about it from beginning to end. Barlaam gave thanks for it to Jesus Christ. For two years the boy remained with his master, who instructed him thoroughly in the doctrine and the love of Jesus, our sweet Lord, and gave him an understanding of all the blessings of God that he was able to teach, so that as long as they were together, Josaphaz lived a life of great holiness. (2685–742)

¶ They lived together all this time until Barlaam received certain knowledge from a message delivered by an angel that it was time for him to leave this life. He prayed that God in his majesty would show him so much pity as to postpone his moment of dying, so that he might attend to Josaphaz's welfare. Then he returned straight to Josaphaz, took him gently in his arms and kissed him very tenderly. Crying piteously, he blessed himself in a clear voice while making the sign of the holy Cross, then went straight to lie down right in the middle of the floor[141] where happy and joyful, and with a cheerful expression, he immediately gave up his soul to the angels, who quickly conveyed it into Jesus's presence and gave it comfort.

When Josaphaz saw this, he felt sadder than he had ever done before. Completely beside himself, he fell across the body in a faint. When he returned to consciousness, such was his sorrow that it was as if he had lost his reason. He tore his hair and his clothes. He harangued death, as if it might bring him some comfort. But why should I make a long story[142] of the grief that overcame him? There is nobody on earth[143] who would not have felt pity for him. Josaphaz took the saintly corpse and carefully wrapped it in the coat that Barlaam had given him as he left the country. He put the holy body in the earth as decorously as he knew how, and then covered it, as it was right for him to do. Night and day he lay at the grave, weeping and crying for God to show mercy and take pity on him. (2744–86)

¶ So long did the boy Josaphaz grieve that he fell asleep there and then, on the tomb where he lay, so that as he slept it seemed to him as if that very same company of grotesque people, of whom he dreamed in the dream that you have already heard about, were right then leading him through a very attractive landscape. There would be no point in trying to find any land more prosperous, more attractive or more pleasant anywhere in this world (you can be quite sure of that). He entered a city, where a company of beautiful people came to meet him, bringing with them two beautiful crowns made out of fine gold, bright and new.[144] And you can be sure that, just as the story says,[145] he had never seen any more beautiful. He asked them whose they were, and the people who were carrying them replied that Jesus was giving one of the crowns to him on account of his virtuousness; and they said that Jesus was sending him the other so that his father might be crowned with it: it was on his account that this crown was being given, because it was through him that his father had been saved. Both of the crowns would be made more splendid if he carried on living so virtuously. (2787–2814)

¶ Josaphaz found it amazing that his father had a crown—and so splendid a crown at that—seeing that, while he himself had been constantly in pain and hardship, night and day, for the love of God the Creator, the king had not suffered in any way at all, except to the extent that he had repented, and yet he was

---

[141] 2758 **floor** *eire*. Rutledge (303) assumes that *eire* here means "life's course" and offers an elaborate justification for this reading (via Dante's *Inferno*). However, *eire* here equals *AND aire*[1], not *eire*[1].

[142] 2773 This line is a duplicate of *Seven Sleepers*, v. 154, and *Josaphaz*, v. 819.

[143] 2775 **on earth** *enclos de mer*: literally, "enclosed by the sea."

[144] 2799–804 Cf. the "diadems" in *Visio Pauli*, cap. 29, trans. Elliott, 631–32.

[145] 2803 **just as the story says** *si cum il* dit: literally, "just as it [or: he] says." The Latin text actually says that the crowns were "such as no human eyes had ever seen" ("quales humani oculi nunquam uiderunt": BJL, 542).

just as highly placed in glory. He turned this over a great deal in his mind[146] until Barlaam appeared to him and asked him what it meant that he should be so disturbed by his father's happiness. He said that Josaphaz should be pleased and delighted that, by his agency, his father had been saved. If, as a result of Josaphaz's own virtuous prayers, the king was now being treated in such a way that he was crowned just as honourably, then never on this account should Josaphaz himself feel any sorrow. "Master," said Josaphaz, "Forgive me. I now believe that I'm greatly at fault."

"Master," said Josaphaz, "For the love of God, tell me where you dwell in this city."

"My dear son," replied Barlaam, "Right in the middle of the city (may God guide me!), in the greatest happiness."

"Master," said Josaphaz, "I entreat you, lead me to your house! Do this much for me now, master: show me the nature of your existence!"

Barlaam told him the whole truth: "My dear son, on this occasion you cannot come to my abode. If, with the help of God and the holy Cross, you bring all your good work to completion, you can be sure that in the end you'll receive the reward of coming to my house and dwelling there in joy forever."

With that, Josaphaz woke up. This dream and this journey weighed very heavily on his spirit. He strove even harder than he was accustomed to, leading a life that was even harsher afterwards than it had been before. No man ever underwent so much suffering. (2815–60)

¶ I think it was thirty-five years that he lived in this way in the desert, from the time that he first renounced his realm and all the barons of whom he was so fond. He was twenty-five years old when he forsook his barons, and he spent the remaining part of his life in the service of God, in the way that I have described. For thirty-five years, he served God well, then rendered up to him his soul. Full of virtue and goodness, he was crowned before God on high. An angel spoke to the man who had directed Josaphaz to the house of Barlaam (for Barlaam had been his good master too);[147] and he commanded him in the name of God to go without delay and do the utmost honour to the saintly corpse. This man went off in great haste and ministered to the corpse as he was supposed to do. He prepared it properly and buried it just where the blessed Barlaam was interred. Then he set off straightaway to tell Barachie, the king, that his good friend Josaphaz had departed out of this world. (2861–86)

¶ The king was sorrowful in his spirit. He had all of his barons summoned and they all went straight to the cave, where the old man led them. The king had this "treasure" dug up, which he valued more than silver or gold. He found the bodies uncorrupted, as if they had just gone to sleep. They gave off a very sweet

---

[146] 2824 **mind** *memoire*: literally, "memory."
[147] 2874 See above, vv. 2708–12.

odour[148] to all the people who were nearby. The king had the bodies taken up with the greatest reverence and enclosed in gold and silver. Then he had this "treasure" that he valued so much ceremoniously conveyed into the city where he resided, and into the church that Josaphaz had ordered to be constructed when he first came there and revived Christianity. Barachie had his body richly interred in the presence of many of the nobles and many of the common people. On the great occasion of this translation, God brought about many miracles by means of his most holy name for the love of Barlaam and Josaphaz, and he still does so right to this very day. (2887–2910)

¶ Gentlemen, now you can clearly understand that whoever wishes to use his time well, loving God to the best of his ability, will be lavishly remunerated for doing so, for by his most holy name, God has the reward for it all ready. Whoever wishes to serve God will receive blessings both on heaven and on earth, because as long as that person lives he will be well liked by people here on earth, and when he dies he will go directly to God. There, where joy lasts forever and has no end, he will be crowned in splendour. When we are capable of attaining such happiness, we would be foolish to be half-hearted and allow ourselves to be deterred by a little discomfort from devoting ourselves to God and his goodness—when with just a little effort we can be rewarded as fully in the end as was the boy Josaphaz, about whom you have been hearing. This is something we fail to do, because we love the foolishness of this life so deeply that, as it seems to me, we would much more willingly listen to tales about Roland and Oliver; much more willingly hear about the battles fought by Charlemagne's Twelve Companions, than hear about the Passion of Jesus Christ. We are so faint-hearted that we put God and his power completely out of our minds. All of us ought to beseech the omnipotent ruler of the air, the sea and the wind, that, in his divine pity, he grant us, by means of his grace, both the desire and the capacity to make it happen that each of us succeeds in pleasing our Lord, so as to win salvation in the end. "Amen, amen!" we should all say to this. This is the end of the excellent Life of Josaphaz, that sweet child. To everyone who has been listening to it, Chardri sends no end of good wishes, both night and day.[149] Amen. (2911–2954)

The End.

---

[148] 2895 This is the "odour of sanctity," a conventional topos in relation to saintly bodies in hagiography.

[149] 2954 **both night and day** *au vespre au matin*: i.e. "continually"; literally, "in the evening and in the morning."

THE LITTLE DEBATE

Here begins the Little Debate.

¶ Fair and noble gentlemen, I am going to entertain you with a pleasing tale about an old man and a young man, telling you how they debated with each other about youth and age, happiness and folly. Each of them recounted his set-backs, his satisfactions, and his worries. The contest between the old man and the young lad[1] was very enjoyable and, as written down here, it is entitled the 'Little Debate'. It offers much comfort to those who are depressed, to anyone disheartened by a headwind,[2] because it contains many truthful sayings replete with good sense and eloquence. Now pay attention and listen! You will hear no lies from me, for a great deal of wisdom can often be found in a young man.[3] (1–20)

¶ There was once a young man of a thoughtful disposition, and adept in subtle thought, who happened to be amusing himself to find pleasure and contentment, and trying to avoid the one thing in this world that, more than anything else, injures a man's health: sadness, which God abhors, for it entirely demeans our whole life. I exclude those who are sick at heart and in body because of the malice of the wicked, and those who are inflamed by a steadfast love. These people I am not criticising, since it is on somebody else's account that they experience whatever unhappiness they do. Rather, I am talking about the hypocritical and the greedy, the proud and the envious, charlatans and thieves, perjurers and fraudsters, and all those who set their minds on wickedly deceiving their neighbours — may God curse them if they do not repent of it! This young man I mentioned to you was very preoccupied: I do not know what about. But in order to distract himself from his unhappy thoughts he went all alone into an orchard.

---

[1] 10 **young lad** *jofne tus*. Koch explains *jofnetus* as a derivation from Latin **juventosus*, "young man"; Merrilees sees it as combination of the adjective *jofne*, "young", plus *tus*, from the Latin *tonsum*, "young man", although such a conjoined form is unattested elsewhere in Old French. Neither of these interpretations is entirely convincing, although the sense is the same in either case.

[2] 14 **headwind** *ventage*. Merrilees suggests that this is "a derivative of *ventus*, presumably meaning 'trifle'" (59); more plausibly, *AND* translates this as "gust of wind."

[3] 19–20 The apparent implication of this is that Chardri himself was relatively young at the time when the *Petit Plet* was composed, although of course it is possible that he was being ironic at his own expense.

He said to himself that sorrow for this fleeting world would certainly never dwell in his heart, nor would he ever make any complaint about it. If God chose not to help him relieve his anxiety, then he was not going to bother about anything except himself—may God help him! Up and down the orchard went this young man, until he decided to stop at a spring where the water was both clear and clean. The water, as it flowed over the pebbles, was pure and beautiful, and its sound so soft and delicate that it resembled a living thing. All around, the grass was luxuriant, sprinkled with little flowers; and there were tall trees extending their shade so far that, no matter how hot it might be, nobody would have felt any discomfort there, even in the hottest summers. Birds of all kinds perched by the river and they sang very sweetly on account of the foliage and the flowers.[4] The young man was delighted by all this, and by hearing the sweet song of the birds. Here he found more happiness than many a wealthy man has found in a rich fief. (21–76)

¶ THE YOUNG MAN: The young man sat down next to the stream to contemplate the natural spring: it brought him so much joy at heart that no king or queen ever had so much. Just then an old, old man arrived, going in the opposite direction. His thoughts were so mournful and sad that his misery clearly showed in his face. As he was about to pass by, he noticed the young man looking so happy; and so he stopped, leaned against his walking-stick and greeted him. In a loud voice the young man replied: "God save you, my good man! Now come and sit down here next to me, and tell me about whatever trouble it is that's making you so sad! It's very clear from your countenance that your heart is troubled and that there's much upsetting you." (77–96)

¶ THE OLD MAN: "That's certainly true," said the old man, "I'm very anxious—may God protect me! And I'm utterly amazed that you have none of the troubles I do, but are so contented instead. It's obvious that you're not at all prudent to immerse yourself in such happiness when it's not going to last long. If you knew what I know, then you'd adopt a different disposition." (97–106)

¶ THE YOUNG MAN: "My good man," said the young man, "this is a very strange accusation you're making against me: that I'm going about having fun in order to restore my spirits. If young people like to have a good time, then you shouldn't blame them too much for their attitude, as long it doesn't get extravagant. You did the same when you were young. It's typical of old people, when they are old, to become utterly hostile to everything they liked when they were

---

[4] 71–72 Cf. *The Owl and the Nightingale*, vv. 15–16, 19–20: "[The Nightingale] sat up one vaire boȝe, / Þar were abute blosme inoȝe, [. . .] Ho was þe gladur uor þe rise, / & song a uele cunne wise" ("[The Nightingale sat] upon a pleasant bough covered with lots of blossom [. . .] She was happy having the branches around her and she sang in all sorts of different modes").

young.[5] I don't know an old man or a young one who has no need for some sort of relaxation." (107–20)

¶ THE OLD MAN: "Young man," he said, "from a good teacher you can still learn how to be wise. What you have said to me is quite true: that once upon a time I was light-hearted. But the older I became, the more I regarded my childishness and cheerfulness as something foolish, and this was because I had turned my thoughts elsewhere.[6] Night and day I was so concerned about living virtuously, and about the end of my life, that the great joy I'd possessed for so long simply became a great annoyance to me." (121–32)

¶ THE YOUNG MAN: "Sir," said the young man, "These thoughts are all well and good. How to live well, how to die well, and how to go to God: these are worthwhile things to think about. But I don't see any point in overdoing misery, except in the case of those old people who, having spent their whole lives wickedly, have reached the time when death is imminent. People like that ought to be sorrowful for the rest of their days. Were I to take the world too seriously while yet young and energetic, then I'd risk overburdening myself with worry and sadness, so much so that I might fall into despondency.[7] I'll go grey soon enough; and, what's more, I might even hasten the end of my life by worrying too much.[8] That would be pseudo-wisdom,[9] if it meant wasting the best part of my life through sheer folly. You know very well what's written—what Cato teaches: 'Intersperse your responsibilities with pleasure and relaxation.'[10] For this reason you shouldn't be surprised if I'm happy and cheerful. There's still plenty of time for me to change my mind."[11] (133–60)

---

[5] 115–18 Merrilees cites *Distiches of Cato*, 1. 16: "When you, grown old, blame what folk do or say, / Think what you did in your own youthful day" ("Multorum cum facta senex et dicta reprendis, / fac tibi succurrant iuvenis quae feceris ipse"). He also observes the comparison with *Josaphaz*, vv. 577–83.

[6] 124–28 Cf. 1 Cor. 13: 11: "When I was a child, I spoke as a child, I understood as a child, I thought as a child. But, when I became a man, I put away the things of a child."

[7] 146 **despondency** *nunpoier.* Chardri is perhaps referring specifically to the deadly sin of *accidia* or "spiritual sloth": on which see Siegfried Wenzel, *The Sin of Sloth: Acedia in Medieval Thought and Literature* (Chapel Hill NC: University of North Carolina Press, 1967).

[8] 149 Cf. Ecclus. 30: 26: "Envy and anger shorten a man's days, and pensiveness will bring old age before the time"; *Distiches of Cato*, 2. 3: "Cease fearing death: 'tis folly day by day, / For fear of death to cast life's joys away" ("Linque metum leti; nam stultum est tempore in omni, / dum mortem metuas, amittere gaudia vitae").

[9] 150 **pseudo-wisdom** *un faus latin*: literally; "a false Latin."

[10] 154–56 *Distiches of Cato*, 3. 6: "Sandwich occasional joys amidst your care / That you with spirit any task may bear" ("Interpone tuis interdum gaudia curis, / ut possis animo quemvis sufferre laborem").

[11] 159–60 It is perhaps implicit that the Young Man ought to be aware of Eccles. 12: 1: "Remember thy Creator in the days of thy youth, before the time of affliction come" and *Distiches of Cato*, 4. 37: "Thyself to promise years of life forbear; / Death, like thy shadow,

¶ THE OLD MAN: "By God," said the old man, "you know how to give force to your words, my son, so as to express what lies in your heart. But there's nothing on earth created by God that can make you sure of your life, or of anything else. We are so wretchedly fragile—alas that we were ever born! For this reason I think it would be silly to be confident of a very long life, for there's no one on earth, whether an old man or a child, who knows the hour of his death;[12] and the suckling child can die just as easily as someone who's lived a hundred years.[13] That's why I'm worried and sad: because the world ebbs and flows, this way and that, up and down. It's enough to make anybody feel confused. If you want to be wise, think about this—and give up your silliness and your folly!" (161–80)

¶ THE YOUNG MAN: "Sir," said the young man, "Only someone who'd never heard any sermonising—someone ignorant of his ABCs as well as all the other letters—would have anything to learn from you. Your tongue is as lavish with precepts as a priest's on Sunday.[14] It's true what you say, that I have no guarantee for my young life; nevertheless, the High King who made us all won't give you one day's respite just because of your sorrow, you can be sure of that—not unless you've served him in other ways. And if I'm to die as a young man, I'd rather go to God smiling,[15] than end my days as an old greybeard, in misery.[16] I tell you,

---

dogs thee everywhere": ("Tempora longa tibi noli promittere vitae: quocumque incedis, sequitur Mors corporis umbra"). See also Caesarius of Arles, *Sermon* 20. 3: "Dicit aliquis: Iuvenis sum, superest mihi tempus aetatis: cum ad maturos annos pervenero, necesse est me de Domini mei timore cogitare" ("Someone might say, 'I'm a young man and the years of my life are still to come: when I reach mature years, then it will be necessary to think fearfully about my Lord"): ed. Marie-José Delage, *Césaire d'Arles: Sermons au Peuple*, Sources Chrétiennes 175, 243, 330 [Paris: Éditions du Cerf, 1971–1986], 1: 486).

[12] 171–72 Cf. St. Bernard of Clairvaux, *Ep.* 105, *PL* 182. 240: "Nil mortalibus vel morte certius vel incertius hora mortis" ("For mortals, nothing is more certain than death and nothing more uncertain than the hour when death comes").

[13] 173–74 Merrilees draws a comparison with the proverb "Aussi tost meurt veiaux com vaiche" ("The calf dies just as soon as the cow": Morawski, *Proverbes*, no. 201). See also Horace, *Odes*, 1. 28. 19: "mixta senum ac iuvenum densentur funera" ("without distinction the deaths of old and young follow close on each other's heels": ed. and trans. C.E. Bennett, *Horace: Odes and Epodes* [Cambridge: Harvard University Press, 1978], 76–77).

[14] 185–86 Cf. *The Owl and the Nightingale*, v. 322: "Þu chaterest so doþ on Irish prost" ("You chatter like an Irish priest").

[15] 193–94 Cf. the Nightingale's certainty (in *The Owl and the Nightingale*, v. 728) that heaven is defined by its "merriness" ("hu murie is þe blisse of houene"), which is answered by the Owl at vv. 854–59: "Wenest þu hi bringe so li3tliche / To Godes riche al singinge? / Nai, nai, hi shulle wel auinde / Þat hi mid longe wope mote / Of hore sunnen bidde bote / Ar hi mote euer kume þare" ("Do you think you can bring them so easily to the kingdom of God, just by singing? No indeed, they'll clearly learn that they have to beg remission for their sins with much weeping, before they can ever enter there").

[16] 195–96 Cf. Proverbs 17: 22: "A joyful mind maketh age flourishing: a sorrowful spirit drieth up the bones."

the longer a man lives, the more sorrows he expects, and the fewer joys, since it's in the nature of aging that the more it drives you forward, the more it sets you back; the more you get older, the more you suffer because of it. Age brings you troubles, and scarcely any profit. Because of their maladies and fatigue, old people have to be looked after by somebody else, just as a nurse looks after a child—ministering to it in every way, putting it to bed and getting it up, looking after it as it eats and as it cries. In just the same way old people have to be looked after later in their lives. Because by then they're not in possession of their senses, they talk drivel without knowing it. And so it would be silly to cling to such a life," said the young man. "Dying would be worth more to me than being alive, if ever I turned into such a wretch—if suffering so oppressed me as to turn my time here into a burden.[17] I'd be showing little appreciation for the joy that God permits me to have right now (as a reward for serving him just as he pleases). I'd be paying[18] him back with unhappiness, with pride and with melancholy—in which case may God grant me a very short life! It would be much better to die young and happy, than as an old man in a miserable state. I've scarcely seen even a single old man who didn't have more ills to put up with, the longer he lived. How can he expect to have any happiness at that time, when he had none of it previously, but instead wasted his whole life on misery and wickedness?[19] You must know there's a saying found in books which many people think instructive:[20] that whoever gives to God what is pleasing to God, but does so without goodwill or pleasure, will never earn any mercy or grace as a result of it: you know that's the truth! Now push off and burden some other young man with your chat, if that's what you like doing! You're far too ready to hand out blame, so from now on leave me alone, and let me amuse myself here without hindrance!" (181–246)

¶ THE OLD MAN: The old man then replied to him: 'May God, who made the world, save me! You know very well how to be clever and daring in defence of an attitude that will do you very little good. Is there no way for anyone to change

---

[17] 220 **my time here** *sujur*. My interpretation of this line differs from that of Merrilees, who translates "which would be with me for an unhappy period of time" (60). Cf. Ecclus. 30: 17: "Better is death than a bitter life: and everlasting rest, than continual sickness."

[18] 224 **I'd be paying** *freie*. Although neither Merrilees nor Koch give any indication of this, *freie* is clearly not from Old French *faire*, but from *fraier* (see *Old French–English Dictionary*, ed. Alan Hindley, Frederick W. Langley and Brian J. Levy [Cambridge: Cambridge University Press, 2000], s.v. 'fraiier¹'). This word is not recorded by *AND*, but it must surely have existed in the French of medieval England in order to produce the modern English *defray* (cf. *OED*, 'defray' v. 1, and 'fray' v. 3).

[19] 229–32 Cf. Ecclus. 25: 5: "The things that thou hast not gathered in thy youth, how shalt thou find them in thy old age?"

[20] 235–36 The allusion is perhaps to Ecclus. 35: 10–11: 'Give glory to God with a good heart: and diminish not the firstfruits of thy hands, in every gift shew a cheerful countenance, and sanctify thy tithes with joy.'

your feelings about what you've resolved, such that you might turn your attention to penitence rather than pleasure?" (247–54)

¶ THE YOUNG MAN: "No way!" he said, "You can be sure that sadness and sorrow have never had any purchase inside my heart. All they ever got there was short shrift! I know so well how to relax, and how to govern my feelings, that only happiness and good humour will ever get admission; I have no time for anything bad." (255–62)

¶ THE OLD MAN: The old man said, "Young man, you can be sure that if you go about boasting like this, a whole lot of terrible disasters might befall you, the like of which you've never experienced before. But now, if you don't mind, and if you've got the time, I'll sit down here next to you. As long as there's no risk of incurring anger or malice or rudeness, I'd like to ask you about your life, and about the frequent occurrence of events that disturb and distract the hearts of men—so as to find out, indeed, if we can by this means discover consolation for worry of any kind." (263–76)

¶ THE YOUNG MAN: "That's fine by me, my good sir," said the young man. "You can say what you wish and you won't see me being offended, nor—God willing!—will you be offended either. But do me this favour: whether what I tell you is sense or nonsense, put up with it equally, since that befits a wise man. If young people utter stupidities, they shouldn't have to put up with an inquisition about it, that's what I think. So go on then," said the young man, "say whatever you please, whether it's sense or nonsense!" (277–88)

¶ THE OLD MAN: "Certainly," he said, "very willingly! But in this world I see so many cruel and harsh events suddenly happening, that I don't know where to begin, and I can't describe it all. One thing I'll say to begin with. Here's the sum of it: I'm going to die. I can't avoid it, you know, and because of it I'm deeply troubled at heart." (289–98)

¶ THE YOUNG MAN: The young man said: "By St. Riquier,[21] I never heard of anyone else who began by putting the cart before the horse[22] in quite this way! Now I'll tell you something to counteract your anxiety: this 'death' that's so

---

[21] 299 The reference to St. Riquier conveniently supplies a rhyme, and the invocation of saints in this way might also be seen as a feature characteristic of epic style, as Koch suggests (207). However, it perhaps also tells us something about Chardri's geographical horizons, for St. Riquier was probably best known as the eponymous founder of a famous abbey in the county of Ponthieu, which became a property of the English Crown in 1279 (Maurice Powicke, *The Thirteenth Century: 1206–1307* [2nd edition: Oxford: Oxford University Press, 1962; reprinted 1991], p. 235; Michael Prestwich, *Edward I*, [2nd Edition: New Haven: Yale Univerity Press, 1997], pp. 316–17).

[22] 301 **putting the cart before the horse** *de la cue feist le chef*: literally, "confusing the tail with the head."

widely feared shouldn't be described as a punishment[23] or something that happens because of misfortune; rather, it's entirely in the normal course of nature. If it's your inclination to be at odds with nature, then I know very well that you're going to be correspondingly disappointed with your whole life, however good—you can be sure of that! But it doesn't achieve anything. You'll be able to say that death has done you an injury only if you have lived happily." (299–312)

[THE OLD MAN:] "That's certainly true!" said the old man, "I find it deeply disturbing that I have to die."

[THE YOUNG MAN:] "My good fellow, it was for this that you were born! No one can escape it," said the young man. "Whatever is given, is taken away.[24] So why are you making such a fuss about it?"

[THE OLD MAN:] "My son, I'm afraid of death: that's why I can't find peace."

[THE YOUNG MAN:] The young man replied: "It doesn't make sense to waste your time on immoderate grieving." And he added, "It's just silly to spend your whole life being afraid of the one thing that can't be avoided: i.e. dying sooner or later. Whoever's afraid of what he can't avoid is getting upset about nothing. Whoever is born, will subsequently die.[25] No one can get around that." (313–30)

¶ THE OLD MAN: The old man then replied to him: "You've presented this advice very convincingly and it gives me great joy that someone so young can be so wise. I take some comfort from it, but nevertheless I'd like to tell you more about my state of mind, in order to hear more of your words of wisdom. You're a great comfort to me, my son. Certainly, brother, my death is inevitable." (331–39)

THE YOUNG MAN: "Is this really sensible, good father?" the young man asked, "That is, that you continue to be so afraid of death that you're unable to accept consolation, but instead keep on repeating that you're going to die? How could you possibly avoid that ford where so many have already crossed over?[26] What's good should never be blamed, but what's bad always should be, and as much as is possible. A man with a bad disposition should always be reproached. Even if you were to die today or tomorrow, you wouldn't be the first, nor would you be the last. So why are you so sad and miserable? All of those who once lived have departed—kings, emperors, all of them have died; and all of those who

---

[23] 303–304 Cf. Palmer, 30–31: "[*Ratio:*] Ista hominis natura est: non pœna" ("This is the nature of man, and nat punysshement").

[24] 315 **Whatever is given is taken away** *Quanke s'en vent, pus s'en revet*: literally, "whatever comes, subsequently goes away": cf. Job 1: 21 ("the Lord gave, and the Lord hath taken away"). This line comes close in phrasing and sentiment to *Seven Sleepers*, v. 817.

[25] 329 Cf. *Seven Sleepers*, v. 819.

[26] 344–45 Cf. Horace, *Odes*, 1. 28. 16: "omnes una manet nox / et calcanda semel via leti" ("a common night awaiteth every man, and Death's path must be trodden once for all" (ed. and trans. Bennett, 76–77).

come after us will bear the burden of death.[27] When you were born, Dame Nature measured out your days and immediately set a limit to your life that you can never exceed. As long as you're here on earth, your life is just a pilgrimage; and, when you die, you'll be returning to your natural state at last."[28] (340–64)

[THE OLD MAN:] "That's just what I'm telling you!" said the old man. "That's what's making me sad."

[THE YOUNG MAN:] "Good sir," said the young man, "there isn't a man on earth who could reproach you with the fact that you'll die either sooner or later—or who won't himself have his own share of dying some time. When the Son of God endured death, it's wrong of you to be afraid of it." (365–72)

¶ THE OLD MAN: "That's very true, my son," the Old Man replied. "According to what you say, it's foolish to be at all fearful when we all bear the same burden. But I often wonder which kind of death might be the most peaceful? If I received many blows from an axe or cuts from a sword, or if I were chopped into small pieces, I'd find that a terrible ordeal."[29] (373–82)

¶ THE YOUNG MAN: The young man replied: "May God, who made the world, save me! I'll tell you my opinion concerning what you've just asked me. No matter how many times you were injured by weapons in this world, whether in peace or in war, you couldn't lose your life more often than once.[30] So I can say for sure that, if a man[31] knew he were going to die of his wounds, it would be foolish of him to be scared that the wounds might be many—for a single mortal wound would do for him just as completely as if he'd had five hundred. Sir, don't think any more about this, since you know that your death is inevitable. Place your trust in the one who can command both heaven and earth, and do in everything whatever he wishes, that he'll guide you in his mercy; and in this way you'll

---

[27] 350–56 Cf. *Seven Sleepers*, vv. 821–26; also Seneca, *De remediis fortuitorum*, ed. Palmer, 32–33: "[*Ratio:*] Nec primus: vltimus omnes me antecesserunt, omnesque consequentur" ("Nother fyrste nor last, all haue gone before me, and al shal folowe me").

[28] 361–64 Cf. Palmer, 30–31: "[*Ratio:*] Peregrinatio est vita, multa cum deambulaveris: deinde redeundum est" ("This lyfe is but a pylgrymage: after thou hast walked a great waye, after thou must returne agayne").

[29] 379–82 Cf. Palmer, 34–35: "[*Sensus:*] Sed saepe ferieris et multi in te gladii concurrent" ("But thou shalt be ofte stryken, and many swordes shall rushe into the").

[30] 387–89 Cf. Palmer, 34–35: "[*Ratio:*] Quid refert an multa sint vulnera non potest amplius, quam vnum esse mortiferum" ("What skylleth it? wheder there be many woundes, there can nomore but one be a death wounde").

[31] 391 **a man** *home* JV; *Jesu* C. Koch departs from the reading of his base-text to print *hoem*. Merrilees acknowledges that JV's "seems to be a better reading", but retains C's *Jesu* on the grounds that it "makes acceptable sense." This does not seem to me the case at all: it is very hard to make theological sense, at least, of a scenario in which Jesus *might* know that he will die of his wounds.

be doing what's wise. Leave off this worrying, for by this activity you're not going to conquer even so much as a single foot of land."[32] (383–404)

¶ THE OLD MAN: "That's certainly true, my brother," the old man replied. "Blessings on that mother who brought forth a son so capable of speaking such well-judged words! But there is still one thing," he said, "that worries me, that makes me deeply unhappy at heart. Now I'll tell you what's on my mind: if I go on a pilgrimage and I'm overtaken by illness, it could well be that it takes away my life—and then I'd be in foreign country,[33] completely destitute, so it seems to me, and I'd have to depart this life without any friends or any kind of help; and my sorrow would be very great, both while alive and in the course of dying. Whether I died there or lived, I'd still be a miserable wretch, finding myself so far from my own country, completely lost without my friends; and none of the foreigners who saw me would take any trouble on my behalf." (405–26)

¶ THE YOUNG MAN: "Good sir," said the young man, "it's no marvel to me that you keep complaining about the frequent occurrence of the misfortunes that fill your heart with bitterness. But it's a very much greater misfortune for you to be so very sad and sorrowful that you have no interest in being consoled; for if you do travel to a foreign country, whether on pilgrimage or on some other business, your good sense ought to be able to keep your youthful heart in check. I call it a 'youthful' heart, because it merely acquiesces in all[34] your whims. A wise man who's reached old age ought to be able to control a foolish heart. Wherever it is that you eventually die, that will be your homeland, and rightfully so. Your body is of the earth and to the earth it will return.[35] So I tell you (and you can be sure it's no joke!)

---

[32] 404 **a single foot of land** There is perhaps a deliberate echo here of Walter of Chatillon's well known epitaph for Alexander the Great, in *Alexandreis*, 10. 448–50: "cui non suffecerat orbis, / Sufficit exciso defossa marmore terra / Quinque pedum fabricata domus" ("Five feet of carved stone / sufficed for his abode in tunnelled earth, for whom the world held insufficient space": ed. Marvin L. Colker, *Galteri de Castellione Alexandreis*, [Padua: Antenor, 1978], 273; trans. David Townsend, *The Alexandreis: A Twelfth-Century Epic* [Peterborough, Ont.: Broadview Press, 2007], 211). Cf. also Juvenal, *Satires*, 10. 168: "Vnus Pellaeo iuveni non sufficit orbis" ("One world is not enough for the young man from Pella", i.e. Alexander), ed. and trans. Jeffrey Henderson, in *Juvenal and Persius* [Cambridge, MA: Harvard University Press, 2004], 380–81; Horace, *Odes*, 1. 27. 1–4: "Te maris et terrae numeroque carentis harenae / mensorem cohibent, Archyta, / pulveris exigui prope litus parva Matinum munera" ("Thou, Archytas, measurer of the sea and land and countless sands, art confined in a small mound of paltry earth near the Matinian shore": ed. and trans. Bennett, 76–77).

[33] 415 Cf. Palmer, 34–35: "[*Sensus:*] Peregre morieris" ("Thou shalt dye in a straunge countre").

[34] 440 **in all** *itute*. The form *itute* is obscure, as Merrilees admits. Koch's conjecture that it should be taken to represent *en tute* appears to be the only possible solution to the problem.

[35] 445 Cf. Gen. 3: 19: "for dust thou art, and into dust thou shalt return."

that you'll die and afterwards rot away,[36] no matter how delicately you were nourished. Then it would be a difficult matter for me to distinguish your flesh from the earth, for I wouldn't know which is which, nor could any man alive. Then, whether it's in India or the land of the Moors,[37] it would be as natural to your body as the land of your birth; you'll never be able to leave it. Thus you should realise that it's silliness to spend too much of your life wondering where exactly you'd want to be deprived of it, or where you'd wish to be buried. You'd sleep just as peacefully in a foreign land as you would in your own — that's what I say."[38] (427–62)

¶ THE OLD MAN: "That's true," said the old man. "May God protect you! But tell me how, even if I don't die, I can lead my life without any sorrow or sadness? If by chance I suffer illness or some other distress in a foreign country where I've gone in order to better myself, I wouldn't know who to complain to. It would make me sad and sorrowful if I didn't see any of the friends whose company I was accustomed to have.[39] Whatever the situation might be, the foreigners wouldn't care much about my distress. That would be a serious concern for me, which might well cause me a great deal of grief." The old man stopped and didn't say any more: he held his peace in order to listen carefully. The young man noticed and understood that the old man was now keeping a careful watch on him, in order to be able to trip him up a little bit (whether in word or deed), so as to deny him his happiness, and in this way obstruct his plans. (463–86)

¶ THE YOUNG MAN: "Now I certainly see, sir," said the young man, "that every day there are many setbacks that might occur to put you into deep misery. If you were a woman or a child, then you'd be so much less to blame for allowing your heart to be so flighty as to worry about such harm. Now I'll tell you what I think: no matter what country you're in, it'll be your own, no doubt of that, even if you're not worth a dime.[40] You'll never be able to wander so far on this earth that he who made both the heavens and the oceans won't be able to see you all the time. You'll never be able to get to such a place. He is the one who made the earth and the sea, the sky and the wind, all together; and he made it all for you to make use of, if only you knew how to accept it.[41] Wherever you go, you'll be turned completely upside-down (you can be sure it's the truth) if you don't do

---

[36] 447–48 Cf. *Seven Sleepers*, vv. 403–404, 1439.

[37] 453 Cf. *Josaphaz*, v. 1982.

[38] 461–62 Cf. Palmer, 34–35: "[*Ratio*:] Non est grauior foris: quam domi somnus" ("It is a slepe nomore greuous without the dores than at home").

[39] 472–74 An illustration of this is provided by Malchus's plight in the *Seven Sleepers*, vv. 1241–54.

[40] 498 **dime** *maille* Cf. *Seven Sleepers*, v. 286; *Josaphaz*, v. 2538; *Little Debate*, vv. 1318, 1500.

[41] 499–506 Cf. *Seven Sleepers*, ll. 1–24, 385–400; *Josaphaz*, vv. 25–28.

what he wishes. Not even in the house of your father,[42] your mother or any other relative, will you have perfect happiness or any help, if you don't serve the Son of Mary, for indeed everyone in this world is your foe.[43] If you're generous, kind, and gentle, all countries are your own country: if you're deceitful and proud, even the place where you were born will be alien to you. Now I'm going to tell you something else that you really can believe. Whoever has exactly what pleases him will live contentedly in any land: in every country he finds nothing there but happiness and security. If you're afflicted with illness or injury, blame only your own disposition. Do good and you'll receive good:[44] if you wish to do ill, you'll taste the consequences. The things that people complain about most, you can be sure, lie within themselves, whether the harm or madness they suffer comes about through faintheartedness or through folly. A fool will always be a stranger: he'll never go about unchallenged. Anyone who's clever, wise and valiant will be liked by everyone wherever he goes. Therefore anyone who makes wisdom his master makes a good life for himself everywhere. And so you should leave off all your sorrowing, for I don't see any wisdom in it." (487–542)

¶ THE OLD MAN: As a result of the young man's words, the old man then got to his feet, saying, "Son, may the Holy Spirit protect you both in word and deed! — for even in this short time you've been able to enlighten me with your deep thinking. Because you've spoken to me so well, I won't hide anything from you now. Now you're going to hear about a particularly harsh misfortune that could occur. This is the particular sorrow I mean: the possibility that I might die young,[45] bringing all the joys of this life to a premature end. And that," he said, "would be very tragic, and a great disaster that would take away my happiness." (543–58)

¶ THE YOUNG MAN: The young man stood up at these words and immediately responded to the old man: "Sir, you shouldn't be deceitful about this, for as a grey-haired old man you shouldn't joke about being born to die young without being able to enjoy this transient life any longer.[46] But you should understand,

---

[42] 511 **in the house of your father** This is perhaps a tacit reference to St. Alexis, the saint who famously spent seventeen years living unrecognised as a beggar dependent on his own father's charity: see Cartlidge, *Medieval Marriage*, 77–99.

[43] 511–16 Cf. Luke 14: 26: "If any man come to me, and hate not his father, and mother, and wife, and children, and brethren, and sisters, yea and his own life also, he cannot be my disciple."

[44] 529 Cf. Ephesians 6: 8: "Knowing that whatsoever good thing any man shall do, the same shall he receive from the Lord, whether he be bond, or free."

[45] 554 Cf. Palmer, 36–37: "[*Sensus:*] Iuuenis morieris" ("Thou shalt dye in thy youth").

[46] 562–66 Merrilees translates this is "for it would be no joke for you to be born thus and to die young (so) that you could not enjoy this ephemeral life more than an old man (would)" (62), which seems to miss the point that the Old Man's fears about dying young can hardly be taken very seriously, when he is already (by definition) no longer young.

whether you like it or not, that not everyone in this world is at ease, nor is everyone miserable; he who was once on top is now at the bottom. The wheel of Fortune turns in such a way that all of us are governed by the same law, which is to the good of some, to the injury of others; some heading up and others heading down. Even someone who is young and valiant, athletic and energetic, won't always be that way, my friend. The game you're playing[47] will turn against you. You'll become ill and depressed, perhaps for just a little while or perhaps repeatedly. And so I say that it would be much better for you, should you feel the want of anything, to die young than to wait for the misfortunes that exceed all bounds. Then you would prefer death: that would be your best consolation. Certainly, it would be better to avoid the ford, than to tumble into it like a fool.[48] It would be much better to die young than to live long in a state of misery. Something else I'll tell you, with no word of a lie: even if you had everything you wanted and never in your whole life experienced any trouble, you'd be very lucky to die in this state: for you can never evade old age, no matter how sweet your life may be." (559–98)

[THE OLD MAN:] "So you consider old age to be an evil?"

[THE YOUNG MAN:] The young man replied, "Not at all, sir. But its sorrows are so numerous that no one on earth could recite them all to you. You'll find in the Bible that anyone who lives so long that he grows frail with old age will suffer distress from all kinds of afflictions.[49] And so I can safely say that it's much better to die when happy and not too far from the cradle, than to wait around for the great misery that so many now endure. When a youngster who has loved God dies, he's quite old enough, you can be sure of that. A child's early death is just as much a matter of destiny as the death of a grey-haired man." (599–614)

¶ THE OLD MAN: "Son," he said, "what you say is true. You're making me optimistic about another issue I want to raise with you. My death is ultimately inevitable, whether it comes sooner or later, whether it comes upon me when I'm happy or I'm sad. But it might very easily happen that my body is left unburied, left lying out in the open for everybody to see.[50] Then many people would be offended by its stench and nakedness; and it would be terribly humiliating for me if my body weren't quickly placed in the ground. The birds would pluck me apart

---

[47] 578 **the game you're playing** *giu parti* (cf. *Little Debate*, v. 644); *gvi parti* C; *ieu parti* J; *gui parti* Merrilees; *ju parti* Koch. For the literal meaning of this phrase, see note to *Josaphaz*, v. 1812. The implication is that life is like a game of chess.

[48] 587–88 This sentiment has the air of a proverb, but I know no parallel for it. However, there is perhaps an implicit allusion to the muddy ford ("Mal Pas") that plays such a prominent role in Béroul's *Tristan* (ed. Norris J. Lacy, in *Early French Tristan Poems*, 1: 3–216, at 162–76).

[49] 603–606 Cf. Ps. 89: 10: "The days of our years in them are threescore and ten years. But if in the strong they be fourscore years: and what is more of them is labour and sorrow."

[50] 621–23 Cf. Palmer, 36–37: "[*Sensus:*] Insepultus eris" ("Thou shalte lye vnburyed").

and the fierce wolves would devour me, and all the dogs as well;[51] and for me that would be a terrible ordeal."[52] (615–32)

¶ THE YOUNG MAN: "Sir," the young man said, "I'll tell you: I won't hide my opinion from you. If you're never buried at all, you shouldn't think that it's any great crime. A hundred thousand saints have been granted joy, who were never buried on this earth: some were drowned, some were burned in the fire, some were eaten by bears or leopards.[53] I'll tell you another thing, and make sure that you listen carefully! When the soul has departed from the body, then it's certainly checkmate[54] for every individual, that's what I think. And even when the corpse remains intact, it doesn't feel anything at all,[55] no more than would a clod taken from the earth. So, I tell you, the body doesn't know whether it's in the earth or lying in the open air. Then there'll be nothing at all that can cause you any displeasure, as long as your soul is at ease." (633–52)

---

[51] 629–31 Cf. Palmer, 38–39: "[*Ratio*:] Quid interest [. . .] an fera me comedat?" ("What forseth it wheder [. . .] a wyld best deuour me?").

[52] 632 Cf. St. Augustine, *On the Care of the Dead*, cap. 7 PL. 40, col. 598: "si cognoscant homines aliquid post mortem suam suis corporibus defuturum, quod in sua cujusque gente vel patria poscit solemnitas sepulturae, contristantur ut homines; et quod ad eos post mortem non pertinet, ante mortem suis corporibus timent" ("if men know that after their deaths their bodies will lack what is demanded by the ritual observances of burial in each man's nation or country, it makes them sad as men; and before death they fear for their bodies what after death has no effect on them").

[53] 637–40 Cf. *Seven Sleepers*, vv. 168–83, and *Josaphaz*, vv. 1287–96, 1621–26. See also St. Augustine, *On the Care of the Dead*, cap. 1, PL 40, col. 594: "Dicitur quidem in Psalmo, *Posuerunt mortalia servorum tuorum escam volatilibus coeli, carnes sanctorum tuorum bestiis terrae: effuderunt sanguinem eorum tanquam aquam in circuitu Jerusalem, et non erat qui sepelerit* [Ps. 78, 2–3]; sed magis ad exaggerandum crudelitatem eorum qui ista fecerunt, non ad eorum infelicitatem qui ista perpessi sunt" ("Indeed, it is said in a Psalm, 'They have given the dead bodies of thy servants to be meat for the fowls of the air: the flesh of thy saints for the beasts of the earth. They have poured out their blood as water, round about Jerusalem and there was none to bury them.' But this is to emphasise the cruelty of those who did these things, rather than the misfortune of those who suffered them"). Augustine also praises the martyrs for not succumbing to the temptation of allowing "faith in the resurrection to stand in dread of the destruction of the body" ("ne fides resurrectionis consumptionem corporum formidaret": cap 8, col. 599). Underlying Augustine's thinking is Luke 21: 16–18: "And you shall be betrayed by your parents and brethren, and kinsmen and friends; and some of you they will put to death. And you shall be hated by all men for my name's sake. But a hair of your head shall not perish."

[54] 644 **checkmate** *giu parti* C, Merrilees; *ieu parti* J; *ju parti* Koch. See note to *Josaphaz*, v. 1812.

[55] 647 St. Augustine, *On the Care of the Dead*, cap. 10, PL 40, col. 599: "quando in carne omni vita carente, nec aliquid sentire posset qui inde migravit, nec aliquid inde perdere qui creavit" ("when a body is wholly devoid of life, he feels nothing who has departed from the body, and he loses nothing who created it").

¶ THE OLD MAN: The old man replied: "It would be very humiliating if no one cared for me even enough to bother to put my body in the earth." (653–56)

¶ THE YOUNG MAN: "Sir," he said, "I'll tell you something clearly, man to man. I've heard it said in many places (and, sir, you really ought to know this) that the burial of bodies was never instituted just for the sake of the dead, but for the sake of the living: you can be sure of this. Because when the corpse decays, it is harmful to the living, with its stench and its putrefaction; and the horror of looking at it makes the living sad at heart.[56] What with the anxiety it creates and the smell, it causes people such profound unhappiness that they might never be cheerful again, and some of them might not live so long as they would have done before. So, good father, you ought to understand that other people have much more reason to be concerned about the burial of your body after your death than you do. Since God has arranged things in this way, it's my view that you shouldn't care very much about it." (657–78)

¶ THE OLD MAN: "Son," the old man said, "that may well be the case: I admit that you're the expert. Even though it's often said, proverbially, that wisdom is found in old men,[57] I'd say it's true that your youth shows much more wisdom than my old age. The blood is warm and the heart light: good sense might very well like to lodge there. I'd regard as an ignoramus any old man who thought he was cleverer than a youngster like you. No matter how much he'd heard and seen, he would still look like a fool. Now, my son, I have something else to say. You should take care not to be troubled by the frequent occurrence of things that cause sorrow in the hearts of those who are wretched right now. The dead have enough sorrow, but the living much more. About the dead we've spoken quite enough and you've bested me in all of it. Now, if you don't mind, let's speak about those who are alive and in great distress, suffering from the pains and profound sorrows continually afflicting people." (679–702)

¶ THE YOUNG MAN: The young man replied: "Feel completely free to say whatever you want, good father." (703–704)

¶ THE OLD MAN: "Thank you," said the old man, "I'll tell you, without any bad temper or discourtesy (God save me from that!), about the accidents that happen every day of our lives to cause us so much sadness. Now I'll begin my argument (for it doesn't matter which of us goes first), and it's like this: even in

---

[56] 660–68 Cf. Palmer, 40–41: "[*Ratio:*] non defunctorum causa: sed uiuorum inuenta est sepultura, vt corpora et visu, et odore feda amouerentur" ("buryall was founde nat because of dead men, but for them that lyue, for th'entent that deed bodies, horrible in syght and smell, shulde be remoued"); St. Augustine, *On the Care of the Dead*, cap. 1, PL. 40, col. 594: "ista omnia, id est, curatio funeris, conditio sepulturae, pompa exsequiarum, magis sunt vivorum solatia, quam subsidia mortuorum" ("all these things—that is, the arrangement of the funeral, the disposition of the burial, the funeral procession—they are more to comfort the living, than to aid the dead").

[57] 681–82 E.g. Job 12: 12: "In the ancient is wisdom, and in length of days prudence."

your healthy body there's always a residue of serious disease that could reduce you to feebleness for the rest of your life without any hope of recovery. Then misery rather than pleasure will constantly be with you. Son," he said, "this is the sum of it: this is how many a noble fellow has to suffer. Now tell me something to address this evil, for it's very widespread." (705–22)

¶ THE YOUNG MAN: The young man said, "Very willingly: now listen for a while. It's no shame if illness overcomes your body: rather it's the will of God that you should be scourged in this way. I'll tell you another thing (and I'm not going to lie to you). You should accept for sure that it's not only when travelling by land or sea, or when in battle, that one's courage and fortitude are tested. I can't refrain from telling you this: they're also put to the test by illness.[58] In the feebleness that you suffer, your heart is being tested: if anyone suffers a great deal and yet is not dismayed by it, then that shows a heart that is valiant through and through. Indeed, good father, you should realise that, if sickness reduces you to weakness, then either you or the sickness must be the winner: you can't co-exist forever. If you don't completely vanquish it, then the sickness will vanquish you[59] — and then the battle will be a tough one. Make sure that your heart doesn't fail. If you despair of anything and your heart fails, then you can be sure that you'll be defeated all the more quickly, whether in battle or by sickness. And so I say that a truly courageous heart is never daunted, not at any price. The blows of a sword in battle are to be feared just as much as the throes of a fever, even one that sets your lips trembling, for you can lose your life just as easily in battle as in sickness." (723–60)

¶ [THE OLD MAN:] "That's true, brother," he said. "It seems to me that by accepting such a point of view I'll be much better able to endure sickness of this kind. But now I'll tell you something else I want to reveal about myself: about something that happens quite often to deprive me of my peace of mind. It's that people don't always place their confidence in me, but rather are deeply suspicious of me, believing that I'm much more wicked and much more conceited than is in fact the case.[60] Because of this there's no limit to the way in which they slander and abuse me. It causes me heartfelt suffering when they accuse me of all kinds of foolishness in ways that I've never deserved." (761–78)

---

[58] 731–38 Cf. Palmer, 40–41: "[*Ratio:*] Venit tempus, quo experimentum mei caperem non in mari tantum, aut in prelio vir fortis apparet, exhibitur etiam lectulo virtus" ("The tyme is come wherein I shulde haue the profe of my selfe. Nat onely in the see, nor at batayle vpon lande a manly man doth apere: but also valiant vertue is shewed in thy sycke bedde").

[59] 745–46 Cf. Palmer, 41–43: "[*Ratio:*] Cum morbo mihi res est, aut vincitur, aut vincet" ("I am at warre with sycknes, eyther it shal be ouercome, or els shall ouercome me").

[60] 768–73 Cf. Palmer, 42–43: "[*Sensus:*] Male de te opinantur homines" ("Men haue an euyll opinon vpon the").

¶ THE YOUNG MAN: The young man replied: "What you say is true." And he
added: "In my opinion, sir, a fool can bring a great deal of shame on a good man
on account of some trivial thing, and severely damage his reputation if the good
man refuses to give him a good word. Now I'll tell you what I think about it. The
wicked put a lot of effort into slandering people indiscriminately, good people
as well as bad. If you didn't worry so much about your good name, their gossip
wouldn't be so important.[61] For this reason you shouldn't be too eager to take
their silliness too much to heart. It's not customary with wise men to be harshly
critical, but if there were a fault that they happened to know about it, then they
ought to correct it gently. If St. Paul or St. Augustine or St. Gregory[62] had something harsh to say about you, then you'd have reason to be concerned, and your
conscience really ought to be disturbed. But it wouldn't be their intention to go
around maligning people, nor would any other wise man do so, for that's not the
lesson they learn from their books. When it doesn't originate with wise people,
this criticism that I'm talking about, then I'd say that it's bound to be caused by
silliness, you can be sure of that. Slander is characteristic of fools, since their
wickedness compels them to say nothing good about other people, since no one
is ever virtuous enough for them. How could someone devoid of any virtue bring
himself to speak well of you? A person who's obviously worthy of hanging deserves no hearing in court; and a thief shouldn't sit in judgment if he were party
to the crime. Thus I pray that no one takes seriously the things that wicked people say and do. You should understand that this is characteristic of them: slandering people, whatever the circumstances, and giving unfavourable testimony at all
times, whether it's justified or not. Because of this they think they're doing someone a good turn when they say nasty things about their neighbours. They think
that they'll be more highly regarded if they maliciously defame other people;
but they can scarcely do any real harm, no matter how many foolish things they
say. Prudent people find it easy to recognise their malice, for they're incapable of
saying anything positive: that's not their habit. Now leave them be, good father,
whatever they've done in the past, since you'll never make a good hawk out of
a kite or a buzzard.[63] Spend your time with prudent people and you won't lose

---

[61] 789–90 Merrilees cites *Distiches of Cato*, 3, 2: "Mind not ill tongues, if you live
straight of soul: / A neighbour's words are not in our control" ("Cum recte vivas, ne cures
verba malorum: / arbitrii non et nostri quid quisque loquatur").

[62] 797–99 For this particular collocation of authorities, see also *Josaphaz*, v. 7. They
are a Christianised version of the moral authorities listed in *De remediis*. See Palmer,
42–43: "[*Ratio:*] Sed mali, mouerer si de me Marius, si Cato, si Laelius sapiens, si aliter
Cato, si duo Scipiones ista loquerentur. . ." ("But suche that be euyll them selfe: I wolde
be angred yf Marius, yf Cato, if wyse Laelius, yf the seconde Cato, yf the [two] Scipions
spake thys . . .").

[63] 837–38 This is proverbial. Merrilees cites Morawski, *Proverbes*, nos. 96, 965,
1514; but see also Geoffrey of Monmouth, *Historia*, 146, and *The Owl and the Nightingale*,

by it, even if you don't gain. As long as you're in the company of a wise person, your mind will be in peace, but if you want to put your trust in fools, then you'll never have any peace on earth.[64] I advise you not to set your mind on preventing their foolishness, since even if they don't speak slander against you, they'll do so against other people, of that I'm sure. A tongue that's wicked and troublesome is never satisfied unless it's wagging maliciously." (779–850)

¶ THE OLD MAN: "My son," replied the old man then, "You're certainly saying the truth (so help me God!). There's no one alive or dead who's ever been able to put a stop to the wickedness of such people. So I sincerely declare that we should leave them to their own devices. But, my son, you should know that there's another thing I'm worried about: which is that, without deserving it, I've fallen deeply into poverty. From every side grievances, sorrows and misfortunes rush upon me. Privation, hunger, thirst, and cold: it's inevitable I'll be inflicted with at least one of them. And it constantly troubles me, you know, that my neighbours are all much richer. They've all got plenty of gold and silver, and everything they want. It's only me who's so deprived: I curse the hour that I was born!" (851–70)

¶ THE YOUNG MAN: The young man replied: "Thank you, sir. But I wouldn't want to hear it said that you ever cursed your life in some attack of folly. Up to now you've listened to me carefully and so far I've clearly warned you against being sad, no matter what happens, and that you should be sensible and moderate. Again I'll tell you my opinion right away, whatever it happens to be, as long as you don't find it annoying to hear my arguments."

[THE OLD MAN:] "Even if it were unpleasing to God," said the old man, "it would be very suitable[65] and pleasing for me." (871–83)

[THE YOUNG MAN:] As the old man fell silent, the young man replied: "Sir," he said, "I'll bet my life that I can say something to address your grief. This poverty that you complain about: you're at fault if you don't like it, since it was with you at the very beginning, when you entered this life. You didn't bring with you anything apart from your poverty. It was your only possession: you didn't even have the wherewithal to be able to cover your buttocks.[66] For this reason, poverty ought to be liked and loved and honoured. God gave poverty great honour

---

vv. 127–38.

[64] 839–44 Cf. *The Owl and the Nightingale*, vv. 293–308.

[65] 883 **it would be very suitable** *mult me set*. Here *set* is not from *saver*, as Merrilees suggests (84, s.v. 'saver'), but from *seer*.

[66] 887–94 Cf. Job 1: 21: "And said: Naked came I out of my mother's womb, and naked shall I return thither." Merrilees cites Cato's *Distiches of Cato*, 1. 21 ("A naked babe since nature fashioned thee, / With patience bear the load of poverty": "Infantem cum nudum te natura crearit, / paupertatis onus patienter ferre memento"); and Morawski, *Diz*, 64, CXCI.

and praise when he dwelt on the earth.[67] Now you're not being very respectful of God when you're so scornful of what was most dear to him on earth, when he came to convert the saints. Poverty is something you can rely on: no one who's got it will ever have to endure regret or loss. If you're cold or hungry or thirsty, you shouldn't worry too much on this account about tomorrow, since he who created you will feed you soon enough.[68] Now you're talking like someone blind or one-eyed. God will give me beef with the horns attached.[69] You've got it all wrong, and do you know how? If you don't know, I'll tell you. God didn't create a single creature for which he didn't also provide a means of sustenance. Otherwise anyone might say that God had made a creature only in order to kill it with hunger or thirst or by some other means: that wouldn't please God almighty. God certainly provided food for every creature when he created it. He didn't abandon it to destitution when he brought it into this life. This can be seen both among the beasts and among the birds that fly, and also among the fish that swim in the sea, for when the day brightly dawns, they don't know how to choose what they're going to feed on.[70] As I've just said, God, who made them all, provides for them all, so that every creature is by nature vigorous and well fed. But you, who are supposed to govern everything that lives on the earth or in the sea,[71] under God's authority and in order to serve him, you don't know how to support yourself. When everything else enjoys plenty, you possess scarcely anything that's good. Do you know why? I'll tell you why, and I can point it out to you in the scriptures: if you're too inquisitive about things, God will think that much less of

---

[67] 897–98 E.g. Luke 6: 20: "And he, lifting up his eyes on his disciples, said: Blessed are ye poor, for yours is the kingdom of God."

[68] 905–908 Ps. 9: 10: "And the Lord is become a refuge for the poor: a helper in due time in tribulation." Also Matt. 6:26.

[69] 910 **beef with the horns attached** *boef par la corne*. Merrilees cites as a parallel Morawski, *Proverbes*, no. 580: "Dieus done le buef, més ce n'est pas par la corne"; and he suggests that the meaning might be something like "God is giving me a gift that has dangers attached." This would hardly support the Young Man's general point in this passage, which is that God will provide. Perhaps in this context "beef with the horns attached" means something like "beef with all the trimmings"—or "the full monty."

[70] 923–26 Cf. Palmer, 48–49: "[*Ratio:*] Nihil deest auibus, pecora in diem viuunt. Feris ad alimenta sollicitudo sua sufficit" ("Foules of the ayre lacke nothynge, bestes lyue without fore cast or care but for the tyme, wylde beastes take no care but for theyr lyuynge and fode").

[71] 931–33 Cf. Genesis 2: 19–20: "And the Lord God having formed out of the ground all the beasts of the earth, and all the fowls of the air, brought them to Adam to see what he would call them: for whatsoever Adam called any living creature the same is its name. And Adam called all the beasts by their names, and all the fowls of the air, and all the cattle of the field."

you.[72] You think that your provision for the future is more important than God and all his power. In this you're all the more at fault for not putting your faith in God on high. Poverty is in itself a splendid thing, something pure and wholesome. If you find poverty uncomfortable, it finds you yourself very much more of a burden, since it's out of your heart that the wickedness comes, if there's any there. If you can't help complaining, as might very well happen, then it doesn't matter as long as your complaint doesn't at any cost reveal your inmost thoughts. As long as that's the case, I'd regard you as someone good and wise, since reason must always conquer grief and drive it back." (884–958)

¶ THE YOUNG MAN: "Good father, I'll tell you something else to make you less anxious about everything. If your neighbour is very rich, then he's either a prodigal or a miser.[73] If he's a miser and avaricious, then he won't get any good out of his property, since (to save his life) he can't bear to spend anything, but instead constantly amasses treasure for the benefit of someone else when he is

---

[72] 939–40 Ecclus. 3: 21–25: "For great is the power of God alone, and he is honoured by the humble. Seek not the things that are too high for thee, and search not into things above thy ability: but the things that God hath commanded thee, think on them always, and in many of his works be not curious. For it is not necessary for thee to see with thy eyes those things that are hid. In unnecessary matters be not over curious, and in many of his works thou shalt not be inquisitive. For many things are shewn to thee above the understanding of men."

[73] 962 Cf. Palmer, 48–50: "[*Ratio*:] Vtrum auarus, aut prodigus: si auarus nil habet, sin prodigus, nil habebit" ("Whether is he a nygarde or a wastfull spender: yf he be a nygarde he hathe nought, yf he be a spender he shall haue nought"). The opposition between avarice and prodigality seems to have been proverbial in medieval culture: see Hans Walther, *Initia Carminum ac Versuum Medii Aevi Posterioris Latinorum* (Göttingen: Vandenhoeck and Ruprecht, 1959), no. 14787; *Proverbia Sententiaeque Latinitatis Medii Aevi* (Göttingen: Vandenhoeck and Ruprecht, 1965), no. 22570. It is perhaps ultimately Horatian: see Horace, *Epistulae*, 2. 2, 192–94, ed. Fairclough, 438–42: "et tamen idem / scire volam, quantum simplex hilarisque nepoti / discrepet et quantum discordet parcus avaro" ("and yet I shall want to know how much the man who is artlessly good-natured differs from the prodigal, how much the frugal contrasts with the avaricious"). See further Neil Cartlidge, 'An Intruder at the Feast? Anxiety and Debate in the Letters of Peter of Blois,' in *Writers of the Reign of Henry II*, ed. Ruth Kennedy and Simon Meecham-Jones (New York: Palgrave Macmillan, 2006), 79–108, at 89–91. To the examples given there should be added Lawrence of Durham, *Dialogi*, III. 407–408, ed. James Raine, Surtees Society 70 (Durham: Andrews, 1880), 42.

dead![74] So I say that splendid wealth isn't worth any more than a haw.[75] If he's prodigal and has plenty, it won't last long, you can be sure of that. Instead your neighbour's wealth will soon go into a recession. A rich man, you know, is much more often troubled and disturbed than a poor man is, since (whatever the rights and wrongs of it) bailiffs, sheriffs, and extortioners[76] pinch him on every side, looking for any excuse to take away from him whatever they can. While the poor man goes about laughing,[77] the rich man has to be able to put up bonds, for the rich have to work much harder all the time in lawsuits and disputes. In this way the heart of the rich man grows bitter on account of his wealth: it deprives him of his appetite and he can't sleep because of his worries. Because of trying to protect his wealth he goes through a lot of bitterness and anxiety. As a result he becomes so sick that it could well be that he loses his life.[78] Therefore I declare that I'd much rather be poor and happy, than rich in such a state." (959–96)

¶ THE OLD MAN: The old man replied: "What you say is true, but now advise me on one other little thing. What if in the past I enjoyed all sorts of pleasures because of being rich, but having become so impoverished on account of some disaster, the memory of my prosperity and my subsequent misfortune continues to cause me grief?" (997–1004)

---

[74] 967–68 This idea is something of a commonplace in medieval culture (cf. Ps. 39: 6). One of the most popular poems in which it was disseminated is the Body-and-Soul poem known as the 'Visio Philiberti' (ed. Thomas Wright, *The Latin Poems Commonly Ascribe to Walter Map* [London: Camden Society, 1841], 95–106), vv. 69–71: "mortem tuam breviter plangit tuus hæres / quia sibi remanent turres, domus, [et res], / et thesauri copia, pro qua modo mœres" ("your heir won't grieve for you very long, because all your towers, houses and businesses are now his, as well as the profusion of treasure that now you're now so sorry to lose"). On this poem more generally, see Neil Cartlidge, "In the Silence of a Midwinter Night: A Re-evaluation of the *Visio Philiberti*," *Medium Aevum* 75 (2006): 24–45.

[75] 970 **haw** *cenele*. This comparison can also be found in *Josaphaz*, v. 2081.

[76] 979 **extortioners** *wandelarz*. The meaning of this word is obscure. There are only three other recorded examples of its use—once in English, once in French and once in Latin. See Merrilees, *Little Debate*, 66.

[77] Cf. Juvenal, *Satires*, 10.22: "cantabit vacuus coram latrone viator" ("a traveller who is empty-handed can sing in the mugger's face"), ed. and trans. Jeffrey Henderson, 368–69; Proverbs 13: 8: "The ransom of a man's life are his riches: but he that is poor beareth not reprehension."

[78] 987–94 Cf. *Distiches of Cato*, 4. 5: "Yourself, when you grow rich, treat well; for pelf / The invalid owns, but does not own himself" ("Cum fueris locuples, corpus curare memento: / aeger dives habet nummos, se non habet ipsum").

¶ THE YOUNG MAN: The young man replied: "It would certainly be very much better to say, good sir, that Fortune had released you from a burden that was far too heavy for you.[79] Do you know why?"

"Not at all, son!"

"I'll readily[80] tell you," he said. "Wealth might no longer be with you, but it did you a great favour by sparing you from dishonour and injury. In this respect it's been kinder to you[81] than to any other man, since in the end this is what it amounts to: either wealth deserts a man or he deserts it, since one of the two of them must come off worse. I won't hide it from you, good father," he said: "a man might triumph over his wealth to the extent that he seeks nothing out of all that he has amassed except a sufficiency: that is, a very moderate amount of food, drink and clothing, so that he can serve God. And perhaps he might use the surplus to make frequent charitable donations to deserving people,[82] rather than hiding away in his strong-room coffers full of gold and silver. Such a man deals with wealth in just the right way, since he barely pays any attention to it at all. But the alternative is much harder, when a man is protective of his wealth. Then it'll conquer him, and do you know how? I'll tell you straightaway. When someone puts all his effort into being rich, amassing gold and silver, and yet has no intention of doing any good with it, that's one of the sicknesses that's found in this world. After all, no one person can spend all his wealth just on clothes and shoes, nor can he eat and drink more often than anyone else in this life. So what will become of the surplus, when neither he nor anyone else is going to have it? In the end, his riches will be his nemesis, you can be sure of that. People he's never even met will do what they like with it, while he'll be damned for all eternity. That's why I say it's good what's happened to you, when you lost all this wealth. As long as your avarice disappeared along with all your worldly goods, then you can be sure that by means of this loss you've been blessed in your poverty. If you listen, I'll tell you something else that's worthwhile: even if you've lost all your wealth, whether by violence or bad luck, you've no reason to regret anything, since everything you possessed was previously lost by someone else, and by many others

---

[79] 1005–1008 Cf. *Distiches of Cato*, 4. 35: "When robbed of wealth, in anguish sorrow not: / Rather rejoice in what falls to thy lot" ("Ereptis opibus noli maerere dolendo, / sed gaude potius, tibi se contingat habere").

[80] 1010 **readily** *sanz mal*. Merrilees translates "without prejudice", but this seems to me neither very literal nor particularly clear. The point is that the Young Man will speak without making any "trouble" about it—i.e. "readily."

[81] 1014 **kinder to you** *vers vus changee / Plus*: literally, "she has changed more for you."

[82] 1025–26 Cf. *Distiches of Cato*, 3. 9: "If you've abundant wealth, as old age ends, / Be generous, not close fisted, with your friends" ("Cum tibi divitiae superant in fine senectae, / munificus facito vivas, non parcus, amicis").

too before you ever had any of it.[83] You were rejoicing in someone else's property, and now you're depressed about the loss of it. That seems to me mere silliness, something appropriate to a fool, but not to a wise man. It would be much better to lose everything and feel secure, than to spend the rest of your life living in fear of loss." (1005–68)

¶ THE OLD MAN: The old man then gave him this reply: "My son," he said, "You've spoken so well that, in regards to this issue, you've relieved much of my anxiety. Now I'm going to report an event that amounts to an infringement of my rights.[84] It's an injury that makes me very sad and deeply disturbs my spirit. Whatever the matter is, whether it's sense or folly, it's right that I should tell you about it. By misfortune, I have lost all of my children.[85] All of my children suddenly died, and that's why I'm grieving. That's a loss I'll never make good: it's much more severe than poverty, for all the wealth of this world means nothing to me in comparison with my children." (1069–86)

¶ THE YOUNG MAN: With that the old man fell silent. The young man turned his head towards him and said loudly: "Good grief! Of all your misfortunes, sir, this seems to me the worst. Why have you concealed it from me, and not mentioned it before?" (1087–94)

¶ THE OLD MAN: "You're right," said the old man. "My children were the most important part of the plans that I used to make. I put all my confidence in them, thinking that I'd have some consolation and someone to remember me when I died, for they would have been the heirs of everything that I had rightfully earned. Now, as it turns out, they're dead; and that's why I have so much sorrow." (1095–1104)

¶ THE YOUNG MAN: "That may well be the case," said the young man in reply. "But let's investigate this further. By God, it seems to me that you, sir, are like an apple-tree full of fruit that deliberately breaks itself for the sake of an apple that was dislodged by the wind.[86] That's what you're doing when you lament the death of a child so inconsolably. It's foolish and repugnant for any mortal to lament the death of another.[87] When he has to depart the same way himself, he grieves that someone is going with him. He's not the only one in this situation.

---

[83] 1060–63 Cf. Palmer, 52–53: "[*Ratio:*] Nempe quam vt tu haberes, alius perdiderat" ("Surely another lost it to th'entent thou sholdest haue it").

[84] 1074 **amounts to an infringement of my rights** *Ki me fet de dreit le tort.* This idiom also occurs in the *Little Debate*, v. 1220, and *Josaphaz*, v. 13.

[85] 1079–82 Cf. Palmer, 54–55: "[*Sensus:*] Amisi liberos" ("I haue lost my chyldren").

[86] 1107–10 Cf. Palmer, 54–55: "[*Ratio:*] Quid si foelicem voces arborem, a qua stante cadunt ipsa poma?" ("what yf thou call a tree frutefull, fro the which standynge [i.e. as it stands] frutes fal downe?").

[87] 1113–14 Cf. Palmer, 54–55: "[*Ratio:*] Stultus es si defles mortem mortalium" ("Thou arte a foole yf thou morne the deth of mortal creatures").

The great are in it too; and also the not-so-great.[88] Understand, there's no king on earth so great, nor any duke or count in his palace, who won't sometime complain of a loss like this (whatever good complaining will do him!). For the son of a king dies just as readily as the son of a beggar. And a king has greater need for his son than some rogue whose libido might well have provided him with seven or eight sons already,[89] because there's no doubt that it's a king's duty to look after his barons by leaving an heir. If he doesn't do that, believe me, the realm goes to rack and ruin, since everyone gets it into his head that he ought to wear the crown. If the king loses his heir in this way, then that's a reason for sorrow—not on his own account, but because of people behaving so badly. When the king dies, the weakest will be driven out.[90] But you, being a peasant as you are, even if you did have only one child and you couldn't stop it dying, you're making such a big fuss about it that it's as if you don't want to be consoled. Good sir, you've got it wrong, for you don't know whether your child would eventually turn out to be a wise man or a prodigal, who, when you weren't in sight, would do exactly what he pleased. If your heir lacked sense, it would be much better if he died young, since otherwise you'd be grieving for his foolishness all his life.[91] Now there's another thing I've got to say to you, sir, in order to preserve your peace of mind better: was it up to you to engender a child whenever you wished?"

THE OLD MAN: "Not at all," said the old man.

THE YOUNG MAN: "Who was it up to then?" asked the young man.

THE OLD MAN: "That was up to God almighty to decide whether to give me children." (1105–62)

¶ THE YOUNG MAN: "What you say is right, by God," he said. "Now I'll tell you what I conclude from this. If God once gave you children in order to give you pleasure, then you shouldn't feel too much sorrow if he now takes them away from you—unless you're wickedly trying to slander God and his purposes. He

---

[88] 1117–18 Cf. Palmer, 54–55: "[*Ratio:*] ducuntur ex plebaea domo funera, ducuntur et ex regia" ("[funerals] be brought forth of a pore rascall house and also forth of a kynges house").

[89] 1126–28 For the social and sexual assumptions being made here, see also *The Owl and the Nightingale*, vv. 509–12: "A sumere chorles awedeþ, / & uorcrempeþ & vorbredeþ— / Hit nis for luue noþeles, / Ac is þe chorles wode res" ("In summer the yokels are driven mad, contorting and deforming themselves [in their lust]. However, this is not out of love, but because of the yokel's mad fury").

[90] 1140 **driven out** *fors parti*: or perhaps, more specifically, "excluded [from the succession]."

[91] 1146–54 Cf. St. Jerome, *Adversus Jovinianum*, 1. 47, citing Theophrastus's "golden book", ed. Hanna and Lawler, *Jankyn's Book*, 154–55: "Aut que senectutis auxilia sunt, nutrire domi qui aut prior te forte moriatur aut pervisissimis moribus sit aut certe cum ad maturam etatem venerit, tarde ei videaris mori?" ("And what kind of support in old age is it to nurture in your house a son who either may perhaps die before you or be of the most depraved habits, or truly, when it he comes to his majority, think you are dying too slowly?").

doesn't have to ask you permission for taking them away, any more than he did for giving them to you. Don't grieve, for that wouldn't be wise: nothing that God does can be wrong." (1163–74)

¶ THE OLD MAN: "That may well be," said the old man. "May God bless you! But now would you discuss with me another event that's caused me much unhappiness? My sorrow never comes to an end: it's the very worst sorrow in the world and it causes me the utmost pain and confusion. It's only fitting that I tell you that I've lost my sweet beloved.[92] She was my loyal wife; and I have every right to grieve for her. She was the very sweetest lady there was and the most generous I ever knew. She was faithful and pure. Her beauty surpassed that of the briar-rose. She had a very large share in every virtue that you could name and she surpassed all other women, just as a sapphire surpasses pebbles.[93] Because of this I loved her as much as I possibly could: indeed, she was my greatest delight. Now she's dead, now she's gone from me, and because of this my happiness is completely shattered and I'm incapable of accepting joy by any means in my heart. I'd sooner die than remain here in such misery after she's gone: that's how I feel. You know, my son: without her I'm going to be desolate at heart. Now you're going to have to console me at length, for I have great need of it." (1175–1204)

¶ THE YOUNG MAN: "Certainly, that's true," said the young man. "In this regard you have a very great need for consolation and reassurance, since I well understand that this death pierces your heart much more deeply than all of those misfortunes that you have collected up to now. Now listen to me, good father," he said. "However much you grieve for your beloved, it's no marvel if fools trust women. Even if she were wise, beautiful, and courteous to begin with, she'd have been exceptionally good if she didn't go bad later on. There's no man alive on earth whom a woman can't deceive by clever pretences. She'd make you think what's weak is strong; she'd make you think what's wrong is right;[94] she'd make you think what's cold is hot; she'd make you think what's lowly is noble; she'd make you think what's white is black; and she'll make you think what's foolish is wise. Whatever you want, a woman will do the opposite, if she's of a bad disposition. When you're embracing your beloved, that's when you've got to watch out for treachery. There isn't a woman under the heavens, whether she's young or old, who won't bring you to ruin if she wishes to hurt you somehow. They know so many tricks[95] that they scarcely thank you even if you do them good. A woman

---

[92] 1182–83 Cf. Palmer, 60–61: "[*Sensus:*] Vxorem bonam amisi" ("I haue lost a good wyfe").

[93] 1192 **pebbles** *gravele*. The Old Man's comparison might be taken to be inspired by the pebbles (*gravele*, 60) in the river immediately next to where he is sitting.

[94] 1220 **she'd make you think what's right is wrong** *Ele vus fet de dreit le tort.* Cf. *Little Debate*, v. 1074, and *Josaphaz*, v. 133.

[95] 1233 **tricks** *wanelaces*. The derivation of this rare word is obscure. It may be an Anglicism, possibly related to the English word *windlass*.

won't give any sign at all of whether she wants to do you good or do you harm. You can trust her and be certain of her only when her wickedness is apparent. I don't say that they're all like that, any more than [I agree with] those who tell me that a wolf is like a dog. You can certainly believe me that not all women are so wickedly disposed. There are many whose dispositions are good—and may God soon increase the number of those who are unencumbered by any wickedness! I'd be very happy and delighted if I could know for sure how many of them possess the disposition that I see in some of the women in this world: women who are full of virtue and kindness, simplicity and good manners, and whose natures are loyal. That's something I can promise you in good faith. Don't be in any doubt about it: there are many more of this kind in England, than in France. Nevertheless, the moon shines everywhere,[96] and in France you can find the odd one. It's only right and proper that every land, whatever it's like, has the odd one. But England has as many of them as a meadow full of flowers. Of all the realms that exist, England is pre-eminent. And in what way, do you think? In every kind of enjoyment and elegant behaviour! If the women there are so well brought up, it shouldn't be any surprise if there are lots of knights there, together with all the other men who follow them, who are superlatively valiant, elegant and noble—except that heavy drinking often mars the decorousness of their lives.[97] But you've lost your lady, that's clearly a fact, and you've praised her for many things, saying she was loyal, beautiful, and good-natured. Now I understand clearly from what your words that you loved your wife with great affection. The English have a good saying about this: a dog, wife, or horse should be praised in proportion to how much affection you have for it. Of whatever kind it is, whether good or ill, there's nothing more admirable than love when it's valued and highly esteemed." (1205–84)

¶ THE OLD MAN: The old man said straightaway: "My son, you should understand that I am absolutely certain and confident (so sure am I of her loyalty)

---

[96] 1257 This was presumably a proverbial saying. The point is that some things remain the same, wherever you go.

[97] 1271–72 On English drinking, see Peter of Blois, *Epistola* 31, ed. Elizabeth Revell, *The Later Letters of Peter of Blois* (Oxford: British Academy/Oxford University Press, 1993), 159–64, discussed in Cartlidge, "An Intruder at the Feast?," 88–97; also the exchange of poems on water and wine by Peter of Blois and Robert of Beaufeu, ed. C. Wollin, *Petri Blesensis Carmina*, CCCM (Turnhout: Brepols, 1998), 274–85 (nos 1.6, 1.6a and 1.7); "The Dispute between the Englishman and the Frenchman," ed. Thomas Wright, in *Political Poems and Songs relating to English History composed during the Period from the Accession of EDW II to that of RIC II*, Rolls Series 14, 2 vols. (London: Longman, 1859–1861), 1: 91–93. See also Rickard, *Britain in Medieval French Literature 1100–1500* (Cambridge: Cambridge University Press, 1956), 167–70; Short, "'Tam Angli quam Franci'," 153–54.

that there never was, nor would there ever have been, any trace of folly in my sweet beloved." (1285–90)

¶ THE YOUNG MAN: The young man replied: "You can quite safely say that with confidence now, since death, as I know, has confirmed your verdict. Even if she were noble and courteous, death has cut short her career, so that she can't subsequently change her heart like February of the thirteen moods.[98] A woman looks like a briar-rose, but she behaves like a wind at sea: now it's in the west, now it's in the east. However much she chatters, she just as quickly goes quiet. There's nothing alive and mortal under the vault of heaven[99] that's so prone to change in every way, as is the heart of a woman, whenever she sees the need.[100] According to whether a woman feels good or bad, first it's up there, and then it's down there; now it's inside and now it's outside. And if it's like this with her heart, then so too with her body." (1291–1310)

¶ THE OLD MAN: "Certainly, son, that's very true, but you haven't under-stood my complaint. The beloved lady that I lost was faithful, and the delight of my life. As you said just now, not all women are the same. Some of them are undeniably virtuous; and the ones who are wicked aren't worth a dime.[101] The wicked ones are so busy that the virtuous ones aren't trusted. But I know for sure, whatever anyone might say, that my beloved surpassed all women in her virtues and her manners, and that she would always have continued on this course,[102] for she had a good upbringing in her youth and she was very faithful to it. What-ever a colt is taught in its youth it will remember for a long time, so they say.[103] But my beloved was endowed by God with such an abundance of every kind of grace, that even if she'd never had such an upbringing, she would have been more worthy, even in just her shift, than any other woman in the world, even if you searched the whole globe. I was as sure of her as I am of myself, and that's the truth. Now she's dead and I'm desolate: so deeply sorrowful that I can never get used to it." (1311–38)

---

[98] 1298 **like February of the thirteen moods** *Cum feverer tredze covenant.* This expression sounds proverbial, but no exact parallel has been found for it (see Merrilees, 69).

[99] 1303 **under the vault of heaven** *desuz la chape del cel*: literally, 'under the sky's cape': cf. *Josaphaz*, v. 202.

[100] 1304–1306 Cf. Proverbs 5: 6: "her steps are wandering, and unaccountable"; Palmer, 62–63: "[*Ratio*:] "Nihil tam mobile quam fœminarum voluntas, nihil tam vagum" ("nothynge is so soone moued as a woman's wyll, nothynge so vnstable").

[101] 1318 **dime** *maille.* Cf. *Seven Sleepers*, v. 286; *Josaphaz*, v. 2538; *Little Debate*, vv. 498, 1500.

[102] 1324 Cf. Palmer, 62–63: "[*Sensus*:] Sed hæc et bona fuit, et fuisset" ("But she was good and wolde haue ben").

[103] 1327–28 This is proverbial, as Merrilees demonstrates, giving several illustrations, including Morawski, *Proverbes*, no. 1765.

¶ THE YOUNG MAN: "Now this is an amazing thing," said the young man, "that you should go around grieving in this way for your beloved, who was so 'faithful'. If you'd paid more attention to me, you'd have left off with this grief. Did she ever have as much love for you, as you had for her?"

¶ THE OLD MAN: "Yes, and much more, you can be sure of that!" (1339–46)

¶ THE YOUNG MAN: "Indeed, that's an amazing thing, for I tell you, good father, in my whole life I never heard of any woman who was of such a disposition as to love when she was loved.[104] You should hear about the typical outcome: as soon as a woman notices that someone loves her, immediately she thinks that she's being treated disrespectfully and straightaway gets all stand-offish, and malicious and angry too. If you say something she doesn't like, she looks on you with an unfavourable eye.[105] But if there's someone who has no liking for her at all, she readily jokes with him, embraces him and kisses him fondly and tries to attract him by putting on an act. Yet if there's anyone she's sure of, you know, she scarcely gives a damn about him. Any woman before you marry her will, without fail, put on a show of being nice to you.[106] When she says to you, 'Be sure, my sweetheart, how deeply I love you!', then her heart is saying 'This is a lie: the dice will fall very differently! He's a fool who puts any faith in the act that I put on, for it doesn't reflect my heart in any way. Trusting my appearance is like trying to hold onto an eel by the end of its tail.'[107] Good father, you should know it's the truth: there's no man ever born who saw anything so flighty as a woman and

---

[104] 1347–51 This is presumably an allusion to the literary topos of unrequited love, as it is found in both medieval love-lyric and romance, but there are parallels for it in antifeminist literature too. See, for example, Andreas Capellanus, *On Love*, ed. and trans. P.G. Walsh (London: Duckworth, 1982), 3. 65, 306–7: "Amorem namque mutuum, quem in femina queris, invenire non poteris. Non enim aliqua unquam dilexit femina virum nec amanti mutuo se novit amoris vinculo colligare" ("You could never find the reciprocated love you look for in a woman. No woman ever loved her husband, nor can she ever bind herself to lover with a reciprocal bond of love").

[105] 1358 **an unfavourable eye** *l'autre oil*: literarily, "the other eye."

[106] 1365–66 Cf. St. Jerome, *Adversus Jovinianum*, 1. 47, citing Theophrastus's "golden book", ed. Hanna and Lawler, *Jankyn's Book*, 150–51: "Nulla est uxoris electio, sed qualiscumque obvenerit habenda. Si iracunda, si fatua, si deformis, si superba, si fetida, quodcumque vitii est, post nuptias discimus. Equus, asinus, bos, canis, et vilissima mancipia, vestes quoque et lebetes, sedile ligneum, calix, et urceolus fictilis probantur prius et sic emuntur. Sola uxor non ostenditur, ne ante displiceat quam ducatur" ("There is no picking out a wife, but we have to take whatever comes along. If she has a temper, if she is foolish, malformed, proud, smelly, whatever vice it is, we learn of it only after the wedding. A horse, a donkey, a bull, a dog, and the most worthless slaves, even clothes and kettles, a wooden stool, a goblet, and an earthen pitcher are all tested first and then bought or not. Only a wife is not shown, lest she should displease before she is wed").

[107] 1374 This is also proverbial: see e.g. Morawski, *Proverbes*, no. 2159.

her moods.[108] How can you be so sure of your beloved as to swear that for the
rest of her life she would never have changed, no matter how things panned out?
But even though I'm just a youngster, I'll tell you a something amazing. Good
father, I've often heard in the past, you know, that women are changeable. I've
seen chaste and faithful wives become whores in no time at all. I've seen those
who were unequalled for sweetness turn nasty in the end. I've seen those who
were good-natured, kind and demure reduce their lovers to a sorry state. Most
of the divorces[109] that ever occurred were caused by women's malice. If there is
anything that causes them displeasure, they gather together in groups[110] to discuss their complaints. One says that her husband is a dreadful scoundrel, and not
because of her. Another says that hers is an old goat.[111] Another's husband is said
to be a malicious villain; while another says she has good cause for complaint,
since he doesn't do with her what he is obliged to do.[112] Thus each woman strains

---

[108] 1378 **and her moods** *e sun curage* Koch and Merrilees emend to *en sun curage* ("in
her moods").

[109] 1393 **divorces** *devorz.*

[110] 1396 **they gather together in groups** *enz en chapitres*: literally, the women discuss
their complaints "in chapters", a term more usually used to describe the general meetings
of the religious orders or cathedral clergy. Chardri is perhaps thinking specifically of
such texts as "Gilote et Jehane," ed. and trans. Carter Revard, in "The Wife of Bath's
Grandmother: Or, how Gilote showed her friend Johane that the wages of sin is worldly
pleasure, and how they both then preached this gospel throughout England and Ireland,"
Chaucer Review 39 (2004) 117–136. See also the examples given in Cartlidge, *Medieval
Marriage*, 171.

[111] 1399 **hers is an old goat** In other words, she accuses him of being a dirty old man:
goats were proverbially lecherous.

[112] 1401–1402 This is an allusion to the "marital debt", the doctrine that marital
partners were mutually obliged to serve each others' sexual needs. For a case in point, see
"Gilote et Jehane," vv. 228–31, 242–44: "Je su jeouene espouse, si ay vn baroun— / mes
trop est il fieble en sa mesoun. / Ce est la verite: il ad vn vit, / trop est il plyant, e trop
petit / [. . .] Trop est femme descu malement, / e forement trahy, qe tiel houme prent /
yl ne puet foutre, ne fere talent?" ("I am a young wife, and I have a husband—but in his
own household he's far too feeble. This is the truth: his prick is just not hard enough, and
much too small. [. . .] A woman is wretchedly deceived and cruelly betrayed who marries
such a man, [if] he can't fuck, or doesn't want to!": ed. Revard, "The Wife of Bath's
Grandmother," but with my translation. See also "De la fole et de la sage," ed. Achille
Jubinal, *Nouveau Recueil de Contes, Dits, Fabliaux et autres pièces inédites des XIIIe., XIV.,
et XV.* siècles, 2 vols. (Paris: Challamel, 1839–1842), 1: 73–82, at 79: "Por ce que mon
mari voi de toz biens laschir, / J'ai usé mon jovent tant comme homme l'a chier, / Quar
poi a de poissons, qui n'a dont taaschier" ("since I see that my husband is lacking in every
quality, I'll use my youth like something that one holds dear: for no one gets any fish if
he hasn't got the means to fish for them"; my translation). Jubinal edits this poem from a
continental manuscript (Paris BN MS f. fr. 837), but it is also to be found in an English
manuscript (Oxford, Bodleian Library MS Digby 86), where it appears as the "Estrif

to cause a row by bringing shame upon her sweet lover. Each of them knows very well what will serve her interests, so that she'll be able to obtain a separation:[113] if she doesn't get it, she thinks that she's been humiliated, and the husband will never get any peace for the rest of his life. I've never seen a woman who loved or cherished her husband so much that, if she spotted anyone more attractive, she wouldn't desire him—you can be sure of that![114] When a woman wants to love, her heart is like fog or smoke or a sea-mist." (1347–1414)

¶ THE OLD MAN: "Thank you, my son," said the old man, "But in the name of God, please moderate your words and your attitude, so that you aren't so insulting to women! 'You shouldn't say everything you think any more than you should say none of what you think!' as the wise man proverbially says.[115] I have lost my beloved sweetheart and that makes me very sad, whatever anyone might say. It's a loss that can never be made good, since I will never possess her equal." (1415–24)

¶ THE YOUNG MAN: "Sir," said the young man, "I'll very willingly make peace with women from now on. For your sake, whatever the matter is, it'll be forgiven from now on. Nevertheless, you should know it's true that many further arguments of this kind exist that might relieve you of your grief, but for your sake I'll pass over them. But now tell me: explain why you'll never find a woman like her. Go looking, and, even if all you want is someone just like your wife was, then you'll certainly find her. Young as I am, I can teach you very well, without any word of a lie, how to choose such a woman. Observe her upbringing and her carriage; her nobility and her self-restraint. You shouldn't, sir, pay any attention to what blinds many in this life: that is, lands and riches.[116] But if you were to

---

de deus dames," ed. Edmund Stengel, *Codicem Manu Scriptum Digby 86 in Bibliotheca Bodleiana Asservatum* (Halle: Orphanotropheus, 1871), 84–93 (although the particular lines that I have just quoted do not appear in the Oxford manuscript). On this text and its origins, see Neil Cartlidge, "Aubrey de Bassingbourn, Ida de Beauchamp and the context of the *Estrif de deus dames* in Oxford, Bodleian Library MS Digby 86," *Notes and Queries* 245 (2000): 411–14.

[113] 1405–1406 Chardri is perhaps specifically referring to the careful description in "Gilote et Johane" of how women can contrive temporary separations from their husbands (for their own sexual convenience) without running the risk of losing their dowries ("Gilote et Jehane", vv. 270–317.

[114] 1411–12 Cf. "Gilote et Jehane", vv. 236–37: "me couient moryr pur anguisse fyn, / si je n'eie l'amour de Jolif Hokekyn!" ("It's killing me! I'll die if I can't win / The love of. . . you know. . . Hotlips Hooligin?": ed. and trans. Revard).

[115] 1419–20 Cf. *Distiches of Cato*, 1. 12: "Shun tattling, and the newest thing to say / Seek not: closed lips hurt no one—speaking may" ("Rumores fuge neu studeas novus auctor haberi; / nam nulli tacuisse nocet, nocet esse locutum"); cf. also *Distiches*, 1. 3.

[116] 1443–45 Cf. Palmer, 62–63: "[*Ratio:*] Inuenies si nihil queris nisi bonam. Dum modo ne imagines, proauosque respexeris, nec patrimonium" ("Thou shalte fynde as good, yf thou seke nothynge but a good wyfe, all the whyle thou doest nat regarde her

take a good look at the woman herself, you certainly shouldn't take her just for
the sake of her possessions, whatever they might be. For when the money's gone,
the miserable fool will come to grief. Wealth will disappear in the end and all
he'll be left with is sorrow, if for him her possessions were such a distraction that
he didn't recognise her true nature; whereas if she's beautiful and well brought-
up, even if her relatives are poor, you can be more confident that your beloved
will never grow proud on account of her dowry.[117] If you wanted to take a wife,
someone perhaps who might make you spend more than your income actually
amounts to, then that would be an unpleasant story for you. When you've married her and she's being led in procession to your house, her dress and its trappings might be worth more than two or three years of your income, not to mention her jewels and her money, on which you'll never be able to set your teeth.[118]
She'll give you a good ticking-off about it, saying 'It's all mine—and it's going
to stay all mine. All this booty comes from my friends,[119] and it gives me great
satisfaction. If you don't keep me in the same fashion from now on, I'll guarantee you that I'll complain about you to my friends, who'll make a bad situation
for you much worse.' In this way all your peace of mind will be thoroughly dis-
rupted. Now perhaps it's the case that it's *your* wealth that supports her; and so
you're taking her with you round the country (as is only right, I think) along with
her maids (in all their finery, you can be sure), and her big, fine, well-fed riding-
horses, and her dresses and all her trappings, while you're in tattered robes and in
debt right up to the elbows.[120] Your wife's finery will be worth more than all the
furniture in the house. If she notices that your neighbour's wife is better dressed,
you can be sure that she'll rail against you remorselessly at all times of the day.
She'll say: 'I wish you were hanged, you evil stinking rascal, and as soon as pos-

---

progeny nor her auncestre nor patrimony"); *Distiches of Cato*, 3. 12: "Do not for dowry's
sake espouse a wife, / Nor wish to keep her if she causes strife" ("Uxorem fuge ne ducas
sub nomine dotis, / nec retinere velis, si coeperit esse molesta").

[117] 1455–58 Cf. St. Jerome, citing Theophrastus's "golden book", ed. Hanna and
Lawler, *Jankyn's Book*, 150–51: "Pauperem alere difficile est, divitem ferre tormentum"
("It is hard to support a poor [wife], a torment to put up with a rich one").

[118] 1468 The implicit image here is of biting coins to test that they are genuine: see
Seven Sleepers, v. 1145.

[119] 1471 The "friends" in this case should probably understood to be the network
of older relatives, feudal superiors, employers and/or godparents who are likely to have
arranged the marriage in the first place. See Neil Cartlidge, "Criseyde's Absent Friends,"
Chaucer Review 44 (2010): 227–45.

[120] 1479–88 Cf. St. Jerome, citing Theophrastus's "golden book", ed. Hanna and
Lawler, *Jankyn's Book*, 150–51: "Multa esse que matronarum usibus necessaria sunt:
preciose vestes, aurum, gemme, sumptus, ancille, suppellex varia, lectice, et esseda
deaurata" ("There are many things which are necessary for married women's practices:
expensive clothes, gold, gems, shopping sprees, maids, all kinds of furniture, litters, a gilt
two-wheeled chariot").

sible, for making me so ashamed in public because of the way you clothe me so badly. Out of the whole sum of what I possess, without any exception, your contribution isn't worth a dime.[121] You make yourself so important with my property that if I have any share in it, you can't bear it. Round here, there's no man so poor that he doesn't treat his wife with great respect—apart from you, you wretch. Cursed was the hour that I married you!' This is a lesson she'll often repeat and she'll keep on cursing you.[122] When you saw her at first, when she was sumptuously clothed, with rings on all her fingers and ribbons with pretty embroideries, together with all the inheritance that devolved on her, little did you think, it's true, that such interest, such bitter interest, would have been stored up for you in her purse. What you've bitten off, you've now got to chew—and you'll have more than enough of it. That's all the joy and pleasure you're going to get for the rest of your days. In this case, if your wife happened to die prematurely, you'd be able to rejoice and live all the more comfortably, having been freed from such an evil situation. Even if you had nothing to complain about, it would still be much better for you if it happened that your wife were gone—that's the truth. Leave off your grieving and remember that you're a man! You shouldn't weep like a sulky child for some apple. You know very well it's true: whoever's in possession of a good woman has had a very lucky throw of the dice."[123] (1425–1534)

¶ THE OLD MAN: "That's very true," said the old man. "My son, I wish you God's blessings and those of St. Peter of Rome in exchange for your consolation and your eloquent words, since even in relation to this difficult problem you've managed to give me reassurance. Now answer one more question and then I'll leave you in peace. This is the sum of it: my best friend has departed from this world and left me behind alone, forsaken and confused.[124] If someone decided to look on me with hostility, I wouldn't know whom to trust. Understand that for this reason my heart is sorrowful and dejected. There's no loss, you know, that compares with the loss of a friend."[125] (1535–52)

---

[121] 1500 **dime** *maille* Cf. *Seven Sleepers*, v. 286; *Josaphaz*, v. 2538; *Little Debate*, vv. 498, 1318.

[122] 1491–1508 Cf. St. Jerome, citing Theophrastus's "golden book", ed. Hanna and Lawler, *Jankyn's Book*, 150–51: "Dein per totas noctes garrule conquestiones: 'Illa ornatior procedit in publicum; hec honoratur ab omnibus; ego in conventu feminarum misella despicior'" ("Then, all night long, the nagging complaints: 'That woman looks so much prettier when she goes out: this one is honored by everyone; when women get together, they despise me as a wretch'").

[123] 1533–34 Merrilees notes that this couplet also turns up elsewhere in V (fol. 98r), in a collection of proverbs.

[124] 1543–44 Cf. Palmer, 58–59: "[*Sensus:*] Amicum perdidi" ("I haue lost my frende").

[125] 1551–52 See e.g. Morawski, *Proverbes*, no. 1357 ("Ne set que pert qui pert son bon ammi").

¶ THE YOUNG MAN: The young man replied: "A friend is a treasure worth more than silver or gold.[126] It's true what you've just said: losing a friend is no small thing. But I don't see any reason for such unrestrained grief—except that you're being self-indulgent. Why do you think you'll be able to bring your friend back to life with all your tears? That can never happen—for how could it? Was he the only friend that you ever had?"

¶ THE OLD MAN: "No," said the old man. "What upsets me is that he was as dear to me as my own right eye." (1553–64)

¶ THE YOUNG MAN: "Sir, I swear," replied the young man then, "It's absolutely amazing that in the middle of the ocean you're relying on somebody else to keep your ship safe.[127] Even the deep sea, that goes all the way round the world, isn't half so wickedly treacherous as this world. Thus the sea is a symbol of the world, particularly of its instability and discomfort.[128] The sea does only what it's supposed to do, but the world deceives us all. You can sometimes escape the perils of the sea: but I don't know how to escape the evils of the world. Therefore I say that the dangers on land in many respects surpass those of the sea. Yet you—when surrounded by a hundred thousand perils—were reassured by a single loyal friend. This is what I was telling you before: you were navigating by means of somebody else. You'd have to be very ashamed if your worth amounts to so little that in the whole of your life you've only ever had just one friend.[129] If you were surrounded by enemies, you'd need hundreds and thousands of friends. Whatever the situation, you'll never have so many of them that you won't need them to help you in your many misfortunes—so that even if one of them fails you over here, there's another one over there to offer you support. In this way you're likely to find help in every quarter." (1565–96)

¶ THE OLD MAN: The old man replied: "That's very true, but I'd really like to know how I can ultimately attain what you've promised and what I desire—for treachery is everywhere, from the depths of the ocean to the heights of the sky; and as a result I don't know how I can always decide between what's good and what's bad. I might put my trust where I'd get a bad bargain. And now, with the loss of my dear friend, I don't know how to decide whom to trust." (1597–1608)

---

[126] 1553–54 Cf. Ecclus. 6: 15: "Nothing can be compared to a faithful friend, and no weight of gold and silver is able to countervail the goodness of his fidelity."

[127] 1566–68 Cf. Palmer, 59–61: "Quid tu in tanta tempestate ad vnum ancorum stabas" ("why dyd thou stande at one anker in so great a tempest[?]").

[128] 1573–74 This idea is also proverbial. Merriless cites Morawski, *Diz*, 94 ("Le grande mer est ce monde cy / Qui moult est plain de grant soucy"). Cf. also Isaiah 57: 20: "But the wicked are like the raging sea, which cannot rest, and the waves thereof cast up dirt and mire."

[129] 1585–88 Cf. Palmer, 58–60: "[*Ratio:*] Forte animum habe si vnum, erubesce si vnicum" ("yf thou haue but one [friend] only, be abasshed").

¶ THE YOUNG MAN: "I'm sure you're wrong, sir, to regret this death so much. You can't possibly have loved him so much that you won't find his equal easily enough, and then you'll have just the same intimacy and sympathy that existed between you and your friend before. Even among five hundred thousand who are deceitful you'll be able to find one you can trust. Therefore you should try to make yourself liked by everybody, for you might well have need of any of them. You have lost your good friend, but did you always have need of him?" (1609–20)

¶ THE OLD MAN: "No," said the Old Man. "But I used to go around boasting about his demeanour, and about the reassurance he gave me. And I've found by experience that there's never been anyone else so loyal." (1621–24)

¶ THE YOUNG MAN: The young man replied, "Sir, even if you were as wise as Solomon, you could still be deceived by a close friend of long acquaintance. Not all of those who indiscriminately flatter you are true friends. Even someone who eats and drinks at your table won't be a reliable friend if you haven't previously put him to the test. It would be dangerous to trust him in anything. Those who promise you most are the ones who'll ultimately deceive you. Those who laugh with you and smile are the ones who'll slander you in the end. They'll be your friends wherever you go, but they'll fail you when the need is greatest.[130] This is just a friendship of convenience:[131] what you possess is what you're worth, and they'll love you only in proportion to that.[132] You can rely on such people only until it's time for all hands on deck.[133] They'll be your friends through and through, but only as long you can still do them good. If ever you need their help, you'll have lost their friendship. It's best not to praise the day before night falls;[134] and only likewise should you praise a friend for his friendship.[135] Your friend whom you like so much, you shouldn't ever put him to the test in times of need, since it could well be that he'll let you down just when you have most need of his help. That's why I tell you you're wrong when you won't be consoled for the loss of a friend who, in a time of need, wouldn't have paid any respect to

---

[130] 1639–40 This alludes to the proverbial "a friend in need is a friend indeed." Cf. Morawski, *Proverbes*, no. 171.

[131] 1641 **of convenience** *de mein en mein*: literally "from hand to hand." Cf. the modern German idiom "eine Hand wäscht die andere" ("one hand washes the other").

[132] 1642 This too is proverbial: cf. Morawski, *Proverbes*, no. 2283. See also Wace's *Brut*, v. 1742, in Judith Weiss, ed. and trans., *Wace's Roman de Brut: A History of the British: Text and Translation* (Exeter: University of Exeter Press, 1999), 44–45.

[133] 1644 **until it's time for all hands on deck** *Deske les eez ben espruvez*: literally, "until you have properly tested the planks."

[134] 1649 Again, this is proverbial. Merrilees cites Morawski, *Proverbes*, nos. 197, 215 and 216; and Samuel Singer, *Sprichwörter des Mittelalters*, 3 vols (Bern: Lang, 1944–1947), 2. 1: 117; 2. 2: 12.

[135] 1650 Cf. *Distiches of Cato*, 4. 28: "Praise sparingly; for him you oft commend—/ One day reveals how far he has been friend": "Parce laudato; nam quem tu saepe probaris, / una dies, qualis fuerit, ostendit, amicus").

you whatever the situation. Investigate your friend and put him to the test and if you find out that he is actually loyal, hang on to him: that would be wise. Tell him everything that's on your mind, and in return he'll tell you everything that's on his, and in this way you become his friend. And if you can make more than one friend, you'll be all the more secure against the dangers of this life, which is so full of treachery. From one moment to the next, from day to day, you should be afraid of that.[136] But you shouldn't grieve. Do you know why? I'll tell you in good faith. The more you that you're happy, the more annoyed you'll make your enemies. If you're unhappy about anything, they'll laugh about that, you can be sure. If my prayers had any force, I'd take away all your sorrow. Look back at your birth and how you lived in your childhood. Your best friend, from the time you were born, was the woman who carried you in her own belly for ten months and endured very great pain on your account. After the moment of your birth, you'll never again have anyone like that. But yet[137] more grief is shown for strangers than sons show for their mothers! It was by means of your good nature and good manners that you won your friend in the first place. It was because of your qualities that your friend first had a good reason to love you. It was through your own worth and generosity that he undertook to love you. With malice and wickedness you'd never get a friend your whole life through. You should appreciate that, if you behave well, it's your virtue that attracts loyal friends. So in this way you're a kind of craftsman, who manufactures friends out of mortal men. If your friend is dead now, you ought to take very great comfort from the fact that the master-craftsman still lives who manufactured so good a friend in the first place. Thus you shouldn't despair as long as you still remember the skill of making friends, whether young or old, just as good as the one you had before. It seems like childishness to grieve for such an inconvenience. At the end of the day you'll achieve nothing by your mourning but misery." (1625–1712)

¶ THE OLD MAN: "Brother, that may well be," said the old man. "This life, which, according to what you say, is so bitter, doesn't amount to anything except making you ashamed of being alive. God bless you, my son: because of your arguments and your words I see this more clearly now than I did before. We shouldn't set any store by the chances of this life, since it seems to me a very great folly to endure misfortune and then to grieve extravagantly for it. As a result of it you might cause yourself so much pain as to create a mortal wound. Now I don't know what else I can say, since you know so well how to outwit me. By my lord St. Peter the apostle, the victory is yours. Compared to your intelligence and articulacy I certainly[138] don't have any at all. I'm not saying this to you simply as

---

[136] 1669–70 The Young Man's point is that it is better to be fearful of life, and its dangers, than to regret a death.

[137] 1687 **But yet** *Issi*. As Merrilees points out (72), it is unusual for *Issi* to have this sense.

[138] 1732 **certainly** *pur dreit*. Merrilees reads *par dreit* "by rights," which seems to me to make less sense in this context.

a compliment. You have a great deal of intelligence and good sense. If anyone tells me that a light-hearted young man can't possibly be intelligent and rational, I'd contradict him unhesitatingly, since without doubt this contest has enabled me to find what I was seeking. Good sense suits a young man very well. From now on I'm going to advise the old that if they want to follow the best course the shouldn't excessively criticise young people for having fun.[139] My son, I surrender! Tell me how I can repay you.[140] Whatever it is, I'll do it, as long as it brings me your goodwill." (1713–48)

¶ THE YOUNG MAN: The young man replied, "Thank you for the kind things that you've just said to me. If I have any intelligence, it was God who put it there, the maker of both body and soul. May God preserve it, if he wishes, so that I might increase in good fortune, joy, and happiness! Sir, may God do the same for you! May he grant you his grace! You should take heart and be happy! God will look after your destiny, just as he looks after these flowers that you see all around you. It's as if this meadow, which you can see so full of flowers, is itself in possession of perfect joy, taking pleasure in its own way. That's why no one can be in the wrong if he strives to cheer himself up. You shouldn't allow yourself to be downcast by anything. Make the best of it, that's my advice! You should ask the Son of St. Mary, who well knows how to rule the whole world, to keep you your whole life in undisturbed joy and contentment, to grant you the power to serve him and do good in his service, and to allow you to make a good end, so that you go directly to him. May you be granted this, and may I granted it as well, and everyone who's listened to this debate! Let's all say together 'Amen, amen'! The Virgin Mary now watch over us! Amen." (1749–80)

---

[139] 1741–44 Cf. *Little Debate*, vv. 111–18; *Josaphaz*, vv. 577–83.

[140] 1746 **how I can repay you** *vostre talent*: literally, "what you want"; but the reason why the Old Man is asking this is that he is suggesting that the Young Man deserves a reward.

Appendix of Extracts

1. *Seven Sleepers*, vv. 1081–1168:
Malchus tries to buy some bread

Atant entra en la cité.
Quanke il vit fu besturné:
Recunust ren de quanke il vit.
Dunc se preissa il mut petit:
Quida ke ceo fust resuerie.   1085
Si oi numer seinte Marie
E iurer par la seinte croiz
Hardiement od haute uoiz.
"E Deu," fet il, "ke pus ieo fere?
Er seir, ne fu si haut en terre   1090
Ke osast iteu chose dire,
Ke l'emperur nel feist oscire.
La croiz fu er seir partut muscé—
V en fu arsé v despescee:
Or est la seint croiz iurree   1095
E ci partut est avree
E Jesus e sa duce mere.
E ke fet ore l'Emperere?
Affolé sui, ceo sai ieo ben,
N'en pus sauer nul autre ren!   1100
Se Deu me saut," fet il adunkes,
"Ephese ne fu ceo vnkes,
Mes autre cité: n'en puis savoir
Ki cest pais deiue auoir."
Atant k'il ala encuntrant   1105
Vn vaslet ki li vint deuant.
"Bacheler," fet il, "si Deu t'ait,
Resteez vus ici un petit:
Si me dites," fet il, "sanz gile,
Cum ad a nun iceste vile?"   1110
"Vaslet," fet cil, "nel sez tu mie?

Par Deu ki est le fiz Marie,
L'en l'apele Ephese la grant,
Ke tut le mund uet cunussant."

Quant Malcus aueit icest oi,   1115
Sachez, weres ne s'esioi:
Ore quide il ben certeinement
K'il n'ad resun ne entendement.
Cheitif se cleime e maluré
E dit dolent, "Mar fui ieo né!   1120
Fees, ceo quit, m'unt encuntré,
Ki issi m'unt enfantosmé.
Mes quant Deu e sa uertu
Vout ke ieo aie le sen perdu,
Hors de la uile m'en uoil aler,   1125
Ke ne me estoce plus affoler;
Car ieo porreie ia tant errer,
Ke ne saureie pas repeirer,
Car ne cunus pas ces rueles,
Ne ces mesuns ki sunt si beles.   1130
Essaer uoil si ahurter pusse
Mes cumpanuns, ke ieo les tenisse:
Si lur dirrai cest auenture,
Ke tant m'est anguissuse e dure,
Mes auant ke ieo m'en aille   1135
Achater m'estot lur uitaille."

Atant s'en vet dolent e murne.
Par la paneterie s'en turne,
V les pesturs vendeint le pain:
Sa munee portoit en sa main.   1140
Le pain esteit mut maniable:
Cil gette l'argent desur la table.
Le pestur regarda auant
E les deners uet regardant:
Vn dener prent, s'il mania.   1145
"E Deu!" fet it, "Quel argent ci a?
Mut est ore d'autre pris,
Ke nus n'usum en cest pais!"
Cil le mustra a sun ueisin,
Ke mut s'esmerueilla sanz fin,   1150
Car unkes itele munee
Ne fu veu en lur cuntree.

Mut i musent de tutes parz,
E les sages e les musarz,
E dient ben, "Por uerité   1155
Cist uaslet ad tresor truué!"
Malcus ceo ueit, si s'esbai,
Pur ceo ke tuz esgardeint sur li;
E dit a sei, "Or m'unt veu,
Ore m'unt ben aperceu,   1160
E ore me uunt recunussant,
Cil pestur, cil vilain recreant.
Or plust a Deu ke ces uileinz tuz
Vssent les ouz creuez trestuz —
E ieo deske a une liuue   1165
V sur cheuail v desur vue!
Jamés en autreteu manere
Ne uendrai entre cest gent lanere.

1085 resuerie] C; reuerye J – 1100 N'en pus] C; Ne pus J – 1103 nen puis] C; ne
pus J – 1104 Ki] Ke CJ – 1110 a] C; J *om.* – 1111 cil] C; il J – 1112 le] C; J *om.* –
1121 m'unt] me vnt J; mut C – 1122 ki] ke CJ – 1123 en] e CJ – 1126 estoce] C;
asteuce J / affoler] C; foler J – 1127 ia] C; J *om.* – 1130 ki] ke CJ – 1132 tenisse]
J; truisse C – 1150 s'esmerueilla] C; s'enmeruyla J – 1160 m'unt] me vnt J; mut
C – 1163 plust] C; pust J

2. *Josaphaz*, vv. 691–776:
Barlaam pretends to be a merchant

Barlaam ne uout plus targer,
Quant il entent le soen mester,
E luue Deu por la nuvele,
Ke li semblont e bone e bele —
Tant kil fist ignelepas   695
Pur poi trestuz changer ses draz:
Deguiser se fist cume marchant.
Si s'en ala demeintenant
Tut dreit uers la curt le rei.
Sa male portout ouec sei,   700
Cum ceo fust sa mercerie.
Le dreit chemin ke meuz le guie;
S'en ala uers la tur l'enfant.
Deuant la porte deportant,
Truua sun plus priué mestre.   705

Cil li demande de sun estre,
K'il fu e dunt ueneit,
E quei el pais quis aueit.
Cil li respunt demeintenant:
"Beaus sire cher, io su marchant,   710
Si fu de mut lontein pais.
Si vus dirrai ke io ai ci quis:
Por vendre meuz ma marchandise.
Ore en sauez ben la deuise.
Si vus dirrai ke io ai a uendre: 715
De Paris deske en Alisandre
N'a meillure pere ke io n'ai,
Ne plus uaille en grant assai,
Plus bele ne plus uertiuse,
Mut la teng pur preciuse.   720
Ele garist tute maladie:
N'a si fol ci k'a Pauie,
K'ele ne feist sage sanz targer.
Deble ne poet nul demurer,
Ke la vertu de la pere   725
N'en cace en tute manere:
Por ceo la pus io tant amer,
Ke io ne la uoil a nul mustrer."
"Si frez," fet il, "mustrez la mei!"
"Nun frai, si vus dirrai pur quei: 730
Ne la poet nul hoem esgarder
Ke ne n'a les ouz mut cler
De peché e d'autre folie,
E ki ne n'est de chaste vie."
Cil li respunt, "Ne mie a gas!   735
Beau frere, ne la mustrez pas!
Jo su pechur e deslaué
Ma uie tute ad tele esté!"
Barlaam dit, "Beau frere cher,
Vus resemblez bon bachiler.   740
Si par vus en la tur entrasse,
Au fiz au rei ben la mustrasse,
Par si ke io n'i perde ren.
Sire, ore vus en cuuenge ben!"
Cil li respunt, "N'en n'eez dute!   745
Deheez ert la barbe tute
Ke de ren vus fra damage!
Ben vus frai icest message,

S'il vus plet ici atendre.
Mes mut tost vus frai entendre   750
De Josaphaz la uolunté."
Atant s'en est cil tost munté,
E uent dreit deuant l'enfant.
Si li dist, "Sire, par Teruagant,
Jo vus dirrai une merueille: 755
Vnc mes n'oi sa pareille.
La hors est un marchant uenu,
Vnc mes tel ne fu veu,
Ki portast si riche tresor,
Ke meuz uaut k'argent v or.   760
C'est une pere meruelluse:
Vnc mes n'oi si preciuse.
N'a si forte maladie
Ke quor v cors ad en baillie,
Ke ele ne garisse trop ben.   765
E si refet vn autre ren:
Ja maufé n'en aura baillie
V la pere n'eist la mestrie.
De tutes les peres ke sunt en terre
Ke l'em peust v seust quere,   770
Passe cele tutes ensemble,
De ben, de beauté, me semble."
Josaphat dit, "Or i alez,
E le marchant tost m'amenez.
Si issi est, ben ert uenu   775
E ert de mei ben receuu."

692 le] C; J *om.* – 696 trestuz] C; tuz J 712 ke io] C; quey ay J – 722 ci] si CJ – 745
Nen n'eez] C; ne neez J – 751–873 J*'s text is missing.* – 756 sa] sai C – 764 baillie]
ballie C – 765 ele] le C – 768 n'eist] C; meist Koch – 773 Josaphat] Osaphat, *with*
marginal correction C

3. *Josaphaz*, vv. 2911–54:
Chardri's conclusion

Seinnurs, ore poez ben entendre:
Ki uout sun tens ben despendre
E amer Deu a sun poer,
Mut en aura riche loer,
Car Deu par sun seintisme nun   2915

En ad tut prest le gwerdun.
Ki Deu uout seruir leaument
En cel ert beneit, e entre gent.
S'il vit en terre, amé serra:
S'il moert, a Deu tut s'en irra.   2920
La ert curuné en haut,
V ia sanz fin ioie ne faut.
Quant poum a cele ioie ateindre,
Mut sumes fous ke uulum feindre
E lesser par un petit ennu   2925
De seruir Deu e sa uertu—
Quant poum par un petit labur
Itant gainner a chef de tur,
Si cum fist Josaphaz l'enfant,
Dunc auez oi ça auant.   2930
Nel fesum pas, kar la folie
Amum tant de ceste vie
Ke plus tost orrium chanter
De Roulant v de Oliuer;
E les batailles des Duze Pers   2935
Orrium mut plus uolenters,
Ke ne frium (si cum io quid)
La passiun de Jesus Christ.
Tant sumes feinz k'en vbliance
Mettum tut Deu e sa pussance.   2940
Prium tuz le omnipotent,
Ki guuerne eir e mer e vent,
Ke par la sue seinte pité
Nus doint itele uolenté,
E le poer, ke par sa grace   2945
Chescun de nus si ben le face,
Ke paé en seit nostre Seinnur
E nus sauuez a chef de tur!
"Amen, amen!" chescun en die:
Ici finist la bone vie   2950
De Josaphaz le duz enfant.
A ceus ki furent escutant
Mande Chardri saluz sanz fin
E au uespre e au matin. Amen.
Explicit.

2912 tens ben] tens en ben **CJ** – 2917 Ki] Ke **CJ** – 2930 ça] **J**; sa **C** – 2932 Amum] **C**; Auum **J** – 2936 Orrium] Orrum **J**; Orrum **C** – 2942 Ki] Ke **CJ** – 2948 sauuez]

J; sauez C / a] C; au J – 2950 Ici] C; E ci J – 2951 duz] C; bon J – 2952 ki] C; ke
J 2953 sanz] J; san C

4. *Little Debate*, vv. 1339–1424:
On love and marriage

"Ore oi merueilles," fet dunc l'enfant,	L'enfant
"Ke vus alez si dolusant	1340
Por uostre amie ke leale fu.	
Si vus mei ussez ben entendu,	
Vus lerriez cele dolur.	
Aueit ele unkes si grant amur	
Vers vus cum uus auiez uers li?"	1345
"Oil, e assez plus, sachez de fi!"	Veillart
"Par fei, ceo est merueille grant,	L'enfant
Car mes ne oi en mun viuant,	
Ben le vus di, mun beau pere,	
Ke femme eust iteu manere,	1350
Ke femme amast quant fud amee!	
Mes oez lur dreit destinee:	
Si ele se aparceit ke l'em la eime	
Dunc por hunie ben se cleime,	
Si tost ne deuenge dangeruse,	1355
V mult enreuere e trop irruse.	
Si ren dites cuntre sun uoil	
Ele vus regardera de l'autre oil.	
Mes celui ki ne la eime de ren,	
A celui juera ele ben	1360
E acolera e suef beisera,	
E per beal semblant ben le atrerra.	
Mes de celui dunt est seure,	
Sachez, ne en prendra gueres cure.	
Chescune femme deuant l'espusaille	1365
Mult beal semblant vus fra sanz faille.	
Quant ele vus dit, 'Seez certein,	
Mun tresduz quor, car trop vus eim!',	
Dunc dist sun quor, 'Vus i mentez:	
Tut autrement cherrunt les dez!	1370
Fous se fie en mun semblant:	
Mun quor ne i est, ne tant ne quant.	
Ki de mun semblant mult se lue,	
Cil tent l'anguille dreit par la cue!'	

Mun beau pere, sachez de fi: 1375
Ja nul hoem ki unkes nasqui
Ne vit ren ke tant seit volage
Cum est femme e sun curage.
Comment porriez dunc aseurer
En ta amie e tant iurer   1380
Ke iamés ne se changereit
Deske a la mort, coment ke seit?
Mes ieo, ki su iofne enfant,
Ore vus dirrai merueille grant:
Mult ai oi, sachez, beau pere,   1385
Femmes changer sa en arere.
Jo ai veu chaste espuse e leale
En poi de vre deuenir cursale
E tele ke de dulçur n'aueit per,
Mult felunesse au paraler,   1390
E mult simple, duce e coye
Mettre sun dru en male voie.
Les plus deuors ke vnt esté
Firent femmes par mauuesté.
Si ren i ad ke lur desplet,   1395
Enz en chapitres moeuent lur plet:
L'une dist ke le soen mari
Est lere fort, si n'est par li;
L'autre dist ke le soen est vn cheure;
L'espus a l'autre e felun e enreure;   1400
Icele dist ke ele ad grant dreit
Ke cil ne li fet ke fere deit:
Issi se peine por un curuz
Chescune hunir sun ami duz.
Ben quide chescune ke ben se auance,   1405
Si porchaser poet la deseuerance;
Si nun, mult se tendra hunie,
Ne il n'auera pes iur de sa uie.
Unc n'i vi femme itant amer
Ne tant cherir sun bacheler.   1410
Si ele veist un plus beals de li,
Ke ele nel coueitast, sachez de fi!
Vent u fumee v nyule en mer
Est quor de femme quant uout amer."
"Beau fiz, merci!" fet li prudum,   Veillard 1415
"Par Deu e sun seintisme nun,
Temprez tun dit e tun curage,

Ke ne lur diez si grant utrage!
'Ne tut dir dire ne tut lesser!'
Dist li sages en reprouer.   1420
Jo ai perdue ma duce amie
Ke mult mei greue keke l'em die:
E la perte ert sanz recouerer,
Car io n'auerai iamés sa per."

1339 dunc] CV; J *om.* – 1342 mei] C; JV *om.* – 1345] auiez] CJ; avez V – 1348
en] CJ; a V – 1349 mun] CV; J *om.* 1350 iteu] CJ; de iteu V – 1351 *The whole line
is missing in* J. 1353 se aparceit] C; parceyt JV – 1356 enreuere] C; areuere J; en
riuere V / e] C; v JV – 1357 cuntre] CV; encuntre J – 1362 atrerra] C; trera J; trer-
ra V – 1365 femme] C; JV *om.* – 1366 fra] JV; frai C 1368 car] C; ke JV – 1369
mentez] CV; mettrez J – 1371 mun] CJ; lur V – 1372 Mun quor ne i est ne tant]
C; Mun ni est taunt J; Lur semblaunt ne vaut V – 1373 mun] CJ; lur V – 1374
l'] CV; J *om.* – 1378 e] C; en JV, Koch, Merrilees – 1379–80 *are reversed in* JV. /
aseurer] C; assenter JV / e tant] CJ; ostant V – 1381 changereit] CV; changerent
J – 1385 sachez] CV; J *om.* – 1388 deuenir] CJ; uenir V – 1389 per] CJ; espeir
corrected by subpunction V 1392 en] CJ; a V –1394 Firent] CV; Furent J – 1395
desplet] C; mesplet JV – 1399 ke le soen est vn cheure] C; kil seon est cheure J; ke
le son est chiuere V – 1400 a] CV; J *om.* / enreure] CJ; riuere V – 1401 grant] CJ;
mut grant V – 1405 ben se] C; mut JV – 1409 n'i] C; ne JV – 1415 fet] CV; fe J

Index of Personal and Place Names

The numbers given here correspond with the line-numbers in Chardri's editions of the *Little Debate* (*LD*) and the *Seven Sleepers* (*SS*), and Koch's edition of *Josaphaz* (*Jos.*).